Information Age Economy

Information Age Economy

K. Sandbiller
Dezentralität und Markt in Banken
1998. ISBN 3-7908-1101-7

M. Roemer
Direktvertrieb kundenindividueller
Finanzdienstleistungen
1998. ISBN 3-7908-1102-5

F. Rose
The Economics, Concept, and Design
of Information Intermediaries
1999. ISBN 3-7908-1168-8

S. Weber
Information Technology
in Supplier Networks
2001. ISBN 3-7908-1395-8

Kurt Geihs · Wolfgang König
Falk von Westarp (Eds.)

NETWORKS

Standardization, Infrastructure, and Applications

With 50 Figures
and 6 Tables

Physica-Verlag
A Springer-Verlag Company

Prof. Dr. Kurt Geihs
Technical University of Berlin
Faculty for Electrical Engineering and
Computer Science, Sekr. EN6
Einsteinufer 17
10587 Berlin
Germany

Prof. Dr. Wolfgang König
University of Frankfurt
Institute of Information Systems
Mertonstraße 17
60054 Frankfurt am Main
Germany

Dr. Falk von Westarp
University of Frankfurt
Institute of Information Systems
Mertonstraße 17
60054 Frankfurt am Main
Germany

ISBN 3-7908-1449-0 Physica-Verlag Heidelberg New York

Cataloging-in-Publication Data applied for
Die Deutsche Bibliothek – CIP-Einheitsaufnahme
Networks: Standardization, Infrastructure, and Applications; With 6 Tables / Kurt Geihs ... (Ed.). – Heidelberg; New York: Physica-Verl., 2002
(Information Age Economy)
ISBN 3-7908-1449-0

Physica-Verlag Heidelberg New York
a member of BertelsmannSpringer Science+Business Media GmbH

Printed in Germany

Softcover Design: Erich Kirchner, Heidelberg

SPIN 10853528 88/2202-5 4 3 2 1 0 – Printed on acid-free paper

Preface

In 1997, scientists from disciplines as diverse as

- Computer Science,
- Economics,
- Economic Geography,
- Information Systems,
- Labor Sciences,
- Law and Legal Sciences,
- Political Sciences,
- Sociology

set out to lay the foundation for a common theory of networks.

The research program "**Networks as a competitive advantage** and the example of the Rhine-Main Region" at J. W. Goethe-University was funded by the German National Science Foundation (DFG) from 1997 until 2000. In three and a half hears, we faced the challenge of interdisciplinarity, i. e. the striving for a common goal amongst most diverse individuals and scientific disciplines. The objective was to gain a deeper understanding of the mechanisms behind social, economic, technical and other kinds of networks. Based upon a mutual understanding of both, the diversity of the network metaphor(s) as well as their common properties, a unified theory of networks should guide public and private decisions concerning the planning, operations and controlling of different kinds of networks and contribute to a responsible and efficient development of state-of-the-art networks.

The enormous impetus of new technologies pointing to a "network society" had us agree on pursuing an interdisciplinary research approach as an adequate means of incorporating the expectation that there is literally no area in the social and economic world unaffected by the recent advancements of information and communication technologies and their application to real world problems.

While on an abstract layer the project's pace was driven by the common belief in the necessity of a common (even unified) theory of networks, it was slowed down by the need to identify mutually agreed upon starting points as well as particular homogeneous research goals. Research approaches turned out to be substantially different between the participating disciplines. Fundamental positions as to the transferability of utility, the applicability of micro-models or the extent to which individual decision making is (solely?) dependent on the institutional embeddedness of the deciding agents slowed down the process.

Particular research results from all the different disciplines are documented in many articles (www.vernetzung.de/eng). As a whole, they provide a broad platform of a variety of views towards networks and define a methodological path for further research. Within the research program, we focused on two topical domains:

- *The process of standardization and its implications on (economic, technical, social) networks*. In this context, a network denotes entities (agents, machines) of a system and their relations. The focus was on understanding and controlling the interaction processes between agents and the mutual implications on network behavior and infrastructure.
- *The role of regional (territorial) agglomeration*. Here, the focus was on the role of regional or territorial organization (e. g. metropolitan areas) in the trade-off between globalization and a supposed increasing importance of regional networks, with the example of the Rhine-Main area.

In two books – reflecting the above distinction – we present a condensed interpretation of parts of our works towards answering the question "how to structure further research". The first volume **Networks - Standardization, Infrastructure, and Applications,** edited by K. Geihs, W. König and F. v. Westarp, aims at contributing to the international discussion about networks and standardization. Therefore, it – as most articles in this part of the program – is completely published in English.

J. Esser and E. W. Schamp edited the second volume titled **The Metropolitan Region in Processes of Networking (Metropolitane Region in der Vernetzung)**. New forms of network-building in different industries as well as in a political context are embedded both in global relations and local context. Still, local or regional networks in a territorial rather than virtual sense are of tantamount importance. That is why this second volume offers various examples of "glocalization processes", i. e. processes with local agents continuously reinforcing their network structure to adapt to international competitive environments and to survive within global schemes of relations. This volume is solely published in German.

We are indebted to the German National Science Foundation for daring to support our broad interdisciplinary project. Although the research program finds its end with these books, the German National Science Foundation still funds some particular research groups that emerged from it. I hope that some of the good spirit of interdisciplinarity together with excellent future contributions from the projects that found new funding will carry on asking the right questions and help us come closer to answers.

Prof. Dr. Wolfgang König

(Speaker of the program's researchers)

Contents

I Standardization

Standardization and the emergence and dynamics of communication networks are strongly interrelated. The following research questions can be identified in this context. What are the relevant standards in networks and what are the interdependencies between them? How do the use and the specification of standards influences the properties of networks? How do standards change with rapidly growing networks of today's world? What is the optimal degree of standardization in networks?

The contributions of this section are focusing on the interdependencies between networks and standardization from an economical and information technological perspective.

The first article integrates two recent approaches, the *decentralized standardization model* and the *network diffusion model of standards*, into an interdisciplinary model of standardization in networks. The second paper gives an overview of real world standardization practice in markets and in large companies, respectively.

Modeling Diffusion Processes in Networks

Tim Weitzel, Oliver Wendt, Falk v. Westarp

Johann Wolfgang Goethe-University
Institute of Information Systems (Wirtschaftsinformatik)
Mertonstr. 17
D 60054 Frankfurt am Main
{tweitzel|wendt|westarp}@wiwi.uni-frankfurt.de

Summary:
In this paper, some of the main results of the research project "Economics of Standards in Information Networks" are presented and integrated into a single framework of technology diffusion. We present an agent-based simulation model that incorporates structural determinants of networks (centrality, topology/density) and individual decision making on the part of prospective technology users under realistic informational assumptions. Based upon these models, decision behavior in terms of the selection of standards and the diffusion of technological innovations in networks can be described; the model can serve as a tool for developing and evaluating various internalization strategies that aim at answering questions like how to consider the determinants of an increasingly global and networked market when choosing corporate strategies.

Introduction

The use of common standards generally makes possible or simplifies transactions carried out between actors or eases the exchange of information between them. Examples are DNA, natural languages and currency or metric standards as well as communication protocols (IP, TCP, HTTP) and syntactic and semantic standards such as XML and EDI. In the context of information and communication systems *compatibility* is important: many different computer networks, operating systems, user surfaces, and application systems have evolved in companies over a number of years. One of the major drawbacks of this heterogeneous legacy is the fact that there is no seamless integration of different data and applications. Recently, this has been discussed in the context of Electronic Business and Enterprise Application Integration (EAI) focusing on the integration of all actors in a value chain. Prominent examples are the various incompatible Electronic Data Preface

Interchange (EDI) standards and efforts aimed at the introduction of Web-based EDI or XML/EDI [Westarp/Weitzel/Buxmann/König 1999].

This paper deals with the selection and diffusion of standards in networks and incorporates the main results of the interdisciplinary research project "Economics of Standards in Information Networks". From 1997 until 2000, the main focus of the research project was

- to identify the drawbacks of traditional theories about network effects (section *Network Effects*) [Weitzel/Westarp/Wendt 2000],
- to gather empirical data about the use of IT standards such as EDI, office software or standard software [Westarp/Buxmann/Weitzel/König 1999], and
- to develop simulation models describing the decision behavior of actors (users as well as vendors) when network effects exist as a foundation for deriving and evaluating internalization strategies (section *The Standardization Problem: A Basic Model* and *Network Diffusion Model of the Software Market*) [Westarp/Weitzel/Buxmann/König 2000; Wendt/Westarp 2000].

Full results can be found at http://www.vernetzung.de/eng/b3/. Among the main outcomes are two simulation models: one describing the way technology users decide about which standard to use and providing a first-best standardization solution for any given network; the other describing the diffusion of technological innovations from a vendor's viewpoint and providing a basis for deriving pricing strategies in software markets. In this paper, these two models are merged, combining the consideration of anticipatory decision behavior in our standardization model with a consideration of the topological properties of networks as described in our diffusion model.

To provide a condensed overview of the major research results of our project, we discuss positive network effects as theoretical foundation for standardization and diffusion problems critically in the section *Network Effects*. In the section *The Standardization Problem: A Basic Model* and *Network Diffusion Model of the Software Market* the basic concepts of both standardization and diffusion models are presented. Based upon these, a fusion of the models is developed in the section *Fusion*. First simulation results show the positive influence on market concentration of anticipative decision behavior for different network topologies. Compared to simple ex-post observations, this also has a positive influence on network welfare.

Finally, future research areas as well as extensions and possible applications of the model are discussed.

Network Effects

Standards in Information Systems

Standardization activities cover a wide range of application domains, as can be seen by the numerous initiatives by standardization organizations such as ISO, ANSI or DIN [Farrel/Saloner 1988]. "Ironically, standards have not been completely standardized“ [Hemenway 1975]. However, there is a general consensus that standards enable and facilitate the interaction between at least two system elements. Standards provide compatibility by specifying extensional structural forms as well as the behavior of the subjects involved. Especially in German speaking countries, standards set by this kind of organization are often referred to as *norms* [DIN 1991]. In this paper, we use the term *standard* to refer to any technology or product (software, hardware) incorporating technological specifications that provide for or require *compatibility*. Thum (1995) presents different definitions of *standard*. An information system or communications network consists of a set of system elements and their information relations. Elements can be human as well as machine actors and usually represent technology users (individuals, business units, enterprises).

Theories of Positive Network Effects

Discussions about the use of standards or the diffusion of technological innovations are often based upon the theory of positive network effects, which describes a positive correlation between the number of users of a network good and its utility [Katz/Shapiro 1985; Farrel/Saloner 1985].

The first groundbreaking contributions to the relatively young research field stem from the early 80s.[1] A common finding is the existence of network effects, i.e. the increasing value of a standard as the number of its users increases (demand side economies of scale) leading in many cases to pareto-inferior results of standardization processes. Katz/Shapiro (1985) differentiate between direct network effects in terms of direct "physical effects" [Katz/Shapiro 1985, 424] of being able to exchange information and indirect network effects arising from interdependence in the consumption of complementary goods.

Kindleberger (1983) describes free-rider problems due to the public good properties of standards. Arthur (1983, 1989) shows that technologies subject to increasing returns (in contrast to constant and decreasing returns) inhibit multiple equilibria and will finally lock-in to a monopoly with one standard cornering the entire

---

1 Of course, there are earlier contributions on the field of standards, e.g. Hemenway 1975; but it was not until about 15 years ago that standards emerged as a separate topic of research.

market. Since this standardization process is non-ergodic (or path dependent) the ultimate outcome is not predictable. Analogously, Besen/Farrell (1994) show that tippiness is a typical characteristic found in networks describing the fact that multiple incompatible technologies are rarely able to coexist and that the switch to a single, leading standard can occur suddenly.

Some contributions distinguish between *unsponsored de facto* standardization processes as described above and diffusion in *sponsored networks*: A quite commonly adopted terminology differentiates between the market-mediated diffusion processes of compatibility standards (leading to de facto standards) and de jure standards resulting from either political ("committee") or administrative procedures. De facto standards can either be sponsored (with certain actors holding property rights and the capability of restraining the use of the standard) or unsponsored (no actors with proprietary interests) [David/Greenstein 1990, 4].

The pattern of argument for standardization processes is always the same: the discrepancy between private and collective gains in networks under increasing returns leads to possibly pareto-inferior results. With incomplete information about other actors' preferences, *excess inertia* can occur as no actor is willing to bear the disproportionate risk of being the first adopter of a standard and then becoming stranded in a small network if all others eventually decide in favor of another technology. This start-up problem prevents any adoption at all of the particular technology, even if it is preferred by everyone. On the other hand, *excess momentum* can occur, e.g. if a sponsoring firm uses low prices during early periods of diffusion to attract a critical mass of adopters [Farrell/Saloner 1986]. In the case of complete information on the part of all actors concerning their symmetric preferences for a certain standard, a *bandwagon* process will overcome the coordination problem, with actors who stand to gain relatively high stand-alone utility or private benefits from adoption (as compared to network effects) starting the adoption process. Nevertheless, in the case of heterogeneous preferences, Farrell/Saloner (1986) show that due to strategic behavior even perfect communication might not be able to overcome excess inertia or momentum. In the case of sponsored technologies the situation is somewhat different. Here there is a possibility of internalizing the network gains which would otherwise be more or less lost by strategic intertemporal pricing, for example [Katz/Shapiro 1986]. There are private incentives to providing networks that can overcome inertia problems; however, they do not guarantee social optimality per se. Common results are the following:

- In many cases, the existence of network effects leads to pareto-inferior market results.
- Demand-sided positive network effects inhibit multiple equilibria and the market will finally lock-in to a monopoly with one standard gaining total market share.

- Instability is a typical property describing the fact that multiple, incompatible technologies are rarely able to coexist and that the switch to a single, leading standard can occur suddenly.
- The start-up problem prevents the adoption even of superior products; excess inertia can occur as no actor is willing to bear the disproportionate risk of being the first adopter of a standard.
- On the other hand, excess momentum can occur, e.g. if a sponsoring firm uses low prices in early periods of diffusion to attract a critical mass of adopters.
- In the case of sponsored technologies there is a possibility of internalizing the network gains which would otherwise be more or less lost by strategic intertemporal pricing. There are private incentives to providing networks that can overcome inertia problems; still they do not guarantee social optimality per se.
- The question arises whether the laissez-faire of decentralized markets should be replaced by centralized state control to ensure favorable diffusion of technologies subject to network effects.

While the traditional models contributed greatly to the understanding of a wide variety of particular (macroeconomic) problems associated with the diffusion of standards, they failed to explain the variety of diffusion courses in today's dynamic information and communication technology markets. Additionally, there are only a few contributions which aim at supporting standardization decisions on an individual level. The examination of network effects is made in a rather general way, which does not cover the heterogeneous properties of the markets with products such as digital television, cellular phones, office software, Internet browsers, or EDI-solutions. Furthermore, the specific interaction of potential adopters within their personal socio-economical environment, and the potential decentralized coordination of network efficiency are neglected. As a result, important phenomena of modern network effect markets such as the coexistence of different products despite strong network effects, the appearance of small but stable clusters of users of a certain solution despite the fact that the competition dominates the rest of the market, or the fact that strong players in communication networks force other participants to use a certain solution cannot be sufficiently explained by the existing approaches.

Common Drawbacks in Network Effect Models

While these traditional models greatly contributed to the understanding of a wide variety of particular problems associated with the diffusion of standards, they seem to be not applicable to real world problems because of the small scope of their framework of analysis. Furthermore, the results seem to be very over-exaggerated and especially over-generalized since, although there is basically no situation without (direct and/or indirect) network effects, the laissez-faire coordination of decentralized markets has outperformed systems of centralized authority in almost every region of the world as well as in most recent management and organizational approaches. Not all markets seem to fail. The frequent notion of indefinitely persisting lock-in situations [David/Greenstein 1990, 8-9] or market failure under network effects in most of the contributions fails to explain practical issues, from the existence of cars to versioning of products, the emergence of new suppliers or more generally speaking any technological progress at all.

In a systematic critique of traditional approaches to network effects we have identified areas that need improvement [Weitzel/Wendt/Westarp 2000]. We propose the hypothesis that assumptions and simplifications **implicitly** and **uncritically** used for modeling standardization problems inevitably lead to the results described, such as market failure under network effects: "...these assumptions are both critically responsible for the results and unappealingly restrictive" [Liebowitz/Margolis 1994] or "...the concept of network externality has, in important respects, been improperly modeled, incorrectly supported and inappropriately applied" [Liebowitz/Margolis 1995a]. Common simplifications are:

- There is no distinction between direct and indirect network effects in the models although it can be shown empirically [Westarp/Buxmann/Weitzel/König 1999] and analytically [Katz/Shapiro 1994] that they have different economic implications. One reason is that indirect network effects are often pecuniary externalities and therefore should not be internalized [Young 1913, Knight 1924, Ellis/Fellner 1943].
- Liebowitz/Margolis (1994, 1995a) and recently Katz/Shapiro (1994) have distinguished between network effects and network externalities. The latter, in accordance with the traditional literature on economics, are characterized by the inability of market participants to internalize these effects. Although an individual actor is not likely to internalize the effect on others of his joining the network when adopting particular standards, in sponsored networks there is no obstacle in principle to prevent a network owner internalizing these effects. In contrast to the problem of internalizing network externalities, the problem of choosing the right network has been the focus of most literature on network externality. Under positive effects, only a monopoly network consisting of the whole population is efficient. Thus, corresponding to the literature on conventional externalities, it is not the relative but the total level of network activity that is affected by the difference between private and social values.
- If optimum networks under network externalities are monopolies, "all networks are too small". This hypothesis only holds where there are constant or falling costs when adding new members to a network. The costs of network size are ignored in almost all models. Thus, even with traditional definitions of network effects, a natural monopoly is not a compulsory social optimum. Instead, there can be optimum network sizes smaller than the entire population and different standards can coexist.

- Besides failing to consider the possibility of an increasing marginal cost of network size, the proposition of indefinitely increasing positive network effects is problematic. If network effects were exhaustible, multiple networks could coexist. Even though IT might be less subject to the physical limitations concomitant with the law of diminishing returns, there might be organizational or managerial problems which would restrain optimal network size [Radner 1992].
- Another limiting assumption is that of similar and actor-independent valuation of networks and the growth of network effects. Heterogeneity can have substantial impact on the evaluation of different networks as well as on the value assigned to new actors. For example, a close colleague of an engineer will add more value to the engineer's network than a sociologist from China. Heterogeneous preferences increase the chance of the efficient coexistence of networks.

The standardization model and the diffusion model described in the following sections serve as first steps towards addressing some of the problems mentioned above by considering microeconomic decision-making by actors embedded in individual informational and communicational environments, the structural determinants of diffusion in networks, and by providing the basis for agent-based simulation models representing real-life actors. This is a foundation for future research on developing and evaluating coordination designs from the perspective of both technology users and vendors.

The Standardization Problem: A Basic Model

The standardization models are a first step towards addressing the drawbacks discussed in the previous section. While modeling basically the same phenomenon, i.e. technology choice under increasing returns, the standardization models were developed to consider:

- individual decision-making, i.e. the particular informational and economical environment of all network actors, especially their heterogeneous costs and benefits and the information sets available
- clear direct network effects, i.e. explicit and separate indirect dependencies will be added in future versions to explicitly analyze their implications
- applicability to real-world problems, i.e. the model as well as its software implementation should be adjustable to both particular problem instances incorporating empirical data as well as generalized networks

Thus, in order to incorporate the individuality of incentives and disincentives in terms of standards adoption (i.e. network participation), an individual valuation of network effects and network costs is crucial. The basic concept of the standardization models is described below.

The Basic Concept

While the use of IT standards can lead to direct savings resulting from decreased communication costs due to cheaper and faster communication, standards often produce more strategic benefits and allow the realization of further savings potential. In short, avoiding media discontinuities eliminates errors and costs. In addition, standardization can enhance the exchange of information so that more and better information can be exchanged between communications partners. Because information provides the foundation for any decision, better information implies better decisions. Economically, this is represented as an increase in information value. On the other hand, standardization produces costs for hardware, software, switching, and introduction or training – in short, standardization costs. Furthermore, the interdependence between the individual decisions to standardize occasioned by network externalities can yield coordination costs of agreeing with market partners on a single standard. More generally, coordination costs embody the costs of developing and implementing a network-wide communications base comprised of a specific constellation of standards which considers the individual, heterogeneous interests of all actors. More precisely, these include the cost of time, personnel, data gathering and processing, and control and incentive systems. Depending upon the context, these standardization costs can vary widely.

Communication between actors can be described as a network. A communications network is a directed graph without isolated nodes. The nodes represent the communications partners (**i**) (e.g. human, machine, firm), characterized by their ability to process, save and transfer information.[2] The network edges represent the communications relationships. In the standardization models, the nodes of a network represent the costs of standardization (K_i) for the respective network actors **i** while the edges show the cost of their communications relations (c_{ij}) with their respective partners that could be saved in case of standardization. These costs include the above-mentioned cost of information exchange, as well as opportunity cost of suboptimal decisions. Because information provides the foundation for decisions in all areas of the firm, better information implies better decisions. From an economic perspective, this can be seen as an increase in the value of information. Cost reductions can be realized only when both communicating nodes **i** and **j** have introduced the same or a compatible standard. This does not mean that no costs whatsoever occur for the transfer of information when both nodes are standardized. Rather, the c_{ij} can be interpreted as the difference between the information

---

2 Note that in previous publications about the network diffusion models which will be introduced in the next section, "i" denotes not network agents but is the index used for products: $i \in \{1, ..., v\}$: For integration purposes, in this paper i denotes agents and q products.

costs before (c_{ij}^{b}) and after (c_{ij}^{a}) standardization along the respective edge, so that $c_{ij}^{b} - c_{ij}^{a} = c_{ij}$. With explicit regard to changes in the information value before (w_{ij}^{b}) and after (w_{ij}^{a}) standardization, the information costs savings potential resulting from standardization can be derived from the equation: $c_{ij} = c_{ij}^{b} - c_{ij}^{a} + w_{ij}^{a} - w_{ij}^{b}$. Thus, the decision problem arises which nodes should be equipped with which standard. In our model, there is a tradeoff between the node-related costs of implementing a standard and the edge-related savings of information costs.

The benefits of implementing a communications standard must be determined for each node i. In order to do so, the costs of standardization (i.e. node costs K_i) must be compared to the savings c_{ij} to be realized along the edges. If the savings are greater than the costs, then the standard will be implemented. The savings of the edge cost c_{ij} can only be realized, however, if the partner node j also implements this same standard, while the node costs K_i occur independently of the decision of the partner node.

In the case described in figure 1, nodes 1 and 2 have information costs c_{12} and c_{21}, respectively. If node 1 or 2 standardizes, it pays the relevant standardization costs K_1 or K_2.

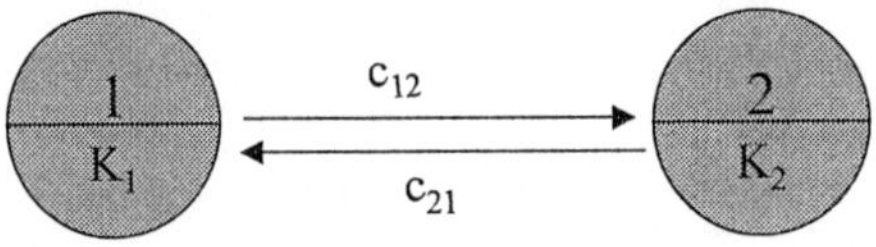

Figure 1: Costs of nodes and edges

If both nodes implement the same standard, they save c_{12} and c_{21}, respectively. If these standards are not compatible however, nodes 1 and 2 pay the costs K_1+c_{12} and K_2+c_{21}, respectively. In this simplified situation with two actors, coordination of the decision leads to a total benefit of $(c_{12}+c_{21}) - (K_1+K_2)$ and prevents the firms from paying standardization costs without realizing cost savings. The more actors involved and the more different standards available, the more difficult this agreement becomes and the less likely the coincidental, completely uncoordinated implementation of a favorable constellation of standards becomes.

From the perspective of the entire network, standardization is advantageous when total savings on information costs exceed aggregate standardization costs. This approach implicitly applies a collective or centralized utility function as a measure of the quality of decisions. We refer to the standardization problem from the perspective of a central decision-making unit (e.g. the state or a parent firm, credited with the aggregate results) as the *centralized standardization problem.* In those cases in which autonomous actors make standardization decisions and are credited individually with the results and responsibility for the effects of these decisions however, this collective measure at the aggregate level of the entire network is unsuitable. The optimization of the individual objectives of each actor with respect to the implementation of communication standards in the absence of a central, controlling unit is described by the *decentralized standardization problem.* Both approaches describe extreme perspectives in the consideration of coordination mechanisms, providing the basis for examination and evaluation of various hybrid forms of coordination. For a more detailed introduction to the models see Buxmann/Weitzel/König (1999).

A Standardization Model for Centrally Coordinated Networks

In centrally coordinated networks, a first-best solution for any given network can be determined using the mixed integer problem formulation in Equation 1. The binary indicative variable x_i takes on a value of 1 if node i is standardized and 0 if not (no investment). If i is standardized (i.e. x_i=1), then standardization costs K_i occur. The standardization costs for the entire network are described by $\sum_{i=1}^{n} K_i \; x_i$. The binary variable y_{ij} equals 0 if both nodes i and j are standardized (x_i=1 $\wedge$ x_j=1). Then, and only then, can the information costs on the edge <ij> be saved.

$$OF = \sum_{i=1}^{n} K_i \; x_i + \sum_{i=1}^{n} \sum_{\substack{j=1 \\ j \neq i}}^{n} c_{ij} \; y_{ij} \quad \rightarrow \quad Min! \qquad (1)$$

$$\text{s.t.:} \quad x_i + x_j \geq 2 - M \; y_{ij} \qquad \forall \; i, j; \; i \neq j \qquad (2)$$

$$x_i, x_j, y_{ij} \quad \in \quad \{0,1\} \qquad \forall \; i, j; \; i \neq j \qquad (3)$$

Equation 1: The basic standardization model in centralized networks

Equation 1.1 describes the costs of a standardization decision. For $x_i = 1$ <u>and</u> $x_j = 1$, the restriction 1.2 in combination with equation 1.1 requires that $y_{ij} = 0$. More precisely, equation 1.2 requires the indicative variable y_{ij} to take on a value of 1 for $x_i+x_j < 2$. If $x_i+x_j = 2$, meaning bilateral standardization, $y_{ij} = 0$ because of the objective function 1.1. For a multi-period multi-standard extension of the centralized standardization model see Buxmann (1996).

The centralized model is based on the assumption that all agency or coordination costs (data, complexity, and implementation problems [Westarp/Weitzel/Buxmann/König 2000]) are resolved (at zero cost) and that there is a central manager who can determine and implement the optimum result network-wide. Its purpose is to serve as the first-best benchmark solution for the evaluation of standardization strategies under realistic information assumptions.

A Standardization Model for Decentrally Coordinated Networks

Given autonomous actors and the availability of a realistic information set, the *decentralized standardization problem* is mainly a problem of anticipating the standardization decisions of others. Each node i needs to anticipate the behavior of the other nodes j (j=1,...,n; i≠j). It is assumed that all nodes i know the various standardization costs occurring in every other node j and the costs along the edges which directly affect them, i.e. the information costs c_{ij} which they themselves pay and the costs c_{ji} assumed by their direct communications partners. Further data, like the information costs between other nodes, are unknown, as estimation is either too inaccurate or too expensive. Assuming that all other nodes standardize, so that savings of c_{ij} are certain, actor i will also standardize when Equation 2 statement is true (the notation is slightly different from that used in our earlier papers in order to facilitate the fusion with the diffusion model introduced in the next chapter):

$$\sum_{\substack{j=1 \\ j\neq i}}^{n} c_{ij} - K_i > 0 \, .$$

Equation 2: Standardization condition

However, actor i does not know the strategies pursued by nodes j beforehand, and vice versa. We assume that the actors are risk-neutral decision-makers.

$$E\,[U(i)] = \sum_{\substack{j=1 \\ j\neq i}}^{n} prob_{ij}\; c_{ij} - K_i$$

Equation 3: The expected utility of standardization in decentralized networks

$prob_{ij}$ describes the probability with which actor i believes that node j will standardize.[3] If E[U(i)] > 0 then actor i will standardize. If actor i were certain of the behavior of his communications partners, $prob_{ij}$ would take on a value of 0 or 1. The decentralized model, however, implies uncertainty. Given our assumptions about the availability of data, p_{ij} can be heuristically computed as follows. Every edge <ij> with costs c_{ij} contributes to the amortization of the standardization costs of the incidental node i. Because the standardization costs K_j and the information costs c_{ji} are the only costs regarding j known to node i, actor i can assume that the

[3] Note that $prob_{ij}$ is used in this article since p denotes price in the diffusion model.

edge <ji> is representative of all of j's edges. Combining all assumed data, node i can then develop the following probability estimate $prob_{ij}$ for the probability of standardization in node j by attempting to imitate j's decision making behavior: $prob_{ij} = \frac{c_{ji}(n-1) - K_j}{c_{ji}(n-1)}$

The numerator describes the net savings possible through the standardization for node j, assuming that all nodes standardize and that the edge <ji> is representative of all of node j's communications relationships (best case). The denominator normalizes the fraction for non-negative K_j as a value from 0 to 1. Should the fraction have a value less than 0, that is c_{ji} (n-1) < K_j, then $p_{ij} = 0$ holds. This suggests equation 4

$$E[U(i)] = \sum_{\substack{j=1 \\ j \neq i}}^{n} \frac{c_{ji}(n-1) - K_j}{c_{ji}(n-1)} c_{ij} - K_i = \sum_{\substack{j=1 \\ j \neq i}}^{n} prob_{ij}\, c_{ij} - K_i$$

Equation 4: Anticipating partners` behavior

As long as the individual actors are unable to influence the standardization decisions of their communications partners, they can do no more ex ante than estimate the probability that their partners will standardize. *Ex post* of course, the communications costs either remain or are no longer applicable, but the situation of uncertainty described here results from the assumption of limited knowledge of available data. The decentralized model allows the prediction of standardization behavior in a network, thereby creating a basis for predicting the effects of various concepts of coordination. Such measures for influencing the decision to introduce standards also generally apply to influencing the development of expectations regarding the future spread of standards (installed base) or to forms of cooperation which would allow partners to jointly reap the profits of standardization through the partial internalization of network effects.

Centrally versus Decentrally Coordinated Networks

A simulation demonstrates the different coordination implications. For a network of twenty actors, c_{ij} and K_i were randomly generated. The average density of the network is 0.3, i.e. in this case the average number of direct communication links of an actor is about six. Over 20 periods, all actors decided whether to adopt a standard or not. The diffusion results for alternative expected values of standardization costs for $E(c_{ij})=1000$ and $\sigma=200$ are shown in Figure 2.

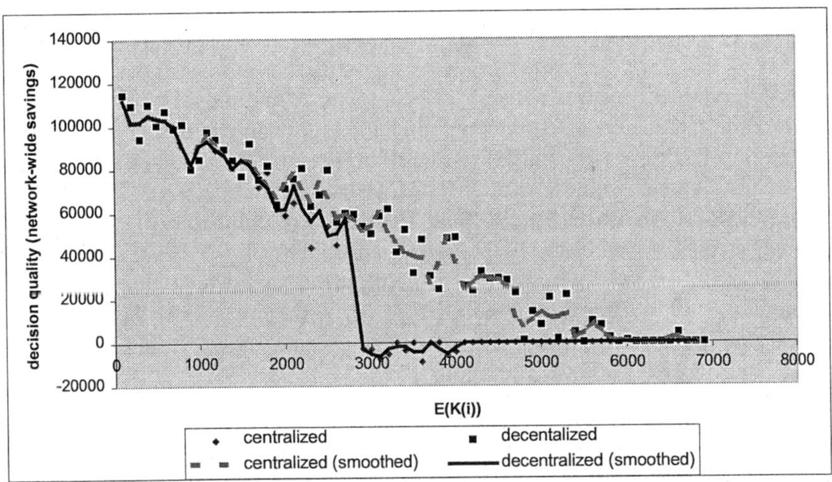

Figure 2: Centralized versus decentralized networks

Cost savings for the entire network resulting from the decision to standardize are graphed against alternated expected values $E[K_i]$ on the abscissa. In keeping with the above assertions, the graph shows that the results in decentrally coordinated networks deviate from those of centralized coordination. We called this interesting yet intuitive result *the standardization gap*. Obviously, centralized coordination implies superior decision quality, given that all the coordination costs of overcoming information and incentive asymmetries are zero. For high standardization costs, neither in centrally nor decentrally coordinated networks is standardization advantageous. With decreasing K_i the propensity to standardize increases; yet decentral coordination, of course, still leaves room for wrong decisions: either advantageous standardization does not happen (start-up problem) or the ex-ante assumptions proved to be wrong and an agent does not find enough standardizing partners ex-post. The reason the standardization gap only closes slowly even for very low standardization costs is losses in early diffusion periods that cannot be compensated for later, since it is impossible to get better results than those from the centralized algorithms.

The standardization gap, i.e. the perpendicular distance between the curves in figure 2, determines a critical value for the costs of coordination above which a centralized solution is no longer advantageous (see Westarp/Weitzel/Buxmann/König (1999) for further details). As a next step, we plan to extend the models towards a multi-period multi-standard framework as a workbench for developing decision support mechanisms for standardization problems, e.g. in EDI networks or intranets. The models will then be used to evaluate different coordination designs aimed at closing the standardization gap.

Network Diffusion Model of the Software Market

Existing models of positive network effects focus on individual buying decisions, the marketing strategies of competing vendors, supply and demand equilibria, and welfare implications. They mostly use equilibrium analysis to explain phenomena such as the start-up problem (Rohlfs 1974, Oren/Smith 1981, Katz/Shapiro 1985, 1994, Wiese 1990, Besen/Farell 1994, Economides/Himmelberg 1995), market failure (Farrell/Saloner 1985, 1986, Katz/Shapiro 1986, 1992, 1994, Gröhn 1999), instability (also called "tippiness") of network effect markets (Arthur 1989, 1996, Besen/Farell 1994, Farrell/Saloner 1985, Katz/Shapiro 1994, Shapiro/Varian 1998), and path dependency (David 1985, Arthur 1989, Besen/Farell 1994, Katz/Shapiro 1994, Liebowitz/Margolis 1995).

While the traditional models contribute greatly to the understanding of a wide variety of general problems associated with the diffusion of network effect markets, a closer look reveals various deficiencies. The examination of network effects is carried out in a rather general way. Furthermore, most of the approaches (e.g. Rohlfs 1974, Katz/Shapiro 1985, Farrell/ Saloner 1986, Arthur 1989, Wiese 1990, Church/Gandal 1996, Oren/Smith/Wilson 1982, Dhebar/Oren 1985, 1986) only focus on the installed base of the whole market [Westarp 2000]. The specific interaction of potential adopters within their individual communication network environment is neglected. As a result, they fail to explain the variety of diffusion courses in today's dynamic software markets. Important phenomena which cannot be explained or even described using the analytical "installed base" are the following:

- the coexistence of different products despite strong network effects (e.g. heterogeneous EDI and ERP markets [Westarp/Buxmann/Weitzel/König 1999])
- the appearance of small but stable clusters of users of a certain solution despite the fact that the competition dominates the rest of the market (e.g. Oracle Applications in the SAP dominated German market, [Westarp/Buxmann/ Weitzel/König 1999])
- the fact that strong players in communication networks force other participants to use a certain solution (e.g. 3Com, Karstadt, Woolworth, Deutsche Bank, and Heraeus [Westarp/Weitzel/Buxmann/König 1999, Westarp 2000]).

In the following, a simulation model of an agent-based computational economy will be developed which addresses some of the important requirements outlined above. Of course, it will take further research efforts to resolve all the general drawbacks of the network effect theory. Nevertheless, the following model can be seen as a first step in the direction of developing an interdisciplinary framework for the modeling of software markets which deals with the relevant real world phenomena.

The adoption decision is modeled discretely, meaning that it is not rational to buy or use more than one unit of the same product or even of different products in the same category. This is an assumption which makes sense especially for information goods like software or telecommunication products. As confirmed by the empirical results, the network effects in the utility function are modeled only as being dependent on decision behavior of the direct communication network of the potential buyer and not on the installed base. This also recognizes the bounded rationality of real-world actors. Therefore, in contrast to the installed base of traditional models, a distinction is made between relevant and irrelevant network effects.

One main hypothesis is that the (macro) dynamics of software markets as multi-actor systems depend not only on the individual (micro) decisions of the participants but also on personal neighborhood structures reflecting the institutional patterns of networks. The influence of various determinants on the diffusion process of network effect products such as price, heterogeneity of preferences, and connectivity, and topology of networks can be tested.

Basic Model

The basis of our simulation is a simple model of the buying decision in network effect markets. The terminology is similar to the model of Katz/Shapiro (1985), but we will interpret the terms differently. Let r denote the stand-alone utility of a network effect product (i.e. the willingness to pay even if no other users in the market exist) and $f(x)$ denote the additional network effect benefits (i.e. the value of the externality when x is the number of other adopters). For reasons of simplification we assume that all network participants have the same function $f(x)$, i.e. their evaluation of network benefits is identical. We also assume that the network effects increase linearly, i.e. $f(x)$ increases by a certain amount with every new user. The willingness to pay for a software product can then be described by the term $r+f(x)$. Let p be the price or the cost of a certain software product/solution, then a consumer buys the solution if $r+f(x)-p>0$. In case of v competing products in a market, the consumer buys the product with the maximum surplus in cases where this exceeds 0:

$$\max_{q \in \{1,\ldots,v\}} \left\{ r_q + f(x_q) - p_q \right\}$$

Equation 5: Objective function for the network diffusion model

If the surplus is negative for all q then no product is bought. Equation 5 implies that only one product is used at the same time. This is a common assumption in many network effect models [e.g. Wiese 1990, 10]. It also seems to make sense for the software market since it would be rather unusual to buy and use two different software products with the same functionality (e.g. Microsoft Office and Lotus Smart Suite) at the same time.

Unlike most of the existing models for markets with network effects, we want to conduct simulations by modeling the software market as a relational diffusion network. In such networks the buying decision is not influenced by the installed base within the whole network, but rather by the adoption decisions within the personal communication network. The significance of this for buying decisions can be demonstrated simply by the following example. Figure 3 shows the communication network environment of consumer *A* who wants to buy a software product that serves his individual needs.

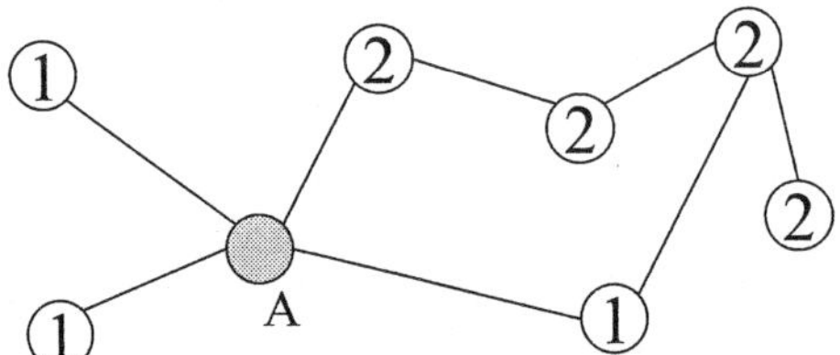

Figure 3: Communication network environment of consumer A

There is a choice of two products (1 and 2) in the market. We assume that both products are free and have identical functionality so that the buying decision only depends on the network effects. Applying traditional models that base the decision whether to adopt an innovation on the size of the installed base, consumer *A* would buy product 2 since the installed base with 4 existing adopters is larger. If we use the relational network approach and therefore only focus on the relevant communication partners of *A*, the consumer will decide to buy product 1 since the majority of his direct communication partners uses this solution.

Of course, this example is of a rather general nature. In the following, we will prove the importance of personal network structure systematically by conducting simulations. Additionally, we will analyze how varying price and the heterogeneity of individual preferences influence the diffusion processes of competing software.

Simulation Design

Our simulations are based on the assumption that network structure, consumer preferences and the prices of the software are constant during the diffusion process. All the results presented below are based on a network size of 1,000 consumers. We also tested our simulations for other network sizes without significant difference in the general results. We conducted 6,000 simulation runs, 3,000 each for low-price and for high-price software, respectively. All entities of our model were implemented in JAVA 1.1 and their behavior was simulated on a discrete event basis.

Network Structure. First, the n consumers are distributed randomly on the unit square, i.e. their x- and y-coordinates are sampled from a uniform distribution over [0; 1]. In a second step, the network's structure is generated by either choosing the c closest neighbors measured by Euclidean distance (*close* topology) or selecting c

neighbors randomly from all n-1 possible neighbors (*random* topology). This distinction is made to support the central hypothesis of our paper, namely: Ceteris paribus (e.g. for the same network *size* and *connectivity*) the *specific* neighborhood structure of the network strongly influences the diffusion processes.

The graphs in Figure 4 give examples of randomly sampled cases of the *close* topology (exemplary for 100 consumers and a connectivity c of two, five and ten respectively). As we see, a low number of neighbors may lead to a network structure which is not fully connected, i.e. its consumers can only experience network externalities within their local cluster. The standardization processes in individual clusters cannot diffuse to any consumer from a different cluster. These "subpopulations" evolve in total separation, and it is therefore rather unlikely that all the isolated regions will evolve to the same global standard. With increasing connectivity (five or ten neighbors), the chances that a network is not connected become rather small, i.e. any sub-group of consumers, agreeing on a specific product, may "convince" their direct neighbor clusters to join them. The "domino effects" might finally reach every consumer even in the most remote area of the network. However, the number of "dominos" that have to fall before a standard which emerged far away in a certain area of the network reaches the local environment of an actor and therefore influences the decision to adopt is typically much higher than in the corresponding graph with *random* topology. Speaking more formally, the average length of the shortest path connecting two arbitrarily chosen vertices of the graph (i.e. the number of neighbors you have to traverse) is smaller for the same connectivity if the graph has a random topology.

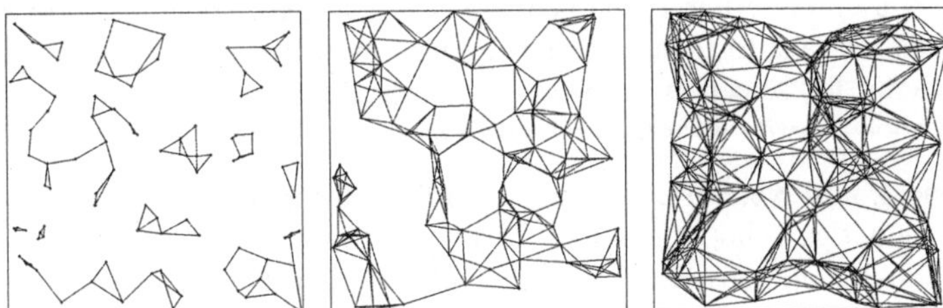

Figure 4: Typical networks with two, five or ten closest neighbors (close topology)

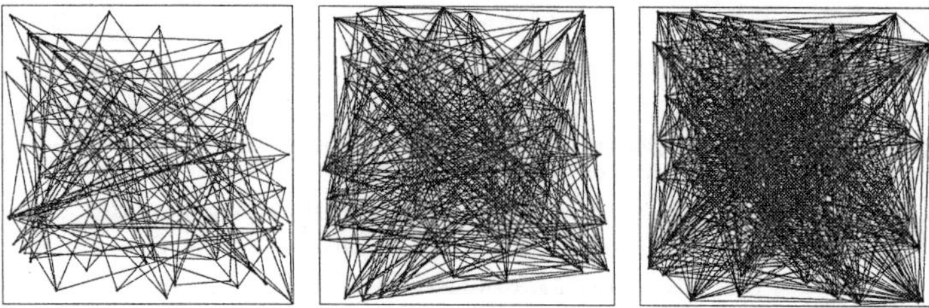

Figure 5: Typical networks with two, five or ten random neighbors (random topology)

Figure 5 shows the graphs with the same connectivity (2, 5, and 10) but *random* topology. The visual impression of a higher connectivity (which is an illusion) results from the fact that we selected "neighbors" to represent an asymmetric relation. That is, when consumer x receives positive external effects from a neighbor y, it is unlikely in the *random* topology that vice versa, y also receives positive effects from x. Of course, within the *close* topology symmetric neighborhood is more common, meaning that there is a higher probability that if y is the closest neighbor from the perspective of x, at the same time x is also the closest neighbor from the perspective of y. In this case the two links are plotted on top of each other and that is why the close topology graphs look less connected.

Of course, most real-world networks represent an intermediate version of these extreme types, but since the costs of bridging geographical distance become less and less important the more information technology evolves, the tendency is clear. Electronic markets will tend to resemble the *random* type of structure (since we select our partners by other criteria than geographical distance), while in markets for physical goods (or face to face communication) physical proximity is still a very important factor for selecting business partners and therefore, the *close* topology will be a good substitute for the real world network structure.

Preferences, Prices, and Network Effects. Regardless of topology, in our simulation, every consumer can choose from all existing software products and knows all their prices. Initially, all consumers are (randomly) equipped with one software product, which may be considered to be their "legacy software" that is already installed and does not incur any further cost.

The direct utility that each consumer draws from the functionality of the *v* different products is then sampled from a uniform random distribution over the interval [0;*util*]. For each consumer and every software product we use the same interval. Thus, a value of *util*=0 leads to homogeneous direct preferences (of zero) while the higher the exogenously given value of *util*, the more heterogeneous the preferences of the consumers become (with respect to the different software products as well as with respect to the neighbors they communicate with).

The weight of the positive network externalities deriving from each neighbor using the same software has been set to an arbitrary (but constant) value of 10,000 (for every consumer and every run).

In order to isolate the network externalities and heterogeneity of consumer preferences from other effects, we decided to fix all prices for the software products to a constant value and all marketing expenditures to zero for the simulations presented here, i.e. consumers decide solely upon potential differences of *direct utility* and the *adoption choices of their neighbors* (see term (1)).

Dynamics of the Decision Process. In each iteration of the diffusion, every consumer decides whether to keep his old software or whether to buy a new one based on the decision rationale described above (see term (1)). The old software is assumed to be discarded once a new product is bought, i.e. it can provide neither the deciding consumer with direct utility nor the neighbors with positive externalities anymore. The adoption decisions are made in a sequential order, i.e. all consumers may always be assumed to have correct knowledge about the software their neighbors are currently running. Although we have not yet established a formal proof, for our simulations this decision process always converged towards an equilibrium in which no actor wanted to revise his decision anymore. We did not experience any oscillation.

Results of Simulating the Diffusion Process

First, a total number of 3,000 independent simulations were run with 1,000 consumers and 10 different software products until an equilibrium was reached. The distribution reached in this equilibrium was then condensed into the Herfindahl[4] index used in industrial economics to measure market concentration (e.g. [Tirole 1993]). In the following diagrams, every small circle represents one observation.

The top diagram in figure 4 illustrates the strong correlation (0.756) of connectivity and equilibrium concentration for *close topology*. Despite this strong correlation, it can clearly be seen that even in networks with 200 neighbors per consumer (i.e. a connectivity of 200) the chances that one product will completely dominate the market are still very low. For *random topologies* (figure 4, bottom) an even stronger correlation (0.781) is obtained. Note that all the correlations illustrated in this paper are significant on the 0.01 level.

Note that the scale of connectivity is extremely different in the two graphs of Figure 6. It is obvious that the likelihood of total diffusion of only one software product is very high in a random topology network even for very low connectivity. Since the diagrams simply plot all circles on top of each other, the visual impression of the very frequent observation of a 1.0 concentration (in the top right corner of the graphs) is distorted. The results will become visually clearer in the 3-dimensional graph of figure 7.

---

4 The Herfindahl index is calculated by summing up the squared market share for each vendor. If all market shares are evenly distributed among our ten alternative products, we get the minimal concentration index of 10*(0.1)^2 = 0.1 while we get a maximal concentration index of 1*1^2+9*0^2 = 1 if the diffusion process converges to all consumers using one identical software product.

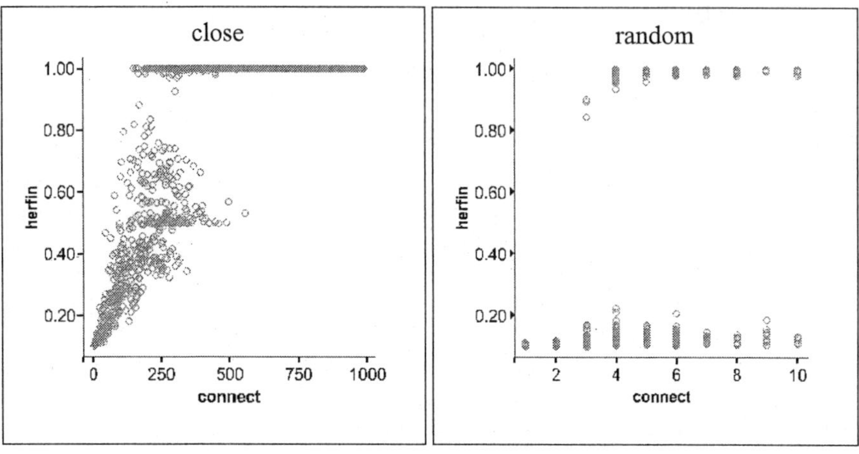

Figure 6: Strong correlation of connectivity and concentration for close and random topologies

In Figure 7 we additionally consider the *heterogeneity of preferences* in the analysis as a third dimension. We did not find any significant dependency of the sampled equilibria on this factor for *close topologies* (Figure 7, left). However, this changes if we sample networks with *random topologies*. Here we found a slight but significant negative correlation of heterogeneity and concentration (-0.141).

Note that the axis for connectivity is again scaled from 1 to 10 neighbors in the bottom diagrams in Figure 6 and Figure 7. It can clearly be seen that for 10 neighbors per consumer (1% of the total population) it is already almost certain that only one product will finally take over the whole market (Figure 7, right).

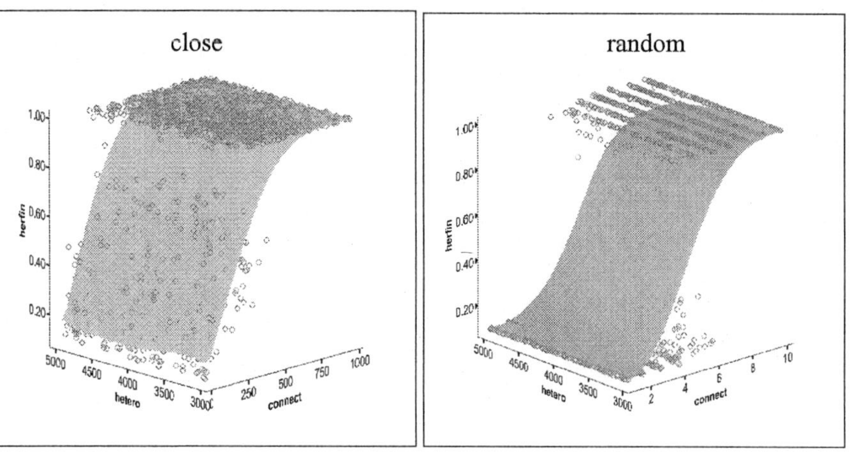

Figure 7: Equilibria in close topology and random topology networks

Comparing this with the top graph where the probability of reaching a concentration higher than 0.2 is almost zero for the same connectivity *strongly* supports our hypothesis that for a given connectivity the indirect domino effects are much stronger for *random* topology networks and thus the diffusion process shows much higher tendencies towards standardization. To test this statistically, we ran a Kolmogorov-Smirnov test [Hartung 1989, 520-524] rejecting the hypothesis that the concentration indices obtained for close and random topologies follow the same distribution on a significance level better than 0.0005 (KS-Z of 2.261). This result substantiates our findings statistically.

A second interesting phenomenon can be seen in the fact that, although the mean concentration for a *random* topology networks of connectivity 5 is about 0.5, there are hardly any equilibria with concentration indices between 0.2 and 0.8, i.e. either the diffusion process leads to one strong product or many products will survive. This is different for *close* topology models where intermediate solutions with two or three strong products can be stable equilibria, obviously being the result of subgroups of consumers (with strong intra-group communication and fewer links to other groups) collectively resisting external pressure to switch their selected product.

Summarizing our findings so far, we display four typical patterns for diffusion processes towards an equilibrium depending on network topology and heterogeneity of preferences (Figure 8). The x-axis shows the number of iterations with every consumer deciding once per iteration. The y-axis illustrates the market shares of the 10 software products. Note that, as discussed above, the *random / heterogeneous* case is one of the rare intermediate cases (in Figure 7, right, it can be seen that there are hardly any equilibria for a connectivity of 5 and a concentration between 0.1 and 1.0).

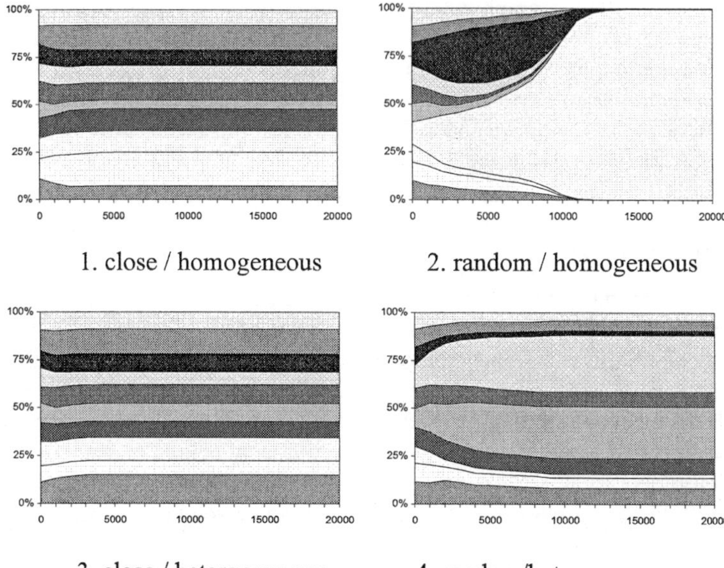

Figure 8: Typical diffusion processes for 1,000 consumers and connectivity of 5 depending on topology and heterogeneity of preferences

The influence of topology on the diffusion of innovations in networks is obvious. While *close* topology is generally the basis for a greater diversity of products since cluster or groups of consumers can be relatively independent from diffusion processes in the rest of the market, *random* topology tends to market dominance of one or few products.

The following list summarizes the results of this and further simulations based on the network diffusion model described above (see [Westarp 2000] or [Wendt/ Westarp/König 2000]):

- *Connectivity* was used to model the source of *personal network exposure* within the diffusion process. It is shown to have a very strong positive influence on market concentration in the low price segment. This correlation weakens the higher the price segment.
- *Heterogeneity of preferences* was modeled by the stand-alone utility. Demand for variety leads to less concentration in high price markets for close and random topologies. In the low price segment, there is no significant dependency between heterogeneity and market concentration for close topologies, but a slight significant negative correlation for random topologies.
- The higher the *price segment* the more diversity of products is found due to the higher switching costs.

- *Closeness* was used to model Intra-group pressure. This parameter is shown to correlate negatively with concentration, meaning that although this pressure enforces group conformity, it also inhibits inter-group conformity. The influence of the network's *topology* on the diffusion of innovations in networks is obvious. While *close* topology is generally the basis for a greater diversity of products (since clusters or groups of consumers may decide relatively independently of diffusion processes in the rest of the market), *random* topology tends to produce the dominance of one or few products.

- *Relative radiality* correlates negatively with closeness and therefore correlates positively with concentration. A low radiality can be interpreted as high intra-group pressure leading to intra-group or -cluster conformity and at the same time to inter-group heterogeneity.

- *Opinion leadership* (position and power) has been modeled by centrality and heterogeneity of node sizes (the latter was used to represent the strength of influence on others). The simulations show a positive correlation between centrality and concentration, showing that some central participants can significantly influence the diffusion process. Differences in power within the network did not have any effect on concentration unless it was combined with centrality.

Fusion

Although using a different notation, the strong similarities of the standardization model and the diffusion model are obvious: The stand-alone utility r_q of the consumer's utility function $\max_{q \in \{1,\ldots,v\}} \left\{ r_q + f(x_q) - p_q \right\}$ may directly be deducted from the price which then corresponds to the individual standardization cost:

$$\underbrace{-(p_q - r_q) + f(x_q)}_{\text{Diffusion}} = \underbrace{x_q \left[\sum_{q=1}^{v} K_q - \sum_{j=1}^{n} c_{ij}\, prob_{ijq} \right]}_{\text{Standardization}} \rightarrow \max_q$$

Equation 6: Decision functions of the standardization and diffusion models

The network benefits of the network diffusion model, however, are modeled as a function of the number of partners using the same product, which is furthermore restricted to being linear and homogeneous for all consumers. In contrast to that, the standardization model allows for differentiating these benefits c_{ij} (while naming them "cost savings") to be a function of the individual link from agent *i* to a specific partner *j*.

Although whenever there is empirical data available representing the bilateral real-world network benefits, the diffusion model should account for this data, we did not experience any significant changes in our diffusion processes when we decided to sample the bilateral benefits derived from a uniform distribution [5000; 15000] instead of taking a fixed value of 10000 units (see above).

A complication in the integration of both models arises from the fact that the decentralized decision function described in section *The Standardization Problem: A Basic Model* cannot be applied to a multi-product world as used in the diffusion model: Recall that agent i estimates the likelihood of agent j implementing the standard to be

$prob_{ij} = \max\left(\frac{c_{ji}(n_j - 1) - K_j}{c_{ji}(n_j - 1)}\right)$. We could extend this estimate to be a function of the product q leading to $prob_{ij} = \max\left(\frac{c_{ji}(n_j - 1) - K_{jq}}{c_{ji}(n_j - 1)}, 0\right)$,

where K_{jq} is the respective cost of buying and implementing product q. Unfortunately, since the other terms do not vary with q, the probability always becomes maximal for the current product used by agent j, since the term K_{jq} equals zero for this product. Thus, every actor expects all his neighbors to be using the current product during the next period, which is exactly the same assumption we have already used in the diffusion model.

The question of whether an agent can do better than this, strongly depends on our informational assumptions:

- Actor i only knows his own cost and benefits and all bilateral cost savings / benefits relating to his direct neighbors (c_{ij} and c_{ji}). Data about other actors' cost and benefits are considered to be unknown since gathering them is too expensive and estimating them is too imprecise.
- Decision making of other actors is unknown ex ante but observable on an ex post basis (incomplete but perfect information).

Up to now, the second assumption of ex post observability has been furthermore restricted to the actors' direct neighbors. If we relax this restriction, i.e. assume that each actor i also knows the identity and the product used by the direct neighbors of his own neighbors (called his 2nd degree neighbors), we may use their current endowment for a more precise forecast of actor i's direct neighbors' decisions.

One possible way to do this is to replace actor i's decision criterion "installed number of product q used in my direct neighborhood" by "expected number of product q used in my direct neighborhood" and trying to approximate this number indirectly by the observable "installed number of product q used in my 2nd degree neighborhood", of course normalized to the number of direct neighbors, since we will not receive ten times the positive network gains, even when each of our ten neighbors has ten distinct neighbors himself. Formally, we may express this expected "installed base" of an actor *i* by

$$E_i(base_q) = \sum_{j \in neighbors(i)} prob_{ijq}$$

with

$$prob_{ijq} = \frac{\sum_{k \in neighbors(j)} x_{kq}}{|neighbors(j)|}$$

with x_{kq} being the Boolean variable indicating whether actor *k* currently uses product *q*.

The decision of each actor is then made as before according to the decision function used in the diffusion model.

The following figure shows that this anticipative behavior (**anticip=true**) from the adapted decentralized standardization model leads to a significantly higher expected market concentration than in the original network diffusion model. This effect is of course stronger in close topology networks, since random topology networks already inhibited a strong tendency towards market concentration with the non-anticipative decision criterion. This observation is not very surprising if we consider the question of choosing an operating system for your new PC: Although you may run into some trouble by installing a Windows 2000 workstation if your company still runs NT 4.0 servers, it may be wise to do so if you observe your company's suppliers and customers switching to Windows 2000 and thus expect your system administrator to be urged to follow them soon.

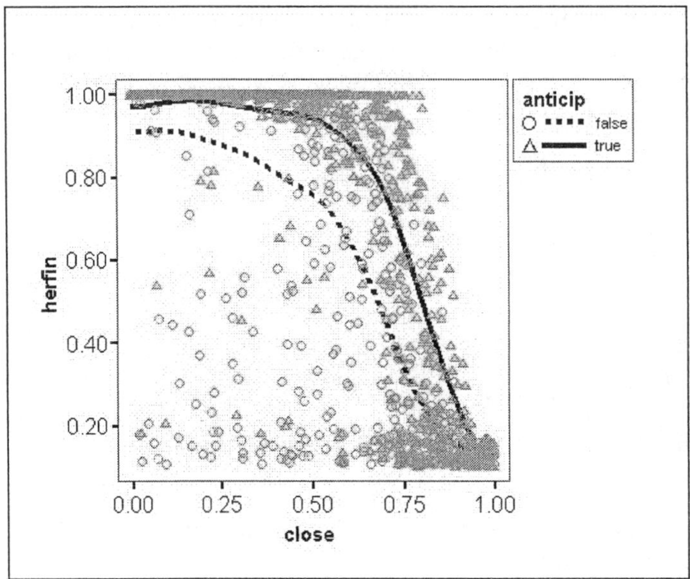

Figure 9: The effect of anticipative consumer behavior on market concentration

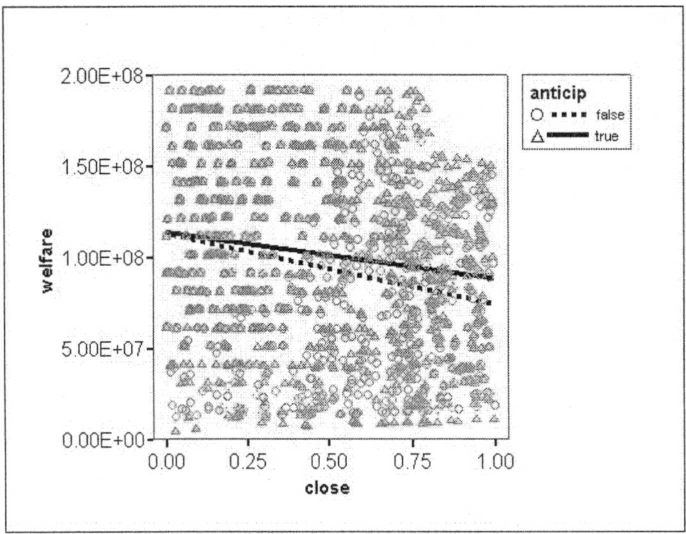

Figure 10: The effect of anticipative consumer behavior on consumer welfare

Figure 10 also illustrates that this anticipative behavior really pays off compared to the ex-post observation of direct neighbors: the figure shows the difference in the cumulative benefit to all consumers measured by the aggregated utility (direct and external effects) minus the total cost of buying the products and maybe buying a new product in the next period, since we have to revise the decision made in the last period.

Open Questions and Further Research

With the integration of the standardization and diffusion models, more sophisticated analysis of coordination problems subject to network effects might contribute to achieving a deeper insight into the determinants of standardization problems. Given the importance of IT standards, software, and communication architectures, the diversity and ubiquity of network effects requires a sound theory of networks.

Promising future extensions of the framework include an analysis of anticipative behavior of a higher order and the efficiency implications of other informational assumptions. Some mechanisms could extend the information set available to any network agent to contribute to individual as well as collective welfare gains, provided information and agency costs are taken into account. In this context, using the models as a "sparring ground", bi-, tri- and multilateral (collaborative) optimization behavior and adequate mechanism designs enabling advantageous behavior can be developed, implemented and tested. Application domains suitable for testing the results are, for example, business networks such as EDI networks in different industries, corporate intra- or extranets, supply chains etc.

One of the most frequently discussed questions still remains open: does the supposed ubiquity of network effects and their particular presence in IT markets imply more regulation in these markets, since markets are said to fail under network effects? As discussed in the section *Common Drawbacks in Network Effect Models*, a sophisticated theory of networks explaining real world phenomena (among others, equilibria transitions) still needs to be established. We hope to be able to contribute some building blocks to that discussion in the future.

References

Arthur, W. B. (1989): Competing technologies, increasing returns, and lock-in by historical events, in: The Economic Journal, 99 (March 1989), 116-131.

Arthur, W. B. (1996): Increasing returns and the new World of business, in: Harvard Business Review, 74 (July-August), 100-109.

Besen, S. M./Farrell, J. (1994): Choosing How to Compete: Strategies and Tactics in Standardization, Journal of Economic Perspectives, Spring 1994, 8, 117-310.

Buxmann, P. (1996): Standardisierung betrieblicher Informationssysteme, Wiesbaden 1996.

Church, J./Gandal, N. (1996): Strategic entry deterrence: Complementary products as installed base, in: European Journal of Political Economy, Vol. 12 (1996), 331-354.

David, Paul A./Greenstein, Shane (1990): The economics of compatibility standards: An introduction to recent research, in: Economics of innovation and new technology, 1, 3 - 41, 1990.

Dhebar, A./Oren, S. S. (1985): Optimal dynamic pricing for expanding networks, in: Marketing Science 4 (4), 336-351.

Dhebar, A./Oren, S. S. (1986): Dynamic nonlinear pricing in networks with interdependent demand, in: Operations Research 34 (3), 384-394.

DIN (1991), En 45020: Allgemeine Fachausdrücke und deren Definitionen betreffend Normung und damit zusammenhängende Tätigkeiten, August 1991, S. 15.

Ellis H. S. and Fellner, W. (1943). External economies and diseconomies. American Economic Review 33: 493-511.

Farrell, J./Saloner, G. (1985): Standardization, Compatibility, and Innovation, Rand Journal of Economics, Spring 1985, 16, 70-83.

Farrell, J./Saloner, G. (1986): Installed Base and Compatibility: Innovation, Product Preannouncements, and Predation, in: The American Economic Review, Vol. 76, No. 5 (December 1986), 940-955.

Farrell, J./Saloner, G. (1988): Coordination through committees and markets, in: RAND Journal of Economics, Vol. 19, No. 2 (Summer 1988), 235-252.

Hartung, J. (1989): Statistik: Lehr- und Handbuch der angewandten Statistik, München.

Hemenway, D.: Industry wide voluntary product standards, Massachusetts 1975.

Katz, M. L./Shapiro, C. (1985): Network externalities, competition, and compatibility, in: The American Economic Review, Vol. 75, No. 3 (June 1985), pp. 424-440.

Katz, M. L./Shapiro, C. (1986): Technology Adoption in the Presence of Network Externalities, Journal of Political Economy, August 1986, 94, 822-41.

Katz, M. L./Shapiro, C. (1994): Systems Competition and Network Effects, Journal of Economic Perspectives, Spring 1994, 8, 93-115.

Knight, F. H. (1924) Some fallacies in the interpretation of social cost. Quarterly Journal of Economics 38: 582-606.

Kindleberger, C. P. (1983). Standards as Public, Collective and Private Goods. Kyklos - International Review for Social Sciences, 36(3), 377-396.

Liebowitz, S. J./Margolis, S. E. (1994): Network Externality: An Uncommon Tragedy, in: The Journal of Economic Perspectives, Spring 1994, 133-150.

Liebowitz, S. J./Margolis, S. E. (1995a): Are Network Externalities A New Source of Market Failure? In: Research in Law and Economics, 1995.

Liebowitz, S. J./Margolis, S. E. (1995b): Path Dependence, Lock-In, and History, Journal of Law, Economics and Organization, April 1995, 11, 205-226.

Oren, S. S./Smith, S. A./Wilson, R. (1982): Nonlinear pricing in markets with interdependent demand., in: Marketing Science 1(3), 287-313.

Radner, R. (1992): Hierarchy: The economics of managing, in: Journal of economic literature, 30, 1382-1415.

Rohlfs, J. (1974): A theory of interdependent demand for a communications service, in: Bell Journal of Economics, 5 (1974), 16-37.

Tirole, J (1993): The theory of industrial organization, 6th ed., Cambridge, Mass.

Thum, M. (1995): Netzwerkeffekte, Standardisierung und staatlicher Regulierungsbedarf, Tübingen, 1995.

Weitzel, T./Westarp, F. v./Wendt, O. (2000): Reconsidering Network Effect Theory, in: Proceedings of the 8th European Conference on Information Systems (ECIS 2000), http://www.wiwi.uni-frankfurt.de/~westarp/publ/recon/reconsidering.pdf

Westarp, F. v. (2000): Modeling Software Markets - Empirical Analysis, Network Simulations, and Marketing Implications, Dissertation, Frankfurt.

Westarp, F. v./Buxmann, P./Weitzel, T./König, W. (1999): The Management of Software Standards in Enterprises - Results of an Empirical Study in Germany and the US, SFB 403 Working Paper, Frankfurt University, Jan. 1999, http://www.vernetzung.de/eng/b3.

Westarp, F. v./Weitzel, T./Buxmann, P./König, W. (1999): Innovationen im Bereich der B2B-Kommunikation - Fallstudien und technische Lösungen zu WebEDI, in: Steiner, M./Dittmar T./Willinsky, C.: Elektronische Dienstleistungsgesellschaft und Financial Engineering, 1999, 263-285.

Westarp, F. v./Weitzel, T./Buxmann, P./König, W. (2000): The Standardization Problem in Networks - A General Framework, in: Jakobs, K. (Hrsg.): Information Technology Standards and Standardization: A Global Perspective, 168-185.

Wiese, H. (1990): Netzeffekte und Kompatibilität, Stuttgart.

Wendt, O./Westarp, F. v./König, W. (2000): Diffusionsprozesse in Märkten mit Netzeffekten, in: Wirtschaftsinformatik, 5/2000.

Young, A. A. (1913). Pigou's Wealth and Welfare. Quarterly Journal of Economics 27: 672-86.

From QWERTY to Nuclear Power Reactors: Historic Battles for the Standard

Tim Weitzel, Falk v. Westarp

Johann Wolfgang Goethe-University
Institute of Information Systems (Wirtschaftsinformatik)
Mertonstr. 17
D 60054 Frankfurt am Main
{tweitzel|westarp}@wiwi.uni-frankfurt.de

Summary:
Key success factors in eleven historic standardization battles are discussed, among them the famous VHS versus Betamax, IBM vs. Apple or QWERTY vs. Dvorak`s keyboard design.

Keywords:
Standard, technology, innovation, success factor

Introduction

There are many popular examples of technologies defeating competing technologies for different reasons. In the 80s, vinyl was replaced by CDs which may soon be replaced by DVDs. We all use VHS video cassettes now, and most nuclear power plants operate using light-water reactors although when those technologies were new, there were a considerable number of alternatives. These are among many historical cases discussed in the literature of standardization problems [e.g. David/Greenstein 1990].

Standardization literature focuses on network effects as a predominant property of modern information and communication technologies, i.e. increasing returns to marginal technology adopters [Farrell/Saloner 1985, Katz/Shapiro 1985, Besen/Farrell 1994]. Path dependencies due to non ergodic diffusion processes of innovations under network effects imply start-up or lock-in phenomena and therefore a possibility of pareto-inferior equilibria or market failure [David 1985, Arthur 1989, Besen/Farell 1994, Katz/Shapiro 1994, Liebowitz/Margolis 1995 a+b]. Although traditional literature offers valuable insights into general macroeconomic phenomena, there are theoretical and practical drawbacks which substantially reduce the models` descriptive as well as normative powers [Weitzel/Wendt/Westarp 2000]. Recent theoretical approaches addressing some of these shortcomings incorporate structural determinants of networks and put more emphasis on the institutional embeddedness of network actors and the particularities of individual decision making under conditions of uncertainty [Wendt/Westarp 2000, Westarp/Wendt 2000, Westarp/Weitzel/Buxmann/König 2000].

In contrast to the theoretical approach to analyzing diffusion processes of standards presented in Weitzel/Wendt/Westarp (2001), this paper looks at eleven of the most famous and broadly discussed cases of standardization, among them the often somewhat emotionally discussed battle between competing video cassette standards, PC operating systems, the browser war or different car engine technologies. Predominant reasons for their success in their respective markets are identified. Based upon these findings, a hypothesis is proposed about a possible categorization of standardization phenomena and success factors. This is a basis for future discussions about different classes of network effects and their economic implications, thus adding to our standardization framework.

Standardization Cases

In this chapter, eleven examples of successful technologies are presented, each of which was considered innovative when they first entered the market. Reasons are identified why particular technologies competing within a market eventually succeeded. Since it is obvious that is most unlikely that there are one or even a few reasons which are solely responsible for gaining a market, we focus on those factors that seem to be of substantial importance in contrasting the competing product(s). Thus, if for example all products competing within one market are available free, price is not considered important in this context, for we do not aim at explaining the success of a whole market as such but rather the particular choice within that market.

Personal Computers: IBM vs. Apple

Why is the IBM PC standard more widespread than its competitors although the latter entered the market earlier? The history of personal computers starts with the invention of the Intel 4004 microprocessor in November 1971 in combination with the RAM chip, also invented by Intel [White 2000a]. The revolutionary quality of this invention that enabled a shift away from mainframe systems is often associated with the well-known quote by IBM's CEO Thomas Watson in 1943: "I think there is a world market for maybe five computers" [White 2000b]. The first Personal Computer (PC), that was sold in parts for self-assembly, was the MITS Altair 8800, made by Micro Instrumentation Telemetry Systems in 1974 based upon Intel's 8-bit 8080 processor [Jones 1999a]; followed in 1976 by the Zilog Z80 with CP/M, the most frequently used operating system for 8-bit computers [White 2000b]. Also in 1976, Steve Wozniak, Steve Jobs, and Ron Wayne Apple developed the Apple I Kit, followed by Apple II in 1977. See e.g. http://www.myoldcomputers.com/ for pictures and other details about these items.

Although computers by Apple, Commodore and Tandy were quite popular within the then quite small community of computer geeks, it was not until the introduction of VisiCalc in 1979 that many people realized the benefits associated with personal computers [Jones 1999a]. Additionally, direct network effects were small, due to the fact that disk drives were incompatible, preventing the exchange of data and software.

It was only now that IBM decided to develop their own PCs based upon the Intel 8008 [Bradley 1990, 36]. In order to reduce time to market, the development of an operating system was outsourced to Microsoft. Due to their experience with System/23 DataMaster, IBM separated keyboard and monitor from the main computing unit on the motherboard. Extension cards made the system extensible and customizable [Bradley 1999, 34]. An important part of IBM's strategy was providing developers with prototypes and interface definitions, resulting in a considerable supply of software programs and periphery when IBM hit the market in 1981 [Jones 1999a]. Within a year, Compaq offered an IBM-compatible computer, and IBM introduced their new XT and AT based upon the more powerful Intel 8086 in 1983 and 1984. At the same time Apple was less successful with its Apple III and Lisa. Lisa was the first PC offering a graphical user interface, but at $10.000 it was simply too expensive [Jones 1999a]. The concept of graphical user interfaces (GUI) with icons and pointers was introduced by Xerox Start in 1981 [White 2000a] and divided the world into two until 1990: after their commercial disaster with Lisa, Apple remodeled their concept and introduced the Macintosh with a GUI and mouse control in 1984 as a direct competitor to the DOS-based IBM PC that did not offer comparable features until 1990 with the advent of MS Windows 3.x. The success of the Macintosh in these years was fueled by supporting Adobe Postscript when introducing the Apple Laser Printer in 1985, enabling WYSIWYG two years ahead of the competition, and by the availability of PageMaker, one of the first desktop publishing programs [Sanford 2000]. Still, Apple were unable to win against IBM-compatible systems. Without enumerating all the follow-up models over the next decade, Apple made some strategically less fortunate decisions than its competitors. In trying to avoid compatibility problems, Apple produced all system parts including printers, monitors etc. themselves. On the one hand, this enabled early plug and play solutions, on the other, Apple was not able to meet market demands due to restricted production capacities, especially in the mid-nineties. Strategies like second-sourcing could have prevented such problems and provided a larger installed base of Apple users. Furthermore, the absence of a consumer strategy, the promotion of cheap Performas instead of powerful PowerMacs, and the fact that Apple products were more expensive than comparable competing products led to financial problems and damaged the company's reputation [Sanford 2000, Katzschke 1987, 54]. With a strategic change towards more open systems and second-sourcing in the second half of the 90s, together with their new generation of products and the widely discussed Microsoft trial, Apple's situation has recently improved again. At the same time, IBM was also unable to maintain its market dominance. In the early 80s, IBM's success was based upon the creation of an open system, in that they tried to involve many suppliers of complementary hardware and software products and the extensibility of the system. Changing that strategy caused IBM to lose their market dominance when in the mid-eighties they tried to counterbalance the loss of uniqueness due to an increased homogeneity of products by introducing the PS/2 system and the Microchannel architecture which was incompatible with the industry standard. IBM could not promote this closed standard in the market and had to go "open" again [Steinmann/Heß 1993, 173-181].

In summary, major success factors in the PC market were openness of standards and flexibility or extensibility of the systems. Success seems to require sufficient providers of platform products, hardware as well as software.

Client Operating Systems: Microsoft Win9x/NT vs. UNIX vs. OS/2

MS-DOS

MS-DOS was released in August 1981 by Microsoft for the new generation of IBM's 16-bit PCs. It was compatible with CP/M and based upon Seattle Computer Product's CP/M-80 "clone" [Koch/Meder/Scheuber/Smiatek 1997, 23]. It became a de-facto standard due to its integration in the IBM PCs. Despite continuous development, DOS remained a single-user, single-tasking operating system with some properties that proved to be problematic for later processor generations, e.g. memory limited to 640 Kbytes. The last DOS release was 6.22 in 1993, version 7.0 was integrated into Windows 95 [Ortmann/Andratschke 1998, 23-25].

Windows 1.x, 2.x, 3.x, 95, 98

Windows 1.0 was released in November 1985 and was basically DOS with a GUI, the equally slightly successful Windows 2.0 followed two years later. The breakthrough was version 3 in May of 1990 that supported Intel's processors of the 286 and 386 generations. It was more user-friendly, easier to install and supported (cooperative) multi-tasking but was still 16-bit and DOS-based, using an outdated file system, memory-consuming and difficult to operate in a network environment [Rojahn 1990]. The main reason for its huge success - it had a market share of 75% when Windows 95 was introduced in 1995 - was license agreements by Microsoft and OEM vendors guaranteeing preinstalled Windows 3.x on almost any new PC [Strasheim 1995]. Windows 95 was a 32-bit operating system, fully compatible with DOS/Windows 3.x, more reliable, easy to use in a network, and supported preemptive multitasking and plug and play; later releases also supported USB and AGP and a new file system (FAT32) [Brenken 1998]. As before, the Windows 98 that followed was fully down compatible.

Windows 3.x was the end of the cooperation between IBM and Microsoft. Microsoft decided against developing a LAN manager parallel to IBM and developed a new operating system: in late 1993, Windows NT was released as a 32-bit multi-user operating system. It came with the same GUI as Windows 3.1 but higher hardware requirements and less available software but was available for more different hardware platforms [Ortmann/Andratschke 1998, 22-23]. In 1994, the more powerful Windows NT 3.5 that supported TCP/IP was released. 1997 saw the release of NT 4.0. It came as a server and a workstation version, had a new file system (NTFS) that was superior to FAT and IBM's HPFS for OS/2, had multi-processor support, multi-tasking and multi-threading and a variety of administration and diagnosis features [Koch 1997, 29-38]. A major success factor for Windows NT was again a huge dispersion of compatible software for two reasons: first, most DOS, Windows 3.x, Windows 95 and OS/2 2.x programs run on NT 4.0. Second, a year ahead of release, Microsoft distributed prototypes to software developers.

Windows 2000, released in February 2000, aimed at combining NT and Windows 9x. A new GUI, plug and play support, and DirectX 7.0 should make NT attractive to users who mainly use their PC for games. But performance lags behind NT, and Windows 2000 requires x86 processors [Siering 2000].

Unix, Linux

The first version of Unix was developed by Ken Thompson in 1969 as a simplified version of MULTICS, a network-based operating system produced in 1965. It was ported to C to be more portable by Dennis Ritchie in 1973. Over the following years, Unix licenses were mainly given to universities as since 1956 AT&T had not been allowed to sell computers in any way. Students took Unix with them to many companies and platforms, resulting in a large variety of different versions. It was only in 1989 that Unix V Release 4 emerged as a quasi standard; it incorporated the Unix dialects of Berkeley University and Microsoft's XENIX [Herold 1998, 12-15; Krienke 1998, 15-19]. Unix is a multi-user, multi-tasking operating system renowned for portability and stability. Its modular design, free availability of source codes and associated number of free tools makes it highly functional and extensible ("keep it simple, general, and extensible") [Herold 1998, 11-19; Krienke 1998, 24-25]. On the one hand, the Unix variety guaranteed availability for a maximum of platforms, on the other hand the absence of a common standard significantly slowed down diffusion and software development.

The most widespread Unix version is Linux, developed by student Linus Thorvalds from Finland in 1991 and since then hugely extended by a worldwide community of developers. Although some GUIs like KDE are emerging, many consider its user-unfriendly user interface a major obstacle to success as a client operating system competing with Windows NT workstation. Besides requiring skilled users, availability of software is a problem. Increasingly, Windows applications are available for Linux platforms, too, but they still lag significantly behind the supply of Windows in both, quantity and quality [Siering 1999].

IBM's OS/2

OS/2 1.x was co-developed by IBM and Microsoft as the beginning of a common operating system of the future. Introduced in 1987, it was superior to DOS in that it was significantly more powerful and supported multi-tasking. But outside commercial users from the banking and insurance industry, OS/2 just didn't sell. The reasons were insufficient availability of OS/2 compatible hardware, too few applications (additionally, DOS-compatibility was too rudimentary), too high a price, and too little marketing on the part of IBM, so that few people knew about it. Due to development problems and Microsoft's surprising success with Windows 3.x Microsoft and IBM eventually split [Koch/Meder/Scheuber/Smiatek 1997, 28-29]. Later versions by IBM consistently improved on performance and even added voice control etc. but couldn't overcome the problem of too few OS/2 applications. Ultimately, OS/2 failed to win against Microsoft although it was superior for some time from a technological perspective, apart from higher prices and more demanding hardware requirements. But IBM failed to support a sufficient amount of software, drivers and the like, be it directly by developing those themselves or indirectly by providing sufficient incentives to potential partners to do so.

Summary

The battle for client-side operating systems reveals that users do not base their buying decision mainly on isolated aspects of technological quality. Obviously, when taking recent market shares into consideration, a "good" operating system needs to cash in on indirect network effects, i.e. compatibility is of utmost importance. Technological properties such as stability, security or performance are a necessary prerequisite for a certain level, which all the systems described seemed to offer beyond a level recognizable by average users, and therefore simply taken for granted. While comparisons often showed Microsoft products to be slightly inferior in these respects, they were clearly superior in what is called user-friendliness. And the release of Windows NT ended the persistent technological dominance of other vendors' products.

In the market for client-side operating systems, compatibility with legacy systems and a wide variety of applications, drivers etc. are key to success. Microsoft managed to involve software developers in their platform and had clearly superior communication strategies, among others the use of pre-announcements before new releases, thus causing users to postpone their buying decisions to wait for a new Microsoft product, leading instantly to a huge installed base.

Another important factor in this market seems to be price. Due to intelligent license agreements, Microsoft's operating systems were readily available on new PCs, dramatically decreasing the willingness to pay for other products that might in addition be significantly more difficult to install and operate, while less software is available. At the same time, this is of course a chance for operating systems such as Linux, if they succeed not only in providing quality solutions at reasonable costs, including post-purchase cost, but also in developing good marketing strategies.

The Microsoft Trial

In the context of the recent Microsoft trial, the discussion of the network effect properties of IT standards has been refueled. The importance of indirect network effects as identified in this chapter is part of the prosecution's argumentation. The U.S. Department of Justice in its Findings of Facts explicitly refers to network effects and installed base effects Fact:

"Consumer demand for Windows enjoys positive network effects.... What for Microsoft is a positive feedback loop is for would-be competitors a vicious cycle. For just as Microsoft's large market share creates incentives for ISVs to develop applications first and foremost for Windows, the small or non-existent market share of an aspiring competitor makes it prohibitively expensive for the aspirant to develop its PC operating system into an acceptable substitute for Windows". [http://www.usdoj.gov/atr/cases/f3800/msjudgex.htm, sect. 39]

Although no definition of network effects is provided in the document, it is obvious that they are addressing those particular effects that are known as *indirect* network effects in the literature. Microsoft is, among others, accused of using its dominant market position in one market to force its products into a complementary market (esp. operating systems and web browsers). This corresponds to the findings in this chapter identifying compatibility with complementary products as crucial success factors. The implications in terms of market efficiency are less clear, though. One aspect to consider in this context is the fact that the discussions about the economic implications of network effects are far from over. Significant problems in finding empirical examples of market failure such that superior products failed to be adopted by market participants who preferred these and knew about their net superiority [Liebowitz/Margolis 1999], as well as theoretical drawbacks of traditional network effect models [Weitzel/Wendt/Westarp 2000], emphasize the fact that no sound theory of network effects has as yet been established that would allow one to make a simple clear point here. In addition, the efficiency implications associated with the existence of direct network effects might significantly differ from those of indirect effects [Katz/Shapiro 1994, Westarp/Buxmann/Weitzel/König 1999]. As long as contributions to network effect theorie(s) cannot explain the transition from vinyl to CD (lock-in) or from no gas stations and no (complementary) cars to a world with gas stations and cars, there is an obvious need for sophisticated and ideology-free discussion about government intervention before governments intervene. Otherwise there is a risk of destroying the most efficient enterprises. Trying to consider network effects does not per se make a marketing strategy unfair.

The Browser War: Netscape Navigator vs. Microsoft Internet Explorer

In 1989, Tim Berners-Lee introduced HTML (Hypertext Markup Language), an application of SGML (Standard Generalized Markup Language), for presenting scientific documents on the Internet with the possibility of referencing physically remote content, i.e. literature references; this is the hypertext part of HTML and the foundation of the World Wide Web (WWW) [Weitzel/Harder/Buxmann 2001]. HTML consists of a fixed set of about fifty so-called tags used to markup content with information on how to present the marked up data. Any web browser should understand these tags and format the particular content so that it can be viewed on a computer monitor.

The first Browsers were Viola and Midas for the Unix clone X-Windows, shortly followed by NCSA's Mosaic in 1993. Mosaic later became Mark Andressens' and James Clark's Netscape. The first version under the name of Netscape Navigator (NN) was released in December 1994. NN 1 was a simple HTML-viewer significantly superior to Microsoft's Internet Explorer (MSIE) that was released without substantial development efforts in August 1995 almost one year later. It is now commonplace to quote Microsoft's hypothesis that the Internet had no future [Wilson 1999]. The quality discrepancy continued through version 2. NN supported Java and frames, had email and a news client (MSIE 2 could only read news but not post). MSIE`s slightly superior performance was not enough to threaten Netscape's market position. With version 3 Microsoft came closer. Most of NN`s features had been incorporated into MSIE 3, in addition to Java and frames, it supported (at least in principle) Cascading Style Sheets (CSS), Active X, HTML-Mails and multiple news servers. NN on the other hand still had better bookmark management and (in a "gold" version") an integrated editor that could be used to save complete web pages including images. At that time, the enormous success of the web implied new functional demands such as virtual shopping malls, E-Commerce transactions, multimedia support and the like. People started looking for more sophisticated ways of presenting web content. But as mentioned above, HTML consisted of a fixed set of tags. Thus, in order to add functionality, Netscape and Microsoft started adding extra tags to the vocabulary of their browsers. In addition, Netscape used JavaScript as its scripting language while Microsoft decided to use Visual Basic Script, Active X and JScript, their own JavaScript implementation. The result of these proprietary extensions were increasingly incompatible web sites. Still, Netscape's market share amounted to 75 % in mid 1996 in contrast to 15 % for MSIE, partly due do NN`s availability for 16 platforms (11 of which were different Unix systems) [Fey 1996]. With the 4.x releases in 1997, Microsoft started taking over the browser market. MSIE 4.x came with Outlook Express and FrontPage Express, supported offline browsing and S/MIME and other further improved features. And from October 1998 on, quality differences became huge, the versions of MSIE 5 released exceeded even Netscape announcements. MSIE 5 supports XML 1.0, XML Namespaces, XSL (Working Draft Version of 18.12.1999), CSS ("direct browsing of native XML"), DOM

Level 1 Recommendation and WebDAV (HTTP 1.1 Extensions, version RFC 2518). In April 2000, almost two years later, Netscape (now under a GNU license) released a beta version of NN 6 (version 5 was skipped). Its XML support is based upon James Clark's famous EXPAT parser, still there is no XSLT support and NN 6 is significantly slower than MSIE 5, or even than NN 4 [http://cws.internet.com/reviews/netscape-netscape6-5.html]. But even the preview of NN 6 is available for Windows, Mac OS and Linux.

Why was MSIE eventually able to drive out NN? Later versions of MSIE proved to be superior in terms of functionality. While the web was young, NN was a great browser; with a maturing audience demanding more sophisticated functionality that was still easy to handle, Netscape seemed to be incapable of coping with the increasing complexity of the technology. All the authors of this article have been happy Netscape users; but compared with the latest MSIE 5, Netscape simply underperformed. What about price? Microsoft tried to compensate for their late launch in the browser market by giving their product away for nothing. They also later integrated MSIE 4.0 into the operating system as part of their new vision that the future is the integration of desktop and Internet. This led to accusations that they were making it impossible for other browser vendors to install their product on a Windows platform. It is noteworthy that NN was also initially free to gain a large market share. Having reached a dominant position, all corporate users had to buy licenses. It was only when MSIE became more successful and Netscape feared losing their dominance, that NN was made freely available again.

Ultimately, a crucial success factor in the browser market was product quality. Not surprisingly, there is a strong positive correlation between (relative) quality and market share.

Electronic Data Interchange: EDI, WebEDI, XML/EDI

For more than 20 years, companies have been using Electronic Data Interchange (EDI) to transmit structured business documents like orders or invoices electronically. As opposed to paper-based communication, EDI is designed to make communication between different systems possible without media discontinuities. But although there is undoubtedly large savings potential, the use of EDI is far less widespread than one would expect. Segev et al. estimate that only about 5% of the companies which could profit from its use actually use EDI [Segev/Porra/Roldan 1997]. The main reason is that small and medium-sized enterprises (SMEs) in particular try to avoid the considerable setup and operating costs of traditional EDI solutions. In addition, the variety of different industry-specific and national EDI standards makes it difficult for businesses to decide which standard to use. Therefore, the use of EDI is mainly reserved for large companies.

Traditional EDI

Electronic Data Interchange (EDI) is the business-to-business exchange of electronic documents in a standardized machine-processable format. EDI enables partners to exchange structured business documents, such as purchase orders and invoices, electronically between their computer systems. EDI is a means of reducing the costs of document processing and, in general, of achieving strategic business advantages made possible by shorter business process cycle times.

In general, the direct benefits of using EDI result from decreased information costs due to cheaper and faster communication. In addition, avoiding media discontinuities eliminates errors due to re-keying of data. The immediate availability of data allows the automation and coordination of different business processes, e. g. enabling just-in-time production. Another reason discussed in the literature on EDI as to why EDI is implemented in enterprises is that it offers better service to the customers [Emmelhainz 1993; Marcella/Chan 1993, 5-6]. It is also common that smaller companies in particular are forced to implement the EDI standard of a larger partner by the threat of giving up the business partnership otherwise, sometimes described as "gun-to-the-head-EDI" [Tucker 1997; Marcella/Chan 1993, 7].

An empirical study we conducted in the summer of 1998 shows that about 52% of the enterprises in Germany who responded, and about 75% in the US, use EDI technology to transfer structured business data. On average, German enterprises use EDI with 21% of their business partners, while 30% do so in the US. With these business partners, 38% of the revenue is realized in Germany and 40% in the US. This confirms the hypothesis that EDI is primarily applied to business with important customers. It also seems that EDI plays a more important role in the United States than it does in Germany [Westarp/Weitzel/Buxmann/König 1999].

Implementation costs for EDI systems consist of the costs of hard- and software, possibly for the adaptation of in-house software, external consulting and the reengineering of business processes. The costs of restructuring internal processes are difficult to quantify and are often underestimated when anticipating the implementation costs of an EDI system. According to the U.S. Chamber of Commerce, the costs of the typical initial installation of an EDI system average at least 50.000 US-Dollars [Waltner 1997]. In addition, these systems are often only compatible with one EDI standard. If an EDI connection is to be established with another business partner, and this potential partner uses a different EDI standard, it becomes necessary either to implement a new EDI system or to expand the existing system to include this new standard. Both measures incur significant costs. In order to enable communication between the EDI systems of companies, so-called Value Added Networks (VANs) are used, which cause additional expenses. The charges for using the VAN depend on the size and the frequency of the data transfers as well as the transfer time [Emmelhainz 1993, 113-116]. A company with about 25,000 EDI messages would pay its VAN-Provider something between 14,000 and 25,000 US-Dollars a month [Curtis 1996].

EDI over the Internet

There is a strong tendency towards using Internet-based EDI-solutions to cut down on cost and to enhance flexibility. The results of our empirical study confirm this. While currently only very few enterprises use WebEDI, more than 50 per cent of the enterprises in both countries plan to implement this technology in the future.

A first step towards the reduction of the costs of EDI solutions is using the Internet as the transportation medium. While the costs for using VAN's lines are often defined by the number of messages sent or by the number of characters transmitted, there is no such calculation on the Internet. For the 25,000 EDI messages mentioned above, transportation over the Internet would cost only about 1,920 US-Dollars [Curtis 1996]. A number of different communication protocols can be used for the transfer of EDI messages over the Internet. Depending upon the task, the exchange can be made via FTP (File Transfer Protocol), HTTP (Hypertext Transfer Protocol) or SMTP (Simple Mail Transfer Protocol), while the data is encoded either with PGP (Pretty Good Privacy), S/MIME (Secure Multipurpose Internet Mail Extension) or SSL (Secure Socket Layer). Low cost in combination with the large number of emerging technologies for the Internet may now make a considerable contribution to the increase of EDI users and in particular allow SMEs to participate in EDI networks.

WebEDI

While at first sight the already available EDI-over-the-Internet solutions address the problem of high up-front and operating costs at least on the client side, there are serious drawbacks. GEIS (GE Trade Web Service), for instance, used to charge up to $6 per document, which some consider “noncompetitive” [Densmore 1998]. More importantly, WebEDI is mostly no more than an HTML-front-end to a shopping system. One user manually enters data into a form using a web browser as communication interface. The server-sided translation to EDI format remains invisible to the client; the translation from EDI to HTML enables the former EDI message to be displayed in the client's browser. But here the integration stops. The client cannot integrate the ‘dead’ HTML-coded data into his inhouse systems.

Thus, there is no machine-to-machine connection and no way the client, i. e. the small partner, can import the EDI data into his inhouse systems.

The obvious advantage of using the Web as a medium for EDI communication is that the only (client side) prerequisite is an Internet connection and a web browser. All communication uses the ubiquitous HTTP-protocol. Security issues can be addressed by using SSL, for example. Thus, all the required infrastructure is most probably available almost anywhere without forcing the partners to invest hefty amounts of money. In this context, form-based EDI proves to be a good idea for large companies seeking ways of having their small customers send their data in a standardized format. But the main advantages of EDI as shown in our empirical study – time savings and improvement of business processes – still cannot be achieved for both partners since there is no system-to-system communication.

XML/EDI

As Jon Bosak, chair of the XML Coordination Group of the W3C, states in his famous article "*XML, Java and the future of the web*" [Bosak 1997] the Extensible Markup Language XML has the potential to be the data format of choice used together with the programming language of choice for the Web, Java, to enable the next step in the evolution of EDI. Generally speaking, the use of open standards can considerably reduce the time and money spent on implementing a solution. By avoiding proprietary formats, the danger of stranding investment in R&D is decreased and future-oriented solutions can be developed. XML in particular can contribute to the opening of EDI networks. While traditional EDI relationships are often long-term and highly integrated relationships, which are worthwhile only with are large number of transactions and for a long term, the willingness to invest into open, compatible IT-infrastructures is stronger at any point of the Value Chain, especially for smaller partners. Traditionally, the establishment of compatibility between different EDI solution-systems was achieved through deep integration of the EDI standard into the applications of the communication partners. However, on the basis of XML, attempts are now being made to avoid the inflexibility which follows from using data which do not comply with the established in-house-system.

Summary

The crucial success factor in the EDI market is the realization of direct network effects or multilateral compatibility at reasonable costs. While EDI per se aims at improving direct communication links, it suffers from compatibility problems and costly operations. Taking EDI to the Internet is a means of reducing communication costs. Using XML syntax to encode EDI messages is a step towards reducing the costs of incompatibility in that XML adds flexibility and offers access to taking advantage of the huge family of web applications.

E-Mail

The first mail programs were quite simple e-mail clients, private users mostly used public domain tools like Crosspoint, Pegasus Mail or Eudora to exchange their electronic messages. They were easy to use and supported the sending and receiving of text messages and later of attachments as well. It was also possible to write mails offline [Herwig 1996; Lindquist 1998]. For corporate users, Lotus cc:Mail was the leading product, shortly followed by Microsoft Mail. These products were all quite similar in the functionality offered, thus other criteria such as platform availability and support of different network and mail protocols or security issues

(PGP, S/MIME) were important when deciding what mail client to use. For corporate users ease of administration was another factor [Herwig 1996].

The integration of e-mail clients in the web browsers version 2 and later reduced the share of public domain programs, resulting in the dominance of Microsoft's Outlook Express that is part of MSIE 4.0 and later [Lindquist 1998]. In corporate environments, MS Outlook and Lotus notes are leading. These offer much more functionality than just mail clients and have evolved into groupware tools. It is interesting to note that the first Notes version entered the market in December 1989, while Microsoft's first groupware solution as a combination of Outlook and MS Exchange Server was only available with Windows 95 [Kuri 1999]. Novell's GroupWise remains way behind these others in terms of market share and functionality. Lotus tried to promote its R5 Notes Private Edition on the private market as well, but they seem to be unable to get users to adapt to the Notes-specific elements; in addition to considerable implementation know-how, users might see disincentives in downloading the 60 MB program (or buying a CD for DM 25,-) since it doesn't offer very much additional functionality when Outlook - which they can handle intuitively - is already on their computer [Kuri 1999].

The Lotus Notes e-mail product (since version 5.0 a client, the server is called Domino) and MS Outlook 98 are quite similar in the functionality offered. In addition to mail functionality, they offer calendar and scheduling functions, address books etc. They support OLE, Active X and HTML. Administration is an important criterion especially in large corporate environments. Many favor Microsoft's centrally maintained Exchange Server in contrast to decentralized Notes. On the other hand, Lotus comes with a superior platform availability [Pompili 1998].

In summary, price is not a factor that can explain the success of particular e-mail clients for private users since all of them are basically free. Because they do not differ too much in terms of functionality either, the private market is quite heterogeneous with Microsoft gaining share due to fact that their product has a look and feel that is well-known to many. In corporate environments, groupware functionality and ease of configuration and administration is important; the two main players Microsoft and Lotus offer similar products at similar prices at similar market shares.

Office Suites: Spreadsheet Programs and Text Processors

Recent office suites all consist of a spreadsheet program and a text processor, they also come with a presentation program, e-mail client and a timer, "professional" editions also include a database program. These components were originally sold separately but later bundled.

Spreadsheets

The first spreadsheet program was VisiCalc in 1979, written for the Apple II and enabling e.g. financial calculations that had so far required huge mainframe computers to be carried out on a PC [Stranahan/Wiegand 1999]. Its success triggered other companies, and Lotus 1-2-3 - released in 1983 with database management and graphical features - was soon to become the most successful spreadsheet program in the DOS world. Microsoft Excel saw the light of day in 1985, notably only for the Apple platform. It was the first computer program with a GUI with pull-down menus and mouse control [Power 2000] and had a market share of 90 % on Apple platforms in 1989. At that time, Lotus 1-2-3 was the leading product in the DOS world [Liebowitz/Margolis 1998]. Although Borland Quattro (Pro) was leading the market even ahead of 1-2-3 for some time later, it could never really influence the battle for the spreadsheet market between Lotus and Microsoft [Storm 1994]. Both Excel and 1-2-3 have been consistently improved, and new functions have been added with Excel continuously getting closer in terms of quality as well as success and taking the lead with version 4.0. Excel 4.0 was better, its competitor at that time significantly lagging behind in terms of quality and release dates, partly due to Lotus` strategic decision to favor the OS/2 platform.

The increasing functional power of the programs led to the extended importance of software assistants and macro languages for automating tasks. Yet the most important criterion - given the wide range of supported functions Lotus and Microsoft were offering in their products - was the possibility of exchanging data between applications, i.e. network effects. All these criteria make MS Excel the superior spreadsheet program, making it the leading product in this market; even the web integration in Excel 2000 is so far unique.

Text Processors

Analogously to spreadsheet programs, the first text processor was released in 1979. But Word Star was to lose the pole position to strong competitors. In 1983 Microsoft released its Word, 1984 saw WordPerfect produced by a subsidiary of Novell that was bought by Corel in 1995, and AmiPro by Lotus, later renamed Word Pro [Stranahan/Wiegand 1999]. As discussed in the chapter "Personal Computers: IBM vs. Apple" a milestone in word processing was Adobe's PDL in 1985 which enabled WYSIWYG authoring. Recent text processors now all offer similar functionality, such as thesaurus, spell- and grammar-checking, math editors, chart and table functions, format assistants etc. that have been added over time. Compatibility to other programs proved to be another very significant feature [Stranahan/Wiegand 1999]. As in the case of spreadsheets, the availability of assistants, macro languages and web integration became important.

Microsoft was again leading in the Apple market, while for DOS computers Word was not able to defeat WordPerfect until the introduction of Windows [Liebowitz/Margolis 1998]. One reason for the analogy between spreadsheets and word processors might be Microsoft's dominance in the Apple world, which prevented others from establishing products in a GUI environment; thus Microsoft were able to gain substantial experience there that they could use when introducing Windows. And many other companies strongly concentrated on OS/2 and failed to make ground in the developing Windows world [Weber 1999].

A problem when searching for key success factors in this area is that on the one hand there are individual products, while on the other there are product bundles in the form of office suites. As before, Microsoft had advantageous OEM license agreements adding to the diffusion of the MS Office Suite. Nevertheless, one criterion differentiating between bundles of otherwise similar functionality proved to be cross-application compatibility [Fichtner 1995] and unified user interfaces, including macros that work between different applications within a suite. A key factor for corporate decisions about using office suites is the know-how and experience of employees with the particular applications and the portability of processed data to other applications [Weber 1997].

Networks: TCP/IP vs. OSI

This story, closely related to the history of the Internet, begins in 1968 when the U.S. Department of Defense founded a project with the goal of developing the foundation for a multiplex computer-to-computer network that was to become the famous ARPANET-project in 1969. ARPANET was originally a network of four computers; its goal was to create an infrastructure that would allow the exchange of military and intelligence information during and after a nuclear war even when parts of the infrastructure had been destroyed. In 1972, ARPANET was presented to the public, and the Internet Working Group developed a Network-Core-Protocol that was further developed by the International Federation of Information Processing into the Protocol-for-Packet Network Intercommunication which was the foundation for the Kahn-Cerf-Protocols which were later known as TCP/IP-Protocols and became part of the Berkeley-Unix-Version 4.1 in 1980 (see "Unix, Linux" on page 37) [Hein 1998, 73-75]. When in 1983 ARPANET was divided into MILNET for military purposes and a "new" ARPANET, TCP/IP became a protocol for the military, resulting in all connected hosts having to switch to this standard. In 1985, the U.S. National Science Foundation (NSF) founded NSFNet, at first connecting scientists and universities all over the United States [Hunt 1998, 3] and later private enterprises, too. The network's growth was impressive, and ARPANET became what is now known as the Internet in 1990 [Lauer 1999, 70].

Independent of the development of TCP/IP, the International Standardization Organization (ISO) developed their OSI reference model in 1984 to describe abstractly the path of data from one application over a network to another application. The goal was to enable communication between heterogeneous computer systems based upon basic services [Kauffels 1999, 69-77]. Although OSI defines seven isolated layers that serve particular goals and that can be implemented independent of one another, it is a conceptual framework; actual communication is based upon protocols implementing functions described in OSI layers. Why are there now few OSI products while TCP/IP is ubiquitous? OSI proved to be too complex and therefore too expensive to implement in a sufficient number of applications. Especially on the application layer, there are very few OSI implementations [Kauffels 1999, 69-78]. In some respects, TCP/IP is a pragmatic alternative to ISO/OSI. TCP/IP consists of two basic protocols: Internet Protocol (IP) for basic addressing, routing, and checking if transmitted data is complete (checksum), and Transmission Control Protocol (TCP) based upon IP to enhance the stability and security of connections (handshake, ports etc.) [Lauer 1999, 83-107].

Since all networks based upon TCP/IP are compatible, the protocols are not only used for the Internet but also for inter- and extranets, adding to its diffusion. Another success factor is the fact that TCP/IP is independent of physical network infrastructures, i.e. it can be used with Ethernet, Token Ring or other networks [Hunt 1998, 4]. In summary, TCP/IP is open, free and enables connectivity in almost any physical environment at comparatively low complexity and costs.

Figure 1:QWERTY (left) and DSK (right) keyboard
(Source: Beacon 2000a)

Keyboards: QWERTY vs. Dvorak`s DSK

One of the most frequently quoted examples of standardization and inferior products winning against better ones is the case of QWERTY, followed by VHS vs. Beta VCR systems. In the following, these historic cases are analyzed, trying to avoid the bias frequently found in such studies. As so often in life, there are more sides to these stories than is intuitively and emotionally self-evident at first sight. Or at least there could be more.

In 1868, Christopher Latham Sholes was awarded copyrights for a simple typewriter. In fact, Sholes was not the first but the 52nd inventor of a typewriter. Back in those days, typewriters faced a major problem: the jamming of type bars when certain keys were struck in close succession. To address this problem, in a trial and error approach, Sholes looked for a keyboard arrangement with letters that were often typed one after the other being physically remote, i.e. that the keys which were most likely to be struck in succession approached the type point from opposite sides of the machine. In 1873 he sold his design, a keyboard with the letters QWERTY at the upper left, to E. Remington & Sons who after adding some mechanical improvements started producing typewriters mostly based upon Sholes' design.

The general problem of jamming type bars was not solved until 1879, when Lucien Stephan Crandall invented the ball head typewriter [David 1985, 334].

In the years that followed, Remington established its typewriters and the QWERTY keyboard as the de-facto standard. One driving force often described in literature as the moment of QWERTY's decisive triumph was victories in speed typing contests, especially by Frank McGurrin, who is known to have been the world's first touch-typist, who not only used all his fingers for typing but had also memorized the whole keyboard [Liebowitz/Margolis 1990, 6]. On July 25, 1888 he beat Louis Taub (who was using a 72-letter keyboard providing all upper and lower keys).

Some decades later, in 1936, August Dvorak patented his Dvorak Simplified Keyboard (DSK). His keyboard arrangement was based upon the idea of ergonomic efficiency. Frequently used letter sequences ought to be close to one another reducing finger movement, the change of hands should be most frequent and balanced, and frequently used letters should be typed with stronger fingers. Dvorak claimed that his keyboard was easier to learn and faster to type with than QWERTY, while not being as fatiguing. However, we all use QWERTY, and in spite of its claims of superiority DSK remained unsuccessful. What went wrong?

The QWERTY case has been used for decades to prove market failure under network effects. It is said that the installed base of QWERTY users suffers from lock-in and does not want to change because changing the keyboard used to type with is associated with the switching costs of retraining. Enterprises buy QWERTY keyboards because typists are available, and typists learn the keyboard design they expect to be successful with in their job search, i.e. a positive feedback-loop. The superiority of DSK was mainly proved by a U.S. Navy research report of 1944, saying that efficiency increases when using DSK would compensate for the costs of retraining professional typists within ten days [Liebowitz/Margolis 1990, 7]. First, if DSK is known to be that superior, why would a rational actor not use it? This question leads to the core of debating the efficiency implications of network effects and the relation between network effects, path dependencies and market efficiency; see Arthur (1989; 1996), David (1985), Katz/Shapiro (1985; 1994) and Liebowitz/Margolis (1990; 1994; 1995a; 1995b). And second, there is more to the story.

One interesting fact, that is often overlooked, is that there is no official Navy Study on that topic. The paper that has for decades served as proof of market failure – and one which is never correctly referenced – is a personal report by an individual naval officer: and that officer was Lieutenant Commander August Dvorak (sic!). That doesn't, of course, make it a bad study per se, but it made Professors Liebowitz and Margolis look deeper into the story. For one thing, the study's methodology is not sound. For example, the test typists for the two systems were of completely different ages and abilities. Then there may be a confusion of 180 and 108 words per minute. And so on. Furthermore, various other studies and simulations conducted by other people (e.g. Earle Strong in 1956 [Liebowitz/Margolis 1998]) came up with quite different results showing no or no significant superiority of DSK compared to QWERTY. The whole story is presented by Liebowitz/Margolis in their instructive paper *The Fable of the Keys* [Liebowitz/Margolis 1990 or Liebowitz/Margolis 1999, 23-39].

One hypothesis is that DSK is theoretically superior - it is an ergonomic approach, after all. But what if that is way beyond the speed humans are physically capable of typing? In other words: who benefits from being able to type 200 words a minute instead of 180 when typing skills restrict one to a fraction of this? This argument somewhat resembles what Liebowitz/Margolis call first-degree path dependence [Liebowitz/Margolis 1995b].

> *"...the QWERTY keyboard appears to be fast enough for almost all uses of it. If you are just driving around town you do not need a 500 horsepower V8" [Poole 1997]*

The Battle for VCR Standards: Beta isn't Always Better

Another famous example of a conflict used to show that markets fail by some standards and not by others is the history of video cassette recording. Most of the literature focuses on VHS and Beta, but the internationally less renowned Video 2000 is especially interesting, as will be shown.

In 1956, Ampex Corporation introduced the first device for audiovisual playback and recording [Liebowitz/Margolis 1995]. The advent of transistors allowed the devices to become sufficiently small for the first plans for private use to evolve in the early 60s [Gerwin/Höcherl 1995, 18]. In 1969 Philips announced the first VCR, with an eventual product release in 1972 that had poor picture quality, 30 minute capacity and cost DM 2.800. It was as unsuccessful as the U-matic, produced by Sony, Matsushita and JVC a few months earlier and offering 63 minutes recording time. Due to the breakup of the Japanese alliance, Sony and JVC/Matsushita decided to develop their own cassette-based video system. In 1974, Sony tried to sell licenses for its Betamax system to JVC/Matsushita who refused, since they considered their VHS system superior. Betamax was released in April 1975, VHS one and a half years later at the end of 1976 [Gerwin/Höcherl 1995, 21]. From a technological perspective, both systems were basically identical; an explicit insight into physical tests and the like is presented in Liebowitz/Margolis (1995b). But they used different tapes. While Sony considered small cassettes more useful, JVC optimized playing time rather than cassette size. Thus, JVC`s first product generation had a playing time of two hours, almost twice the Sony time. Both tried to sell licenses to the other; Sony turned down requests by Hitachi and did not license Betamax to Toshiba, Sanyo and Zenith until February 1977. In contrast, JVC was giving away VHS licenses to Hitachi, Sharp, and Mitsubishi for nothing even before its official market introduction. In addition, JVC offered to sell their partners complex system parts already assembled at JVC [Gerwin/Höcherl 1995, 21]. Maybe more important, JVC managed to win RCA, the only American television provider bigger than Zenith, as a license partner. Interestingly, RCA had already turned down an offer by Sony; they considered recording times of two hours - a whole movie – to be the key to the American market [Liebowitz/Margolis 1995].

When RCA entered the market with VHS in 1977, it soon became obvious what consumers demanded. In the following years, the battle for video cassette standards was a battle for recording time. When Betamax offered two hours, VHS already had four, when Beta had five, VHS had eight - though always at the cost of decreased picture quality.

Then, in 1979, Philips and Grundig announced their Video 2000, a system with impressive advantages: The cassettes were double-sided, thus offering recording times of 2x4 hours, later with longplay 2x8 hours, Video 2000 had a real time counter, stereo sound and superior picture quality, at least with the introduction of chromium-dioxide tapes. Production prices for Video 2000 tapes were about 20-30 % above the competition; but due to longer recording times the price per minute was significantly lower. The main reason for not setting the eventual standard was Grundig`s license policy, involving only European partners and completely neglecting the important U.S. and Japanese markets. When Video 2000 finally hit the market in 1980, it faced an already established Japanese competition which was in the midst of hefty price wars [Gerwin/Höcherl 1995, 22-24]. And a deal in 1983 restricting the import of Japanese VCRs to Europe remained ineffective.

Maybe the real problem of Video 2000 was the establishing of a video rental market in the late 70s. At that time, VHS though younger than Beta dominated the market due to their licensing strategy which was more focused on establishing an installed base. The new rental tapes were all VHS, triggering VHS recorder sales and vice versa. This is basically the same mechanism Microsoft is accused of using when their dominance in a market (operating systems) gives them advantages in complementary markets (web browsers). Grundig understood these principles and tried to establish their own video rental system, but the European market was too small and Grundig was too late [Gerwin/Höcherl 1995, 24-29].

Nuclear Power Reactors

To produce nuclear energy, most reactors use thermal fission. In the reactor core uranium isotope U-235 is shot with neutrons leading to its fission (or splitting, breakdown) into two unequally sized nuclei that are the major contributors of heat and two or three neutrons are produced which bounce around inducing a chain reaction. The thermal heat produced heats water and the steam drives a turbine that powers a generator that produces electricity [Gonyeau 2000].

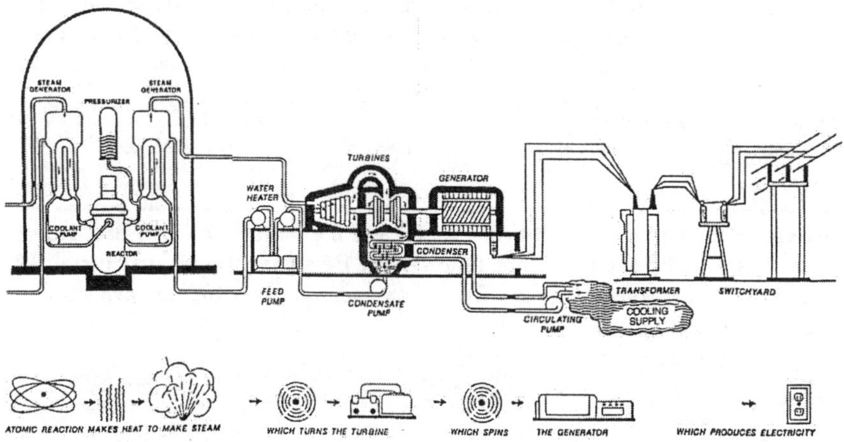

Figure 2: Thermal reactor [Gonyeau 2000]

Two things are crucial, the moderator and the coolant. Since pure U-235 is rare there is most likely to be some U-238 in the reactor core as well, attracting fast neutrons but not being split by them. In order for the neutrons to split the U-235, they have to be slowed down. For this purpose, a moderator is used. Usually, a coolant is used to transport the heat produced, sometimes cooling the moderator, too. The reactor types discussed below use different types of coolants and moderators: Light Water Reactors (LWR) use light water (H_2O) as coolant and moderator, Heavy Water Reactors (HWR) use water isotope D_2O and Gas Graphite Reactors (GGR) use gas (mostly helium or carbon dioxide) as coolant and graphite as moderator. There are other types (see e.g. http://www.cannon.net/~gonyeau/nuclear/rx-types.htm) but these are sufficient for an intuitive discussion of technological diffusion processes.

Nuclear history basically starts in the 40s with the development of nuclear weapons. But the military soon saw a wider range of applications for nuclear energy. The U.S. Navy was seeking for ways of equipping their submarines with a longer lasting energy supply system. After World War 2 Captain Hyman Rickover had the duty of evaluating atomic energy for that purpose. Although there have been no elaborate studies of the advantages and disadvantages of the different methods of producing nuclear energy, Rickover decided in favor of light water technology since it had caused the least trouble so far and met the Navy's demands. He asked Westinghouse to develop a prototype. It was called Mark I and its successor Mark II passed all tests on board the Nautilus in 1954. Another system was used two years later on board the Seawolf but this reactor, constructed by General Electric and using liquid metal as coolant and beryllium as moderator, caused various substantial problems [Cowan 1990, 559-560]. Thus, the Navy decided to use LWR technology.

After the first Russian nuclear explosions in 1949, the U.S. changed their restrictive information policy towards their former allies concerning nuclear energy, since they feared that Russia could become too attractive a future partner for European countries as a technology provider. Civil use of nuclear power became a top priority, and Rickover was again asked to lead the project of developing the world's first stationary reactor. In the meantime, other countries started to become interested in nuclear power and began their own research. The U.K. (first bomb in 1953) and France became Europe's nuclear leaders. Interestingly, the prevalent technology in Europe was gas graphite reactors, and the first European nuclear reactor was in fact a gas graphite reactor in the U.K. in 1956. The first American reactor became fully operational one year later and was an LWR [Cowan 1990, 545-548].

In 1954, the U.S. founded the Atoms-for-peace project to collaborate closely with Europe's Euratom from 1958 on. Of course, American (financial and technological) funding was available for LWR technology research. As a consequence, an LWR was built in Garigliano, Italy, and the development in the U.S. caused Europe to reconsider. In 1969, France (!) decided to switch to LWR technology due to fear of technological isolation, followed by Great Britain in 1977. When Canada had their first HWR in 1967 there were already 10 LWR; five years later with Canada's second HWR there were 27 active LWR [Cowan 1990, 549-556].

Why did the world decide in favor of LWR? Reactor technology is a complex topic. The informational lead of the U.S. Navy in the LWR area also meant substantial informational gaps for civil uses. It was especially smaller countries that did not want to spend money on their own nuclear research who decided in favor of the best-researched and soon - due to the learning curve - less expensive technology. In view of subsequent developments, however, LWR's superiority is not undisputed. Few studies show LWR to be a superior technology, it is more the opposite. HWR and GGR are possibly safer. Due to their construction they offer longer reaction times in case of accidents; they are more efficient because on average they are more time per period fully operational and have a longer life cycle which results in electricity costs from LWR that are about 20-25 % higher. GGR in particular have a higher thermal efficiency and are less subject to the safety risks associated with LWR.

Automobiles: Gas vs. Gasoline

Discussing alternative ways of individual transportation is a new phenomenon. Especially during the years after World War II, much effort and hope was put into gas turbine engines. In 1945 Chrysler was appointed by the U.S. Navy to develop a regenerative airplane engine. A prototype presented in 1948 generated positive results, however the project was stopped due to budget cuts. But Chrysler continued its research into a gas turbine for automobiles. One problem was the high fuel turnover due to the fact that the turbine wasn't constantly running at high velocity as in an airplane. Having solved this with the help of a temperature exchange mechanism Chrysler produced a Plymouth Sedan with a gas turbine engine in 1953, resulting in a mini-series of 50 cars in 1963. Gas turbine development was quite slow over the following years, but was triggered by two events: First, strict governmental exhaust regulations (1966-1970) and second, the energy crisis of 1973. Cars should now be able to run on different types of fuel, a genuine property of the gas turbine. But reducing NO_x emissions demanded new materials for high temperature areas within the turbine which was an expensive research task. What are the reasons that in this situation the development of gas turbine engines wasn't promoted in such a way as to take over the whole market? First, the money to be spent on further research had to be earned by selling traditional combustion engine cars which in turn were improved in the process. Thus fuel efficiency soon increased and technologies were developed to reduce emissions, which met the U.S. requirements.

The additional costs of equipping a car with a gas turbine are estimated at DM 3000-7000 for a car and DM 8000-10000 for trucks. Due to lower fuel costs, cars reach a breakeven after 22000 kilometers, trucks after 45000. A problem, of course, is the very rudimentary network of filling stations. In 1998, there were eighty in Germany, but the annual expected growth rate is 30% [Bundesumweltministerium 1998].

A Classification

The eleven cases presented are now classified according to their prevalent success factors. First, we propose groups of success factors:

- Technology: This category consists of stand-alone properties such as stability (little down time, few crashes), security (integrated security mechanisms) or performance (speed, capacity) and describes technological quality.
- User utility: This category describes a product's advantages in terms of functionality, flexibility (adaptability, customizability) and user-friendliness and determines the extent to which it makes a user's tasks easier.
- Compatibility: This category describes the suitability of supporting tasks with different actors involved over a network, i.e. compatibility, supported standards, open standards, and portability or platform independence.
- Network effects: This category comprises diffusion of a technology (installed base), support by other vendors and availability of complementary technologies.

- Cost: This category describes price or cost aspects of technologies and is considered important if some products competing for a market are given away for free or are significantly less expensive than others or if the cost savings potential is significant [Westarp/Weitzel/Buxmann/König 1999].
- Information: This category consists of criteria independent of the core quality of a product but influencing users' decisions, i.e. the availability of information concerning installed bases, learning effects or switching costs.

Grouping the described standardization cases with respect to the success categories above, five groups of technologies can be identified:

- Hardware (IT): IT hardware describes computer hardware (IBM vs. Apple)
- Hardware (other) describes other (physical, mechanical) products such as keyboards, VCRs, power reactors, and car engines.
- Software (stand-alone) describes products that do not necessarily require to be connected to a network, like operating systems or text processors.
- Software (network) is composed of products that derive their prime utility from being part of a (communications) network like e-mail clients or web browsers. Web clients have evolved to become much more than just website viewers but in the context of the history of their diffusion this seems to be quite irrelevant.
- Network protocols are a prerequisite for using network software.

Since we could only propose the success factors which were particularly important in the historic cases (relevant or not) and not their degree of relevance, measures like cluster analysis are inappropriate for grouping the cases. Thus, to evaluate the grouping based upon the binary data the M-coefficient is used which is appropriate for evaluating the closeness of data on a nominal scale. The M-coefficient describes the similarity of objects with regard to their properties [Backhaus/Erichson/Plinke/Weiber 1996, 264-272]. In a paired comparison between objects - the standardization cases - the M-coefficient is determined by simply dividing the number of matching criteria by the number of all criteria (bilateral importance of a particular property is as valid as bilateral unimportance). An x in the table marks relevant criteria in the particular cases.

		Hardware (IT)	Software (stand-alone)		Software (network)			Protocol	Hardware (other)			
		IBM / Apple	OS	Office	e-mail	IE/ NN	EDI	IP OSI	Keybrd.	VCR	Reactors	car engn.
Technology	stability		x	x				x				
	security		x		x			x				
	performance		x		x					x		
user utility	user-friendliness	x	x	x	x	x						
	functionality		x	x	x		x			x		
	flexibility	x	x	x			x	x				
Compatibility	compatibility		x	x	x	x	x					
	Supp. standards				x	x	x					
	open standards	x						x				
	portability				x	x		x				
Network	support by other vendors	x						x	x	x		x
	indirect network effects	x	x			x			x	x		x
cost	cost	x	x	x	x	x	x	x		x		
Information	installed base	x	x	x				x	x	x	x	x
	learning effects							x	x		x	x
	switching costs	x	x	x					x	x		x

Table 1: Success factors for different technology classes

If a criterion (row) appeared to be relevant for the success of a technology (column) as defined above, the corresponding field is marked with an x. If this criterion was relevant in more than one case within a technology group, that field is also shaded gray. Adding up criteria marked x in two or none of the respectively compared technologies and dividing by the total number of criteria (11) results in table 2, showing the different M-values in their range from 0 to 1 with 0 indicating no similarity and 1 identity. Grey shaded areas in table 2 indicate similarity values for the grouped examples.

	IBM/Apple	OS	Office	e-mail	IE/NN	EDI	IP, OSI	Key-boards	VCR	Reac-tors	Car engn.
IBM/Apple	1										
OS	0,563	1									
Office	0,625	0,813	1								
e-mail	0,25	0,563	0,5	1							
IE/NN	0,5	0,438	0,5	0,688	1						
EDI	0,438	0,438	0,688	0,688	0,688	1					
IP, OSI	0,563	0,375	0,438	0,313	0,313	0,375	1				
Key-brd.	0,688	0,375	0,438	0,188	0,438	0,375	0,5	1			
VCR	0,688	0,625	0,563	0,438	0,438	0,5	0,375	0,75	1		
Reactors	0,5	0,313	0,5	0,375	0,5	0,563	0,563	0,813	0,563	1	
Car engn.	0,688	0,375	0,438	0,188	0,438	0,375	0,5	1	0,75	0,813	1

Table 2: M-coefficients

Evidentially, the similarities marked are the greatest within their respective groups, thus supporting the proposed grouping design.

To summarize the findings derived from looking at historical standards battles based upon the proposed categorization, the following tendencies can be identified:

When deciding on what general hardware to use, users do not primarily focus on core quality or price but rather on direct (installed base) and indirect network effects (complementary products) or switching costs. As with IT hardware, core technological product quality is not a relevant criterion for differentiating between products, most probably because it is in most cases considered sufficient anyway.

In the technology groups stand-alone software, network software and protocols, costs seem to be a primary users focus. It seems to be very difficult to conquer these markets with products that come with a positive price. In addition, compatibility and user-friendliness are very important. Stability, switching costs and explicit installed bases were only considered crucial in the case of stand-alone products. Not too surprisingly, complementary products seem to be the most important aspects when deciding on client-side operating systems.

Due to their use in communication networks, a crucial success factor for network software is portability and the support of different standards, in great contrast to stand-alone software products. It is interesting that for the network protocol case -

and only here - all criteria seem to be significantly important. On the other hand, no factor was completely irrelevant when choosing a product. When a criterion was not marked as relevant, as mentioned before, this only means it was not primarily responsible for defeating its competitors. In other words, they were not a major part of the objective function, but success was subject to their being fulfilled.

References

Arthur, W. B. (1989): Competing technologies, increasing returns, and lock-in by historical events, in: The Economic Journal, 99 (March 1989), 116-131.

Arthur, W. B. (1996): Increasing returns and the new World of business, in: Harvard Business Review, 74 (July-August), 100-109.

Backhaus, Klaus/Erichson, Bernd/Plinke, Wulff/Weiber, Rolf (1996): Multivariate Analysemethoden, 8th ed., Berlin, Heidelberg, New York 1996.

Beacon, Mavis (2000a): History of typing, http://www.mavisbeacon.com

Beacon, Mavis (2000b): Seek and ye shall find, http://www.mavisbeacon.com/history_seek.html.

Besen, S. M./Farrell, J. (1994): Choosing How to Compete: Strategies and Tactics in Standardization, Journal of Economic Perspectives, Spring 1994, 8, 117-310.

Bosak, J. (1997): XML, Java and the future of the Web. http://sunsite.unc.edu/pub/sun-info/standards/xml/why/xmlapps.html.

Bradley, David J. (1990): Wie alles einmal anfing..., in: c't Magazin für Computer Technik, Nr. 10, 1990, 34-40.

Brenken, Dirk(1998): Auf der Waagschale, lohnt sich der Umstieg auf Windows 98?, in: c't Magazin für Computer Technik, Nr. 13, 1998, 80-83.

Bundesumweltministerium (1998): Bundesumweltamt (Hrsg.): So geht's auch ! Gasantrieb, Bonn, Berlin 1998.

Cowan, Robin (1990): Nuclear Power Reactors: A study in technological lock-in, in: The Journal of Economic History, Vol. L, No. 3 (Sept. 1990), 541-567.

Curtis, C. (1996): EDI over the Internet: Let the games begin, in: Internetweek, Issue 627, September 9, 1996, http://www.techweb.com/se/directlink.cgi?CWK19960909S0076.

David, P. A. (1985): Clio and the economics of QWERTY, American Economic Review, Papers and Proceedings, Vol. 75, 332-337, 1985.

David, Paul A./Greenstein, Shane (1990): The economics of compatibility standards: An introduction to recent research, in: Economics of innovation and new technology, 1, 3 - 41, 1990.

Densmore, B. (1998): EDI vs. The new kids, in: Computerworld, April 6, 1998, http://www.computerworld.com/home/Emmerce.nsf/All/980406edi.

Emmelhainz, M. (1993): EDI: A Total Management Guide, New York 1993.

Farrell, J./Saloner, G. (1985): Standardization, Compatibility, and Innovation, Rand Journal of Economics, Spring 1985, 16, 70-83.

Fey, Jürgen (1996): Es kann nur einen geben, in: c't Magazin für Computer Technik, Nr. 10, 1996, 96-100.

Fichtner, Matthias (1995): Zweck Ehen, in: PC Professionell, Nr. 6, 1995, 155-175.

Gerwin, Joachim; Höcherl, Ingrid (1995): Video 2000: Strategische Produktpolitik bei internationalem Wettbewerb, in: Brockhoff, Klaus (Hrsg.): Management von Innovationen: Planung und Durchsetzung; Erfolge und Misserfolge, Wiesbaden 1995, 17-44, 217-244.

Gonyeau, Joseph (2000): Virtual Nuclear Tourist, http://www.cannon.net/~gonyeau/nuclear/index.htm.

Hein, Mathias (1998): TCP/IP, 4. Auflage, Bonn 1998.

Herold, Helmut (1998): Linux-Unix-Grundlagen, 4. Auflage, Bonn 1998.

Herwig, Claus: E-Mail macht die Post zur Schnecke, in: PC Professionell, Nr. 2, 1996, 122-141.

Hunt, Craig (1998): TCP/IP Netzwerk-Administration, Deutsche Übersetzung von Peter Klicman, 2. Auflage, Köln 1998.

Jones (1999a): Personal Computers: History and Development 1999, http://www.digitalcentury.com/encyclo/update/pc_hd.html.

Katz, M. L./Shapiro, C. (1985): Network externalities, competition, and compatibility, in: The American Economic Review, Vol. 75, No. 3 (June 1985), 424-440.

Katz, M. L./Shapiro, C. (1994): Systems Competition and Network Effects, Journal of Economic Perspectives, Spring 1994, 8, 93-115.

Katzschke, Dirk (1987): Big Mac, in: c't Magazin für Computer Technik, Nr. 9, 1987, S. 54-58.

Kauffels, Franz-Joachim (1999): Lokale Netze, 11. Auflage, Bonn 1999.

Koch, Olaf G. (1997): Windows NT 4 Workstation - das Kompendium Platin Edition, Haar 1997.

Koch, Olaf; Meder, Norbert; Scheuber, Peter;Smiatek, Thomas (1997): OS 2 Warp Version 4 - das Kompendium, Haar 1997.

Krienke, Rainer (1998): Unix für Einsteiger, 2. Auflage, München 1998.

Kuri, Jürgen: Mächtiger Mailer, in: c't Magazin für Computer Technik, Nr. 16, 1999, p. 58.

Lauer, Thomas (1999): Internet, München 1999.

Leist, K.; Graf, K.: Straßenfahrzeuge mit Gasturbinenantrieb, in: Forschungsberichte des Wirtschafts- und Verkehrsministeriums Nordrhein-Wesfalen, Nr. 242, Köln.

Liebowitz, S. J./Margolis, S. E. (1990): The fable of the keys, Journal of Law and Economics, Vol. 33, 1990, 1 - 25.

Liebowitz, S. J./Margolis, S. E. (1994): Network Externality: An Uncommon Tragedy, in: The Journal of Economic Perspectives, Spring 1994, 133-150.

Liebowitz, S. J./Margolis, S. E. (1995a): Are Network Externalities A New Source of Market Failure? In: Research in Law and Economics, 1995.

Liebowitz, S. J./Margolis, S. E. (1995b): Path Dependence, Lock-In, and History, Journal of Law, Economics and Organization, April 1995, 11, 205-226.

Liebowitz, S. J./Margolis, S. E. (1998): Path Dependence, in: The New Palgraves Dictionary of Economics and the Law, 1998, also: http://wwwpub.utdallas.edu/~liebowit/palgrave/palpd.html.

Liebowitz, S. J.; Margolis, Stephen E. (1999): Winners, Losers & Microsoft, Oakland 1999.

Lindquist, Christopher: E-Mail-Clients, http://coverage.cnet.com/Content/Reviews/Compare/Emailclients/.

Marcella, A./Chan, S. (1993): EDI Security, Control, and Audit, Norwood 1993.

Ortmann, Jürgen/Andratschke, Wolfgang (1998): Windows 1998, Bonn 1998.

Pompili, Tony (1998): Groupware, http://www8.zdnet.com/pcmag/features/groupware/.

Poole, K. T. (1997): Entrepreneurs and Path Dependence, http://k7moa.gsia.cmu.edu/entrepd.htm.

Power, D.J. (2000): A Brief History of Spreadsheets, http://www.dssresources.com/history/sshistory.html.

Rojahn, Matthias (1990): Neu eingekleidet, die deutsche Version von Windows 3.0, in: c't Magazin für Computer Technik, Nr. 8, 1990, 124-128.

Sanford, Glen (2000): History, http://www.apple-history.com/history.html 2000.

Segev, A./Porra, J./Roldan, M. (1997): Internet-Based EDI Strategy, working paper 97-WP-1021, http://haas.berkeley.edu/~citm/wp-1021.pdf.

Siering, Peter (1999): Halloween - Linux macht Windows NT zu schaffen, in: c't Magazin für Computer Technik, Nr. 6, 1999, 184-186.

Siering, Peter (2000): Der letzte Zug - Windows 2000 auf dem Prüfstand, in: c't Magazin für Computer Technik, Nr. 4, 2000, 180-187.

Steinmann, Horst/Heß, Gerhard (1993): Die Rolle von Marktsignalen bei der Etablierung von Kompatibilitätsstandards im Rahmen der Wettbewerbsstrategie, in DBW 53/2, 1993, 166-187.

Storm, Ingo T. (1994): Kernfrüchte, in: c't Magazin für Computer Technik, Nr. 12, 1994, 108-109.

Stranahan, Paul; Wiegand, Gerhard (1999): Software History and Development, http://www.digitalcentury.com/encyclo/update/software.html.

Strasheim, Christian (1995): Die Entdeckung des Pomp - Windows contra OS/2, in: PC Professionell, Nr. 10, 1995, 126-156.

Waltner, C. (1997): EDI Travels The Web - EDI over the Web offers companies cheaper E-commerce and messaging via browsers, in: Internetweek, Issue 668, June 16, 1997, http://www.techweb.com/se/directlink.cgi?CWK19970616S0066.

Walzer, P. (1991): Die Fahrzeug-Gasturbine, Düsseldorf 1991.

Weber, Volker (1997): Bürofanten, in: c't Magazin für Computer Technik, Nr. 6, 1997, 124-131.

Weber, Volker (1999): Office Neunundneunzig, in: c't Magazin für Computer Technik, Nr. 3, 1999, 88-90.

Weitzel, Tim/Harder, Thomas/Buxmann, Peter (2001): Electronic Business and EDI mit XML, Heidelberg 2001.

Westarp, F. v./Buxmann, P./Weitzel, T./König, W. (1999): The Management of Software Standards in Enterprises - Results of an Empirical Study in Germany and the US, SFB 403 Working Paper, Frankfurt University, Jan. 1999, http://www.vernetzung.de/eng/b3.

Westarp, F. v./Weitzel, T./Buxmann, P./König, W. (2000): The Standardization Problem in Networks - A General Framework, in: Jakobs, K. (Hrsg.): Standards and Standardization: A Global Perspective, Idea Publishing Group.

White, Stephen (2000a): A Brief History of Computing, http://ox.compsoc.net/~swhite/history.html 2000.

White, Stephen (2000b): A Brief History of Computing - Timetable, http://ox.compsoc.net/~swhite/timeline.html 2000.

Wilson, Brian (1999): Internet Explorer, http://bonik.infor.ru/indexdot/history/ie.htm.

II Infrastructure

A network is constituted by actors and relationships. Actors interact with each other according to the defined relationships. From a technology viewpoint, a networking infrastructure is required in order to enable the interactions. Such infrastructures are composed of hardware and software components which facilitate the development and operation of interoperable application programs. A major technical challenge is to find appropriate programming abstractions as well as user interfaces that hide the complexity of the underlying system. Thus, the technical infrastructure should ease the coordination of the interactions between the actors in the network.

From an organizational viewpoint, legal regulations applied to business relations serve a similar purpose. A set of legal regulations allows actors, i.e. business partners, to establish contracts, provide their services and exchange goods, and perform whatever kind of action their business relation requires - all in a well defined and coordinated manner. Hence legal regulations define a kind of infrastructure as well. This part of the book presents two technical articles which address distinct application requirements as well as one article discussing the legal regulations of Public Key Infrastructures (PKI). While the technical articles primarily deal with issues of mobility in computer networks and Quality of Service management, they nevertheless presume application environments where interactions between actors require distinct precautions, such as authentication of users and data confidentiality, among others. PKI provides the necessary infrastructure - the legal environment - in which authentication and encryption of data can be established between actors using electronic means for their communication.

Supporting Mobility through Computer Networks

Anselm Lingnau, Michael Matthes, Oswald Drobnik

Johann Wolfgang Goethe-University
Institute of Biologie and Informatik (ABVS/Telematik)
D 60054 Frankfurt am Main
{lingnau|matthes|drobnik}@tm.informatik.uni-frankfurt.de

Introduction

The development of concepts for the efficient support of mobility through computer networks is an important topic of current research. One major focus of this research deals with making convenient services for computer-based wireless communication available in addition to existing voice-based mobile communication systems. This integration of wireless and IP-based communication requires efficient transport mechanisms. Widespread existing and future standards for radio communications such as GSM, GPRS, and UMTS, but also HyperLAN and IEEE 802.11 in the area of in-house computing, form the basis of mobile computing. But so far, techniques for IP-based communication have been geared towards the characteristics of fixed networks, and they must be adapted to the properties of wireless links if they are to be used efficiently for mobile data communication. Furthermore, the basic IP protocol is not immediately suitable for use by mobile subscribers and devices. Extensions to existing protocols are required in this area as well. Besides enabling mobility for users of data communications or network access devices, there is another important research issue in computer networking which deals with mobility: mobile software components. This includes concepts like mobile agents that can move autonomously in a heterogeneous computing environment in order to perform tasks such as database queries on behalf of their users, thereby increasing communications efficiency in computer networks. Mobile agents also offer a powerful approach to the personalization, flexibility and scalability of network services both in telecommunications and traditional computer applications. Both these research areas deal with different aspects of computer-based mobility, but they are both equally crucial to the future development of applications intended to run in mobile environments. Such applications must be able to adapt to dynamically changing environmental conditions which can, for example, be caused by user mobility. They also need to offer interfaces for interaction with mobile software components. The technical means of mobility support must be designed from various points of view and on various levels of computer-based communication. This entails the extension or development of protocols suitable for handling mobility properties. In particular, concepts which enable the technical aspects of communication to correlate with the user-centered areas of application support are required. An important issue in this context is the increasing convergence of services in the telecommunications and computer fields, such as the merging of voice and data services in mobile communications (telephony, telefax, SMS, e-mail, WAP, ...) or the fusion of „traditional" television and the World-Wide Web by means of set-top boxes and internet-based multimedia services. The rapidly increasing popularity of mobile devices such as cellular phones and the imminent introduction of new wireless communication standards such as UMTS, which are especially geared towards multimedia support, imply that the issue of mobility support is of paramount importance to the emerging communication society. The development of mechanisms for mobility support will result in extended opportunities for actors to establish and maintain relationships by means of computer networks. In addition to describing the aforementioned areas of research in more detail, this contribution attempts to point out various approaches to convergence as a basis of future networking infrastructures and to underline their significance for the emergence of such relationships.

After a brief introduction to various aspects of mobility, we begin by examining technical support for mobility through devices and protocols before proceeding to system support for mobility at the level of mobile processes and mobile agents. Finally, we discuss the convergence of mobile hardware/protocol and mobile software concepts leading to mobile applications that are "aware" of the relevant requirements and constraints in order to make the best use of mobility on behalf of their users.

Aspects of Mobility

Overview

Today, the use of information processing and communication techniques plays a crucial role in business. The increased performance and miniaturization of computation and communication devices permits actors to take part in communication and business processes regardless of their current location—they can work outside their regular workplace, or even on the move. Mobile communication technology gives them a great amount of flexibility and ensures their integration in ongoing business. However, there may be situations in which the reachability of mobile actors is not guaranteed, or in which the possible extent of communication support is influenced by the availability of mobile terminals and communication infrastructures [Reichwald/Möslein/Sachenbacher/Englberger/Oldenburg 1998, Varschney/Vetter 2000].

In view of the wide range of aspects of mobility the mobility of cooperation partners and their support by suitable communication mechanisms are the center of attention. Efficient support for mobility needs to provide increased flexibility for actors and must thus cover:

- optimal reachability and communication capability regardless of the current location,
- capabilities for initiating communication contacts regardless of the current location,
- decrease in the response time of remote mobile users,
- movement during communication connections,
- access to company-internal databases as well as external databases of other companies or service providers,
- consistency guarantees for data, for example by means of distributed transaction systems.

Compliance with these requirements integrates mobile actors into internal business processes and facilitates contact with cooperation partners.

Research and development of efficient support mechanisms for computer-aided cooperation takes place within the context of *computer-supported cooperative work* (CSCW). Different types of cooperation can be identified, and these require suitable procedures for their support by computer. Generally, business processes consist of asynchronous and synchronous cooperation phases. Another distinction is based on the spatial distribution of the cooperation partners. Furthermore, cooperation can be carried out indirectly, for example by the forwarding of documents as part of a predefined workflow, or directly, for example in a face-to-face session [Borghoff/Schlichter 1999].

The various cooperation mechanisms which are needed for the different cooperation phases make different performance requirements of the underlying communication infrastructure. The implementation of a face-to-face session via a video conference system presupposes, for example, a certain minimum bandwidth and minimum delay during data transfer, so that an acceptable quality of live video and audio can be provided. Modern packet-oriented high-speed networks with their high throughput rate and low transfer delay permit the use of cooperation support applications that demand high communication bandwidth. However, within the widespread IP-based networking infrastructure there are still no mechanisms to enforce application-dependent requirements for a certain *quality of service* (QoS). The approach to quality of service which is effectively used in most current computer networks follows the "best effort" principle.

The performance of a communication infrastructure can vary over time. If, for example, congestion occurs during a computer-aided cooperation session so that effective cooperation is no longer possible, it could become necessary to abort the session and to settle for asynchronous communication instead. Integration of mobile actors into business processes implies having to deal with varying communication conditions, for instance if participants are in motion during a synchronous cooperation phase, and the communication connection can be subject to fluctuations [Kleinrock 2000].

Furthermore, mechanisms are needed to preserve the consistency of data during asynchronous phases, since mobile actors usually operate on copies of data which require synchronization after processing. Computer-aided cooperation support must cover both indirect communication (asynchronous information exchange) and direct communication. For this, cooperation applications must interact with the infrastructure to adapt their behavior to the dynamically varying conditions within mobile environments.

Different Kinds of Mobility

From the point of view of system support for mobility, several different kinds of mobility can be distinguished:

- *user mobility*,
- *device mobility*,
- *software mobility*.

The mobility behavior of users can be characterized in different ways. We distinguish the following kinds of mobility behavior which influence the actual ability to participate in ongoing working processes [Kristoffersen/Ljungberg 1998]:

- *Wandering*: an activity characterized by extensive local mobility—for example, wandering between different offices in a single building.
- *Traveling*: an activity that takes place while moving in a vehicle—for example, editing a paper on a laptop computer while commuting by train.
- *Visiting*: An activity that happens in one (remote) place for a prolonged but limited period of time—for example, a consultant working in a customer's office during the course of a project.

These different kinds of mobility behavior need to be supported by different technologies, protocols and mobile devices. In general, there are two types of mobile devices:

- *portable devices*: devices which are not active while they are moving and have to be explicitly integrated in current communication infrastructures—for example, laptop computers without a wireless modem connection.
- *mobile devices*: devices may be active during movement and provide connection to communication infrastructures at that time—for example, cellular telephones or wireless PDAs.

Wandering behavior demands mobile equipment, and visiting requires portable equipment at least. Working with portable devices is often referred to as *off-line working*, which means that, most of the time, there is no connection to a communication infrastructure. Off-line, the user often needs to work on previously-obtained working copies of documents, which must eventually be made (or kept) consistent with the original documents. Therefore software mobility requires explicit management actions.

There are also *active software components*: Sometimes it could be useful if some computational work could take place on a remote computer, e.g., a user could send a software agent to a database to handle a query on his behalf and then go off-line. When coming on-line again, the user would receive the query results. Thus, on the surface, there are two kinds of mobile software:

- *software data*: various kinds of documents.
- *active software*: programs, mobile agents.

It turns out that this distinction is somewhat fuzzy given *active documents* such as network messages that can encapsulate protocols, word-processing documents containing workflow management logic, etc.

The decision which kind of mobile equipment to use is driven by the selection of tasks that a mobile user expects to perform. As work proceeds, there could be changes in the environment (e.g., loss of a communication link) or in the work pattern (e.g., some information needs to be researched on-line while working on a presentation on the train) that imply a change of mobility support equipment. Thus methods need to be developed which both support the mobility scenarios outlined above and also allow for transitions between these scenarios that are as seamless as possible.

Technical Challenges

Mobility introduces new management issues. Two basic problems need to be solved to guarantee effective mobility management: *location management* and *movement detection* of mobile users. Signaling and network management involves being able to locate and track users and to provide a means of changing the current network access point—the entity such as a wireless base station or a network socket—even while a connection is active (*handover procedures*) [Fieger/Zitterbart/Keller/Diederich 1999]. The location problem arises because the system needs to know where a user is at any given time in order to forward incoming data appropriately. Therefore the network must be able to track mobile devices while they are moving. The current location of a user needs to be updated periodically by the network management system, and it could become necessary to change a device's network access point in response to its user's movements. Therefore the properties of the current access link (e.g., its signal-to-noise ratio) must be monitored continually in order to determine the station of the mobile communication network that is best suited to provide access for the mobile station.

Mobility does not directly imply the use of wireless technologies, while, on the other hand, wireless technology does not necessarily support mobility. The most convenient way of taking advantage of mobility support is via wireless interfaces. But mobility within a wireless environment, in particular, requires special considerations, since, compared with classic (wired) telecommunications systems, wireless communication technology tends to be restricted. In particular, radio channels are inherently unreliable, and the available bandwidth is usually limited. The unreliability of radio links is responsible for their error-prone characteristics and is mostly caused by the following phenomena:

- *path loss*: Signal power decreases as the distance from the sender increases.
- *shadow fading*: Obstructions, such as buildings or trees, along the propagation path may cause significant signal attenuations.
- *multipath fading*: Due to various objects and reflectors, signals aren't propagated to receivers along the most direct route, but are instead scattered in many directions. Therefore, multiple versions of the signal, coming from different angles and with different attenuations and delays, are received.
- *movement*: The channel impulse response may change over time due to movement of the mobile station or to movement in the environment, such as passing vehicles or people.

There are various error control techniques which are used to improve channel reliability, such as *forward error control* (FEC), where the transmitter adds redundant symbols to the information stream that are used by the receiver to correct transmission errors.

The currently-available bandwidth is also affected by interference from other wireless services (e.g., broadcast radio or television). Because the available radio spectrum is limited, a major research issue in wireless networks is to develop bandwidth-efficient techniques to increase the number of users who can be accommodated for a given available bandwidth. A major breakthrough in this context was the invention of the cellular concept.

Quality-of-Service Aspects

Different mobile application scenarios make different quality-of-service requirements of the communication infrastructure. For example, a synchronous videoconferencing application needs high transmission bandwidth to accommodate several simultaneous multimedia streams as well as a low transmission delay for real-time display and audio. Asynchronously transmitted media like e-mail do not require such a high level of system performance [Dutta-Roy 2000].

Future mobile communication systems (e.g., GPRS, UMTS) provide [I'm not sure of the use of the present tense here: if they're FUTURE, how can they be providing things now? one would normally say 'will provide']several services to obtain a specific performance quality. Usually the following quality-of- service criteria are supported:

- *service priority*: There are several levels of priority (e.g., low, normal, high) to define the precedence of specific services and to control the transmission of data packets, for example to control the packet dropping in cases of congestion.
- *reliability*: This term includes aspects like packet loss, sequence preservation, and the probability that packets will be corrupted in transit. Here, for example, different methods of error detection and correction can be applied.
- *delay*: In packet switched networks, the total delay of a packet depends on the sum of the delays in every intermediate system on the transmission path. Different priorities could favor the forwarding of specific packets to a greater or lesser extent.
- *jitter*: The variation in the transmission time of data packets. For example, jitter can be caused by variations in the processing time needed to forward packets in intermediate systems or to reorder packets that have arrived out of sequence because they took different paths to the receiver.
- *throughput*: This is the effective data transfer rate measured in bits per second. The required bandwidth can be specified by the expected peak and mean throughput.
- *security*: Security services include, for example, protection against eavesdropping or unauthorized access, access control, or protecting the privacy of the user.

In many cases, service guarantees are provided by means of different *service classes* that aggregate suitable combinations of attributes within the preceding categories.

Mobile Devices and Protocols

Approaches to Mobility Support

To add mobility support to traditional applications for communication and cooperation, new communication protocols must be developed or existing protocols adapted. Owing to the ongoing miniaturization and performance increase of mobile devices (e.g. cellular telephones, WAP-capable cellular telephones, PDAs, ...), communication protocols need to support several different types of device in order to provide mobility support in heterogeneous communication environments. For mobility support, there are two main kinds of communication procedures to be considered: voice communication (such as GSM) and data communication (Internet, local area networks). There are several standards with different kinds of service quality supporting access for mobile devices, which can be roughly divided into *mobile communication systems* and *wireless local area networks* (LANs).

Some of the better-known current or imminent mobile communication systems include:

- The *Global System for Mobile Communication* (GSM)
- The *General Packet Radio System* (GPRS)
- The *Universal Mobile Telecommunications System* (UMTS)
- The *Wireless Application Protocol* (WAP)

Some wireless LAN concepts are:

- IEEE 802.11, *HiperLAN*, *Bluetooth*, *IrDA*,
- *Mobile-IP*, *Cellular-IP*.

The most convenient and flexible way of accessing the communication infrastructure is through a cellular telephone, due to the wide coverage of current wireless telephony systems. But today only low-bandwidth connections are supported (for example, 9.6 kbps in GSM). Therefore the cellular network's computer-based cooperation support capabilities are limited. Newer standards offer higher bandwidths (for example, up to 115 kbps in GPRS, and up to 2 Mbps in UMTS) and so allow better and more complex cooperation support. Furthermore, the newer standards are based on packet-switched instead of circuit-switched networking and are optimized for data communication as well as voice.

The wide availability of modern mobile communication infrastructures makes it possible to initiate and perform computer-supported cooperation independently of the participants' current location. However, in specific locations radio-based or infrared-based systems can be used to give mobile devices wireless access to local area networks (LAN) which may be connected to the global Internet. The most important such standards are IEEE 802.11 and HiperLAN. These approaches allow higher bandwidths (up to 54 Mbps) but are only available locally. Typical application scenarios include trade shows, airports, train stations or hotels that provide Internet access to travellers or guests. In-house intranets with flexible wireless access to the company's internal network infrastructure are also becoming more and more widespread.

Although UMTS has been put forward as the most important future mobile communications standard, advances in wireless LAN standardization have resulted in interesting alternative approaches [Walke 2000]. For example, an access network based on HiperLAN together with a high-speed wired network infrastructure could provide mobile bandwidth which would exceed theUMTS currently offered. It remains to be seen to what extent these new developments will influence the imminent changeover from GSM-based mobile communications to UMTS, in view of the large investments in UMTS licenses by most mobile system service providers.

Mobile Devices

Mobile devices are necessary to participate in day-to-day business even if one is absent from one's workplace. Optimally, mobile devices should be compact, lightweight and easily portable for traveling. Furthermore, they should make it possible to initiate connections with cooperation partners at all times (*ubiquitous computing*) and be similar in performance to the devices used in the normal work environment.

Some typical portable or mobile devices include:

- *Portable computers (laptops, notebooks)*: These are more or less completely equivalent to "traditional" computers like those found in offices—they feature high computational and graphics performance and large secondary storage (hard disk) and can include or access various peripherals such as CD-ROM or DVD-ROM drives, audio output, high-speed networking, printers, or video beamers. Portable computers allow a full range of applications including multimedia presentations, financial modeling, database retrieval, desktop publishing and authoring, software development etc. They can also be equipped with various kinds of mobile communication devices, including infrared or wireless LAN access, analog or ISDN modems, and GSM modules. *Sub-notebooks* occupy the territory between notebooks and PDAs (see below); they are less powerful and flexible than notebooks but offer more convenient data entry facilities than PDAs.

- *Cellular telephones*: These are the most ubiquitous type of mobile communication device and have achieved a very high degree of coverage in many countries. Cellphones support voice communication and certain restricted data applications such as *short message service* (SMS); in conjunction with laptop computers or PDAs they can offer access to data services such as fax and Internet services like e-mail or the World-Wide Web. A fairly new service is the Wireless Application Protocol (WAP), a global standard for providing Internet communications and advanced telephony services on digital mobile phones.

- *Personal digital assistants (PDAs):* Small, special-purpose computers for mobile use. PDAs serve as diaries, address books, notepads, e-mail clients, dictaphones or news readers. On account of their size they normally forgo large displays and typewriter keyboards in favor of pen-based input; another important design feature is ease of synchronization between the PDA's contents and a standard desktop PC. [Comerford 2000].

It is possible to use several of these appliances separately, depending on current communication demands, or to connect them for special use, for example to access the Internet from a PDA via a cellular phone's integrated "soft modem".

Protocols

Most mobile or portable devices let their users work *off-line*: before they leave their office, the necessary data is copied to the mobile device, which they can use to work on the data while they are away. When they come back, the results are *synchronized* with the original data. For instance, PDAs generally support this for addresses, diary items and other bits and pieces of information (PIM: Personal Information Management). Synchronization can also take place during the journey by means of a suitable communication medium, such as a modem-equipped cellular phone. Wireless communication links are the most convenient method of connecting a mobile device with a fixed networking infrastructure.

For compatibility with computer-based cooperation applications in the wired network, wired-network procedures and protocols must be used. Generally that implies using the TCP/IP protocol stack. However, wired-network protocols are optimized according to the characteristics of fixed networks and are therefore only of limited utility across radio communications links. Therefore, using such protocols over wireless links is possible, but not necessarily optimal [Wolisz 1999]. For example, the reliable protocol TCP guarantees the delivery of packets. The reliability mechanism in TCP is based on fixed-network traffic characteristics and reacts accordingly in the event of packet loss. Packet loss on a wired network is most often due to congestion, which is appropriately handled by TCP. While packet loss through incorrect transmission can be neglected in a fixed network, in radio-based systems packet loss usually happens because of errors on the "air interface", the wireless link. Air as a transmission medium cannot be shielded as efficiently against interference as a cable or optic fibre. Possible sources of interference include microwave emitters, electrical devices, or other radio sources. The disadvantages of wireless compared to wired networks can be summarized as follows:

- Higher error rates due to interference on the radio link (for example by electronic devices or radio sources) .
- Restrictive regulation of the radio frequency spectrum; frequency use must be coordinated between commercial wireless service providers and other utilizers of the spectrum such as television networks, aviation or military radio traffic. This usually entails international treaties.
- Lower throughput (today several Mbps locally, but only 9.6 kbps generally, e.g., via GSM).
- Higher delays and jitter.
- Less security against eavesdropping, because the air interface is accessible to everyone.
- Always a shared medium, requiring adequate medium access methods.

Due to these properties of the transmission medium, wired-network protocols do not function optimally in wireless networks, but need to be adjusted in a suitable manner.

One problem in this context is detecting whether a communication link between two devices includes wireless sub-paths. The protocol stack is divided into several mostly independent layers, such that, for example, TCP—as a transport-level protocol—is not informed of the physical condition of the transmission path as evident on lower protocol layers. Furthermore, several different techniques (mixed wireless links, or cable links) can be used by a single connection, because the entire path from a sender to a recipient is usually divided into several parts. Here multi-layer covering mechanisms must be developed to enable optimum integration of radio-based devices into existing communication infrastructures.

Flexible integration into existing infrastructures, however, covers only one aspect of the support of mobile cooperation. To be optimally integrated in the collaborative process even while traveling, accessibility of the cooperation partners must be guaranteed regardless of their current location. This is called *location transparency*. As the points through which a device attaches to the communication infrastructure change, the current address under which the device is reachable must always be updated. Nodes on the Internet are identified by a unique *Internet protocol* (IP) address, which allows the current location of the node within the Internet to be determined. Thus data transmission from a transmitting station to a receiving station is possible over the TCP/IP protocol. When a mobile device is connected to the Internet via a local service provider, it is assigned a temporary IP address by means of which it can be reached as long as its access point does not change. In order to initiate a communication with other cooperation partners, this temporary IP address must first be made public. If the other cooperation partners are also moving about, this may be difficult.

The Mobile-IP protocol is an extension of the IP protocol and allows for mobile IP-based devices. Mobile terminals can be reached under the same IP address regardless of their whereabouts (in the main office or elsewhere). Therefore, establishing contact with cooperation partners only requires finding a suitable schedule, not their location. Furthermore, with mobile IP the access point to the communication infrastructure can be changed even while communication connections are active, without having to reconfigure any applications or the mobile devices themselves (*seamless roaming*). Mobile-IP supports "real" mobile work as opposed to temporary, limited cooperation connections, i.e., "portable" devices become "mobile" devices.

We will now examine in more detail some of the mobility support techniques mentioned earlier on.

Mobile Access

GSM, GPRS, UMTS

The *Global System for Mobile Communication* (GSM) is the most successful mobile communication system in Europe. In contrast to the preceding analog systems, GSM is a second-generation digital system [Eberspächer/Vögel 1999]. The goal of GSM development was to supply a system that offers uniform service for voice communication within most of Europe while ensuring compatibility to existing wire-based speech transmission systems (ISDN and other PSTN systems). GSM technology is focused primarily on speech transmission: voice information is digitized, compressed and transferred digitally, and reconstituted as speech within the recipient's GSM device. The GSM voice data compression method is "lossy", which means that, to improve compression rates, some information is removed during compression according to a psycho-acoustic model of human hearing. At the other end, this loss will not actually be noticeable, or will at least remain within acceptable boundaries. This lossy compression scheme, however, is problematic for data communication. Transmitting binary data such as e-mails with this compression mechanism would distort the information in such a way that the original data could not be reconstructed. For data communication across GSM, a special procedure was developed which operates at a transmission rate of 9.6 kbps.

Since data communication is becoming more and more important in relation to voice communication, an extension of the GSM system was adopted, the *General Packet Radio System* (GPRS). It is a purely packet-oriented transmission scheme, which is ideally suited for communication applications based on the TCP/IP transmission protocol. This system will be deployed during the second half of the year 2000. It provides much higher data transmission rates than GSM—the GPRS standard specifies four different codecs, which offer different data rates, and with different coding schemes data rates within the range of 9.05–72.4 kbps or 13.4–107.2 kbps can be obtained.

The *Universal Mobile Telecommunications System* (UMTS) is destined to become the successor of the second-generation radio systems such as GSM, and thus can be called a third-generation system. A data transmission rate of 384 kbps is going to be implemented within the whole coverage area, and within certain regionally-limited locations, so-called *hot spots* like airports, train stations and shopping centers, transmission rates of up to 2 Mbps are to be offered. UMTS is therefore 40 to 200 times faster than today's digital mobile communication networks. Compared to current wireless standards, UMTS operates very flexibly, i.e., it detects voice and data transmissions automatically and adapts the data rate according to the type of information being sent or received.

These high data rates make new mobile applications possible, such as improved e-commerce or "mobile multimedia" applications like video conferencing. It is also feasible to implement the "mobile Internet" with multimedia contents. Since the introduction of the *Wireless Application Protocol* (WAP), WWW content is already accessible to common mobile devices, but only the newer mobile communication systems such as UMTS allow multimedia contents to be included as well.

IEEE 802.11

The IEEE 802.11 standard defines protocols for wireless local networks. It specifies *ad-hoc networks* and *infrastructure networks* [IEEE 802.11 1999]. An ad-hoc network is a simple network where communications are established between multiple stations in a given coverage area without the use of an access point or server. An infrastructure network uses an access point that controls the allocation of transmission time for all stations and permits mobile stations to access the wired network. It also allows mobile stations to roam between radio coverage cells.

The IEEE 802.11 standard specifies the *physical layer* (PHY) and *Media Access Control* (MAC) layer. The physical layer can choose from two *radio transmission* (RF) methods and one *infrared method* (IR). The radio transmission standards are *Frequency Hopping Spread Spectrum* (FHSS) *and Direct Sequence Spread Spectrum (DSSS)*. Both are defined to operate in the so-called ISM (Industrial, Scientific, Medical) frequency band which is defined in the 2.4 GHz range. In most countries, operation in this band is unregulated and free of charge. The physical layer data rates reach from 1 Mbps to 11 Mbps (IEEE 802.11b). One infrared standard which operates in the 850-to-950 nm band and provides data rates from 1 to 2 Mbps is supported. Data security is accomplished by an encryption technique known as the *Wired Equivalent Privacy* (WEP). Its purpose is to protect data transmitted over the radio channel using a 64-bit key and the RC4 encryption algorithm.

The HiperLAN Family of Standards

The *High Performance Radio Local Area Network* (HiperLAN) has been developed by the *European Telecommunications Standards Institute* (ETSI) [Walke 1998]. It provides high data rates and thus supports multimedia applications. The operation of the HiperLAN is defined in the 5 GHz band, which is available for use in many countries.

HiperLAN specifies a family of standards including *HiperLAN Type 1* (HiperLAN/1), *HiperLAN Type 2* (HiperLAN/2), *HiperAccess* (initially called *HiperLAN Type 3*) and *HiperLink* (initially called *HiperLAN Type 4*). HiperLAN/1 is aligned with the IEEE 802 family of standards (e.g., IEEE 802.3 —Ethernet) and is very much like a modern wireless Ethernet. HiperLAN/1 supports a data rate of 23.5 Mbps. HiperLAN/2 is a standard which can be used world-wide. It achieves a very high transmission rate (up to 54 Mbps at the physical layer, and up to 25 Mbps at the Convergence layer). HiperLAN/2 also enables quality-of-service support, automatic frequency allocation, power saving and security (authentication and encryption) support.

Mobile Internet

The mechanisms introduced in the previous section explain how transparency of communication connections on protocol layer 2 (MAC layer) can be achieved. But on the Internet connections are part of protocol layer 3, the network layer. For mobile users to be permanently reachable and able to roam while using IP-based communication applications, connection transparency for TCP/IP must be available. The Mobile-IP protocol [Perkins 1997] was developed so that TCP/IP connections with mobile devices could be initiated and kept going during roaming. With Mobile-IP, a device can change its location and Internet access point without communication connections being aborted or reconfigured at the TCP level.

The Mobile-IP protocol is based on the Internet Protocol (IP), which governs the forwarding (routing) of packets on the network level, and extends these for the purposes of mobility. The routing of packets depends on the address information in the header of an IP packet, which routers use to pass it on to a certain designated IP subnet. Once the packet reaches that subnet, it can be received by the addressee. If a station which is addressed is not in its subnet, for example a laptop that has been taken on a business trip by its owner, no connection with this station can be established using the normal IP routing mechanisms. Mobile-IP provides mechanisms for the routing of IP packets to mobile stations which are temporarily connected to another (IP) network. A mobile station may also communicate with other stations while and after it changes its point of attachment to the Internet without reconfiguration becoming necessary. While visiting foreign networks, mobile stations maintain their permanent IP address as the target address of incoming communication connections.

The Mobile-IP components need to be available only in those stations which are intended to support mobility. Normal communication connections can be initiated with stations which do not specifically support Mobile-IP. In addition to roaming, Mobile-IP offers access to the usual services on the home network.

The mobility support in Mobile-IP is based on two different types of so-called *mobility agents*: *Home Agents* and *Foreign Agents*. These agents must be located on each IP subnet which is intended to support mobile stations. A home agent belongs in the subnet that a mobile station's permanent IP address is part of (its *home network*). While the mobile station is absent from its home network, its home agent relays incoming packets to the station's current location. Therefore the mobile station must always register its current location with its home agent. *IPIP encapsulation* or *tunneling* is used to forward the station's IP packets over standard IP; routers take into account only the address in the surrounding IP packet and forward it to the mobile station's current location. Before applications on the mobile station can process the packets, they must be *decapsulated*.

If a mobile station is currently connected through a *foreign network* rather than its home network, it is assigned a temporary *care-of address* by that network's foreign agent. On the foreign network, the mobile station can be reached by way of this care-of address. On the home network, packets arriving for the station are passed on by the home agent to that address. There are two types of care-of addresses:

- *Foreign agent care-of address*: The mobile station uses the address of the foreign agent as its forwarding address. The decapsulation of packets takes place via the foreign agent.
- *Co-located care-of address*: The mobile station receives an IP address from the foreign network's address pool for the time of its stay. The decapsulation is carried out by the mobile station itself.

With co-located care-of addresses there is no need for foreign agents if another service for the dynamic assignment of IP addresses exists on the subnet, for example a server for the *Dynamic Host Configuration Protocol* (DHCP) [Droms 1997].

Furthermore, mobility agents have the following functions:

- Support for movement detection of mobile stations,
- Management of mobile stations: registration, deregistration,
- Authentication: security mechanism for the identification of mobile stations and the management of access control.

The current efforts of the IETF are concerned with security aspects and accounting modalities in order to adapt Mobile-IP for commercial use. This occurs in the *AAA Working Group* (Authentication, Authorization, Accounting) [AAA 2000].

Besides the Mobile-IP protocol, which is particularly suitable for *macro mobility*, further mobility-supporting protocols have been developed at different research establishments. On the IP-layer, there is, for example, *Cellular-IP* [Campbell/Gomez/Valkó 1999], which is particularly suitable for *micro mobility*. Also, at the TCP level, various extensions have been developed, for example *TCP-Redirect* (TCP-R) [Funato/Okada/Tokuda/Saito 1999] or *Indirect-TCP* (I-TCP) [Bakre/Badrinath 1997].

Current research in mobile data communication focuses on the development of transport mechanisms that take into account the impact of wireless network segments on the efficiency of TCP/IP connections [Matthes/Krieger/Drobnik 2001].

Mobile Software: Processes and Agents

Mobile Processes

In former times, software was moved between computers by means of punched cards, magnetic tapes or floppy disks. When networking first became a viable proposition, moving *processes*—running programs as opposed to executable files—between computers aroused considerable interest. *Process mobility* is particularly useful in the contexts of *load balancing* (a heavily-loaded network node can offload some of its work to other, less loaded machines), *fault resilience* (processes migrate away from partially-damaged machines, or are moved off by system administration personnel prior to shutting down a network node for maintenance) or *data access locality* (to increase performance) [Milojičić/Douglis/Wheeler 1999]. Process mobility was implemented in various research operating systems [Barak/Wheeler 1989, Douglis/Ousterhout 1991] but never gained much acceptance in commercial systems. More recently, process mobility has been supported not at the operating system level, but at the user level (e. g., [Milojičić/Zint/Dangel/Giese 1993]). This reduces the complexity somewhat but still has not resulted in greater user demand than that for techniques such as remote invocation or remote data access. However, process mobility has experienced a "revival" in the context of *mobile agents*—processes that move of their own accord.

Mobile Agents

An "agent" is "anyone who acts on behalf or in the interest of somebody else" [Meyer 1971]. In computer science and artificial intelligence, *agent-based systems* have recently gained considerable attention, although nobody has yet managed to come up with a reasonably succinct definition of what an "agent" is actually supposed to be as far as software is concerned. For the sake of this discussion, we will stipulate that an *agent* is a computer program whose purpose is to help a user perform some task (or set of tasks). To do this, it maintains persistent state and can communicate with its owner, other users, other agents and its environment in general. Agents can do routine work for users or assist them with complicated and/or unusual tasks; they can also mediate on users' behalf between incompatible programs and thus generate new, modular, problem-oriented and work-saving solutions. An overview of agents and, in particular, the important topic of agent communication is given by Genesereth and Ketchpel [Genesereth/Ketchpel 1994].

Tasks that appear amenable to agents include electronic mail handling, where an agent helps with prioritizing, forwarding, deleting, archiving etc. of mail messages [Etzioni/Weld 1994]; scheduling of meetings (the people involved run agents that will negotiate a suitable date and time, reserve a conference room etc.) [Remmel 1996]; monitoring the stock exchange; filtering an information source such as

Usenet news for interesting items according to various rules or heuristics; or distributed knowledge management.

In a network of communicating computers, *mobile agents* are agents that can move about under their own control. This usually takes the form of special instructions or library calls that are embedded in the program text of a mobile agent, instructing it to "`go foo`", where `foo` is another node in the network. This means that the agent should cease running on the current node and be transported to node `foo` in order to continue operation there with its internal state (mostly) intact. Generally, this requires the use of a suitable *mobile agent infrastructure* on all nodes that are intended to support the execution of mobile agents.

The main strength of mobile agents lies in areas such as distributed database querying and information retrieval, active networking, network management, distributed software updates, or remote device control. Whereas the traditional client-server approach relies on mechanisms such as remote procedure calls to enable communication between clients and remote servers, mobile agents migrate to the server(s) in question to conduct a dialogue there by local interaction. This serves to reduce communication costs drastically, both as far as network load and latency are concerned. In general, agents can "meet" one another and communicate in order to carry out their assigned tasks. There are various surveys of mobile agent technology worth reading, for example [Pham/Karmouch 1998], as well as a "classic" paper which examines the question of whether mobile agents are worthwhile at all [Harrison/Chess/Kershenbaum 1995].

Agents in general, and mobile agents in particular, consist of *program code* defining an agent's actions and its associated internal *state*, e.g., the values of various global variables used in the code and the dynamic invocation stack of procedure calls and local storage defining the actual point in the program execution that the agent has reached. To *migrate* an agent involves moving both the code and the state to the desired location. *Strong* or *transparent migration* means that the dynamic stack is moved along with the contents of the agent's global variables; moving just the global variables is called *weak migration*. Strong migration is desirable from an agent author's point of view, since it makes it possible for the agent's execution to continue just as if the migration instruction ("`go foo`") was just another program statement or library call, while in the case of weak migration the agent is usually re-started at the beginning. However, strong migration is much harder to implement than weak migration; in particular, for languages like Java it can be very difficult to retro-fit to the existing language implementation [Fünfrocken 1998, see also Sakamoto/Sekiguchi/Yonezawa 2000 and Truyen/Robben/Vanhaute/Coninx/Joosen/Verbaeten 2000 for alternative approaches]. Furthermore, strong migration adds nothing to the expressive power of mobile agent implementation languages, since even if the agent code is re-entered from the beginning with global variables intact, it is always possible to reconstruct the appropriate execution context by suitable branching according to the value(s) of global variables. Therefore, strong migration, while nice to have, is strictly a convenience for the agent programmer.

Infrastructures for Mobile Agents

To be useful, a mobile agent needs to interact with its host system, users, and other agents—it must access information that the host offers or negotiate with users or other agents about the exchange of information or services. Agents must also be able to move within heterogeneous networks of computers, and it must be possible to restrict mobile agents to only those hosts that have actually been designated to host them (mobile code which executes on a computer without having been invited by that computer's owner is usually called a "worm", and viewed as a bad thing). Also, users must be able to submit new agents for execution, configure them, find out how they are getting on with their tasks, and revoke or destroy them if required. This makes it necessary to provide a suitable framework for agent operations—a standardized *mobile agent infrastructure*. Such an infrastructure must offer basic support for agent mobility and communications among agents as well as between agents and users. It must also protect the system it runs on from unauthorized access by mobile agents, enforce suitable limits or quotas on the use of system resources, and safeguard the agents' integrity as well as possible.

A great number of mobile agent infrastructures have been proposed and implemented [Hohl 2000]. Most of them are used for research, although some, such as ObjectSpace's *Voyager* [ObjectSpace], Mitsubishi Electric's *Concordia* [Mitsubishi], *Odyssey* by General Magic [General Magic], or IKV++'s *Grasshopper* [IKV++] are available commercially. (Many of the others can also be obtained via the Internet, most notably *Mole* from Stuttgart University, *Ara* from Kaiserslautern University, Dartmouth College's *D'Agents*, MIT's *Hive*, or *ffMAIN* [Lingnau/Dömel/Drobnik 1995], which was developed at the Johann Wolfgang Goethe-Universität by two of the authors of this contribution. Sources for these and many others are listed in [Hohl 2000].) Mobile agent infrastructures may, for example, be classified by the languages they support for implementing agents, by the kind of communication mechanisms used to enable agent communication, or the potential and methods for human users to interact with (their own as well as "foreign") agents.

The most popular language for agent implementation currently seems to be Java [Horstmann/Cornell 1997], even though the Java language and canonical implementation contain various shortcomings that can make life difficult. For example, the "portability" of Java byte code between various computer architectures has been wildly overrated: "With the current set of runtime environments, writing portable Java is very much the same as writing portable code in other languages: there are lots of little annoying things that differ from platform to platform." [Sienkiewicz 1998]. Requiring the language implementation to support threads, as Java does, also places high demands on the underlying operating system and impedes the implementation of Java-based agent infrastructures on small or portable devices such as PDAs. In fact, "Java" environments for small devices usually restrict themselves to supporting arbitrary non-standardized subsets of the language in order to achieve reasonable efficiency, which of course is detrimental to the "write once, run anywhere" maxim central to Java. At the same time, depending on the details of the implementation, the amount of code that must be moved from one location to another for a Java mobile agent can exceed that of an equivalent agent implemented in a very high-level language such as Tcl by more than an order of magnitude [Möbs 1998]. Nevertheless, the moderate success of Java as a language for enlivening World-Wide Web pages through "applets", which are after all a form of mobile code, seems to have enticed many researchers to adopt Java as their language of choice for mobile agents. Other languages used for mobile agents include Ajuba Solutions' Tcl [Ousterhout 1994], General Magic's Telescript (now defunct due to lack of commercial success) [White 1996] or even (interpreted) C [Peine 1997]. In particular, Tcl, as used in, e.g., *D'Agents*, Cornell University and the University of Tromsø's *TACOMA*, or *ffMAIN*, has proved to be a very suitable language for the implementation of mobile agents. Ideally, of course, a mobile agent environment would support agents written in a multitude of languages in order to make it possible to select the one best suited to the problem which the agent is required to solve.

Mobile Agent Communication and Coordination

In order to fulfill their assigned tasks, mobile agents need to communicate with other agents, with human users—their "owners", as well as others—, or with servers or data sources that form part of their execution environment. Concentrating first on agent-to-agent communication and coordination, we can differentiate between *spatial* and *temporal coupling.* In spatially coupled coordination, agents must explicitly name their communication partners, while in spatially uncoupled coordination this is not required. Spatial coupling usually implies temporal coupling, which means that communication between agents is synchronous—it happens at the same time for both partners. This is also called *direct coordination.* Direct coordination is not suitable as a general agent communication mechanism, because it places very high demands on networking protocols (explicitly named, mobile communication partners must be located elsewhere in the network) and network reliability; therefore it is usually restricted to local interaction in a client-server style. This approach is taken by most of the Java-based mobile agent systems, such as *Odyssey.*—In Java, the *remote method invocation* mechanism (RMI) is often used to allow mobile agents to communicate by invoking another agent's methods directly. (Java agents are usually implemented as objects in the Java language and thus support "attributes"—private data—as well as "methods" to access and modify these attributes.) The main problem here is finding out what sort of methods another agent supports and how they are supposed to be invoked. While syntactical issues like method names, method parameters and the types of a method's return value and parameters are reasonably straightforward to figure out using the language's introspection facilities, accurately describing and communicating the *semantics* of a given method to its prospective callers remains an open problem. One possible approach [Minar/Gray/Roup/Krikorian/Maes 1999] entails the use of the WWW Resource Description Framework (RDF, [Lassila/Swick 1998]) but falls short of a universal solution. Instead it is foreseen that the problem will be handled at the application level in a more-or-less ad-hoc fashion. Other problems with the direct approach include the fact that Java (like most object-oriented languages) maintains no explicit notion of "object ownership", so if two agents share access to the same object and one agent wants to migrate, it is unclear what ought to happen to the object—does it leave with agent *A* or stay with agent *B*? Telescript, as a language specifically designed for mobile agent implementation, does support object ownership, and when an agent migrates it takes along all the objects that it owns.

Spatially uncoupled but temporally coupled coordination is also called *meeting-based* coordination. Here, agents do not need to name their communication partners explicitly, but interaction takes place in the context of a known *meeting point* that agents enter in order to communicate. Here again, interaction is often restricted to agents which are present locally. The problem with meeting-based coordination is that it is easy to miss a meeting because the scheduling and routing of mobile agents is difficult to foresee. Typical mobile agent systems using meeting-based coordination include *Ara* [Peine 1997] and *Mole* [Straßer/Baumann/Hohl 1997].

An approach to coordination which is temporally uncoupled, and spatially coupled only to a certain degree, can be termed *blackboard-based* coordination. With this method, agents use a shared data space (an *information space* or *blackboard*) local to each agent server to deposit and retrieve data items (messages). This means that an agent does not need to name its communication partner(s), but agents need to agree on identifiers (*keys*) to use for messages [Lingnau/Drobnik 1996]. The advantage of this approach is that agents can leave messages without knowing when or by whom they will be picked up, which is appropriate in a system model where neither the locations nor the schedules of prospective communication partners are easy to discover or influence. Blackboard-based coordination is used in *ffMAIN*, and it also occurs in *Ambit*, a proposal for a formal model for mobile computations [Cardelli/Gordon 1998]. *ffMAIN* augments the blackboard scheme by access control lists and MIME types for blackboard items [Lingnau/Drobnik 1998]. In *ffMAIN*, it is possible to access the information space from outside the agent infrastructure by means of a WWW browser. Thus agents can interact with human users by means of suitably formatted (e. g., HTML) items in the information space.

Finally, in *LINDA-like* [Gelernter 1985] coordination, spatial coupling is removed as well as temporal coupling by using associative pattern matching on the items in a local tuple space themselves, which avoids the need to name them explicitly. In other respects it resembles the blackboard-based coordination model. Systems using LINDA-like coordination include *Jada* [Ciancarini/Rossi 1997]. *MARS* [Cabri/Leonardi/Zambonelli 1998] is an interesting system based on *reactive tuple spaces*, where the tuple space itself is programmable to a certain extent. These *reactions* can access the tuples, change their contents and influence agent access semantics. This makes it possible to institute specific policies for agent interactions as well as safeguard server integrity. Reactive tuple spaces can also help decouple coordination from the details of agent computation.

Mobile Agent Security

For software environments based on mobile agents, security is a most important topic. After all, many computer users have heard of malicious mobile programs such as "worms" and "viruses" [Shoch/Hupp 1982, Denning 1989, Spafford/Heaphy/Ferbrache 1989] that can potentially cause great damage to computer programs and data as well as much aggravation and extra work for people. Therefore it is important to deploy mobile agent systems that are *secure*.

Security, as applied to mobile agent systems, has a number of facets that must be examined. First, mobile agents roam large networks such as the Internet, which comprises computers belonging to a huge number of administrative domains. An agent server on the Internet is a potential host to mobile agents from diverse sources at various levels of trust. Therefore a mobile agent infrastructure must be able to restrict the operations that agents may perform according to the level of trust that is extended to them. For example, untrusted agents may be forbidden to open arbitrary files or network connections on the hosting computer, since this would enable them to, e. g., obtain a server's password database and send it to another site for off-line cracking. On the other hand, certain agents or classes of agents may be trusted to open and read certain files (but not change their contents), etc. This is a problem of *authorization*. Conversely, one often-quoted application of mobile agents involves "electronic commerce": agents migrating to various sites in order to negotiate for and purchase products or services on their users' behalf. In this scenario it is important that the service *provider* should not be able to analyze an agent's code in order to deduce its negotiation strategy and adjust its own behavior accordingly. To put it more crudely, agent servers ought not be able to steal (electronic) money from agents, to interfere with their code or state (such as sites to be visited next), or to let them disappear without trace.

Technically, it is much easier to safeguard a host from malicious agents than to safeguard an agent from a malicious host. Techniques for the former include *sandboxing* as well as executing untrusted code in separate execution contexts. In Java-based systems, sandboxing is usually implemented through a *security manager* class which allows access to various operations (such as opening files or network connections) to be controlled through methods that either authorize or forbid the operation in question. An agent infrastructure programmer can subclass or re-implement the Java security manager to tailor its operation to the application at hand. Recent Java versions allow for different *protection domains* within the same Java virtual machine, and this increases the flexibility of this approach somewhat [Möbs 1998]. In comparison, Tcl uses the concept of *safe interpreters* to execute untrusted code [Borenstein/Rose 1993]. Here, the system generates a completely new execution context (a "safe Tcl interpreter") in which "dangerous" operations do not exist to begin with, and hence cannot be misused by malicious agents. It is possible to redirect calls from within a safe interpreter to a trusted interpreter, which makes it possible to vet, e. g., a filename to be opened for harmlessness. This model is similar to the approach taken in operating systems, where user applications can make "system calls" which are executed at a higher privilege level, and makes it easy to design and implement much finer-grained security policies than the sandbox model. Furthermore, in the safe interpreter model it is straightforward to operate agents at a level of "least privilege". For example, if an agent needs access to a SQL database, rather than allowing it to open arbitrary sockets to contact the database server, or even to let it access the database server socket exclusively, a special command (a "system call") can be made available to the agent which takes an SQL query and returns its result. This minimizes the possibilities of misuse of the database by an agent sending it arbitrary SQL commands, and adds a second "level of defense" to the system in addition to the SQL database's access control mechanisms.

Assigning privileges to agents—authorization—relies on *authentication* to establish which agents are trustworthy and to what extent. Since it is impossible in general to deduce from an agent's code whether that agent is malicious or not, the usual approach is to summarily declare certain users' agents as trustworthy. User (agent programmer) identity can be established, e. g., by public-key cryptography [Schneier 1996]. In this scenario, a user *signs* an agent digitally with his private key before the agent is deployed to the network. Agent servers can then use the agent originator's public key to identify the agent as authentic and—by means of suitable hashes on the agent code—ensure that the agent itself has not been tampered with. (This of course presumes that the agent code does not change of its own accord while it is being moved.) Unfortunately it is impossible to safeguard an agent's state in the same manner, since the agent state changes during migration and cannot be digitally signed with the originator's key. However, an agent server can sign the agent state before the agent migrates to the next server, and so the integrity of the agent state can be ensured at least during transmission. In the same fashion, an agent's code and state can be encrypted to protect it from eavesdroppers during transmission, even though it needs to be decrypted on an agent server before it can be (re-)executed. (Sander and Tschudin [Sander/Tschudin 1998] propose a scheme for "executing" encrypted agents but this approach imposes very severe restrictions on the agents.)

Protecting agents from malicious hosts is much more difficult due to the fact that an agent server has full access to the mobile agent's code and state. This cannot be prevented using current computer technology, but misuse of agents can be made more difficult by deliberately "obfuscating" their code to make them less understandable. Together with a time limit after which the results obtained by such an agent are no longer trusted (an "expiration date") this makes it less likely that an agent's code will be analyzed and its properties exploited [Hohl 1998]. There are also techniques that help ensure that a result obtained from an agent was actually computed by that agent rather than introduced by a malicious server [Biehl/Meyer/Wetzel 1998]. However, this still does not prevent an agent server from making as many spare copies of an agent as necessary and negotiating with them until the most satisfactory result (for the server) is obtained, even if the original agent's code is too obfuscated to be directly understandable. Obfuscation techniques also carry the risk that the obfuscated code's semantics aren't equivalent to those of the original code.

An easy answer to the problem of untrustworthy agent servers is for agents not to go there in the first place. For example, critical negotiations could take place on a server that is trusted by all involved parties—in effect, a "notary public". Electronic marketplaces could be established under independent trusteeship as part of a municipal or regional infrastructure for electronic commerce. Since mobile agents cannot at this point be protected from malicious servers by technical means, for the time being it seems that administrative means, although imperfect, must remain the answer.

Convergence: Mobile Hardware, Mobile Agents, Mobile Applications

Mobile Applications

For actors in business processes to take advantage of the possibilities offered by modern mobile communication infrastructures, mobility and computer-supported cooperation services need to be integrated within *mobile applications*, resulting in systems that are suitable for direct end-user interaction. As detailed above, mobile applications must be able to cope with the characteristics of mobile environments in order to allow full computer-supported cooperation with mobile partners. This means that *mobile awareness* concepts must be made part of groupware systems at different levels dealing with communication links, individual applications, and specific working processes.

Several kinds of applications lend themselves to mobile scenarios. In particular, this section outlines collaborative applications which benefit from mobility support.

Today, probably the most popular and common form of mobile collaborative work supported by information processing and communication technology is *teleworking*. Within a business, opportunities for teleworking arise in various areas, in management just as in field service, in sales, customer advisory service and support, technical maintenance, and transport and logistics services. Mobile technology makes it possible to access relevant information in the office regardless of distance or location, or to keep centrally-stored mission-critical data such as customer data, price lists or contract conditions consistent at all times with the information available to representatives in the field. On the other hand, by acquiring data locally and transmitting it quickly to a central site, turnaround times are shortened and process quality is improved. This creates a competitive advantage [Reichwald/Möslein/Sachenbacher/Englberger/Oldenburg 1998, Picot/Reichwald/Wigand 1998].

Virtual collaboration projects are focused on particular goals but involve large numbers of participants communicating through computer-based technologies, for example via the Internet [e.g., Berghoff/Schuhmann/Matthes/Drobnik 1998, Brand/Mahalek/Sturzebecher/Zitterbart 1999]. A recent example is the "open-source" development of large software systems such as the Linux operating system, which has evolved through the Internet-based collaboration of thousands of programmers from all over the world. Volunteers can participate in the collaborative development process independently of their geographical location. With mobile communication, participation is possible at any time and from anywhere.
Distance learning enables "education on demand" through the storage, access and distribution of multimedia courseware over communication networks. Digital libraries make it possible to access multimedia files and transfer them over computer networks. Researchers all over the world can share large amounts of data and information conveniently and reliably. Even commercial companies are currently developing and installing distance-learning systems that implement *corporate universities* for in-house continuing education and advanced vocational training [e.g., Cheng/Yen 1998].

A new buzz-word in the world of Internet business is *m-commerce*, "mobile commerce" in contrast to mere "e-commerce" [Varschney 2000]. With commercial Internet-based applications accessible from their networks, most mobile communication providers foresee a great demand for services such as mobile advertising, mobile financial services (stock trading, electronic banking, telepayment) as well as location-specific mobile shopping services.

Mobile Agents in a Mobile Environment

At first glance, mobile hardware and low-level system concepts such as mobile communication protocols and mobile software paradigms such as mobile agents seem to be orthogonal concepts: mobile agents can operate well in a fixed-network infrastructure, while mobile devices do not require software mobility in order to be useful. However, it turns out that the mobile agent concept is ideally suited for a mobile hardware environment: with the limited bandwidth currently available on wireless links and the necessity of conserving power both during wireless transmissions and the operation of a mobile device itself, having to stay on-line for a lengthy remote query operation to complete is often not feasible or desirable. Instead, it would be much more convenient to send a mobile agent from the mobile device into the wired infrastructure to handle the query. After submitting the agent, the user can take the device off-line; the result of the query will be held until the device connects to the network once more. In fact it is not even necessary for the mobile device to be able to support a full-blown mobile agent infrastructure—given a mobile agent system such as *ffMAIN*, which allows users to configure and submit agents via the World-Wide Web, a generic web browser is all the software that is required on the part of the mobile user. Current PDAs support web browsers as a matter of course, and the approach may even be feasible via WAP on a suitably-equipped cellular telephone.

Mobile Awareness

Groupware supports various modes of communication for the support of teams whose members participate in the work process at different locations and times. Another task of groupware is the management of the work process itself. New challenges result from traveling team members who collaborate through mobile devices: on one hand, it must be determined to what extent a mobile group member can influence ongoing work, and on the other hand the mobile participants' reachability status must be considered. For example, it is crucial whether the currently-available resources support synchronous audio/video communication, or whether only asynchronous text-based communication via e-mail or file exchange is possible, e.g., because group members are not reachable directly, or are working off-line. These important considerations are summarily called *mobile awareness*. Both group members and the groupware itself must become "aware" of individual group members' mobility and the resulting effects, and mobility support must be available at the technical level (e.g., mobile devices, quality of connections) and at the application level (e.g., context-dependent participation in the working process, reachability).

Applications in mobile environments need communications services which are able to trace a user's location and to route data to them. These services have to adapt to varying conditions on the transmission path as well as changing links and link attributes. Due to user mobility, these characteristics can change drastically and are difficult to predict. Furthermore, even if the communication service tries to adapt to changing conditions, the application still needs to deal with reduced bandwidth, temporary losses of connection etc., and the user should be aware of current communication conditions and take into account varying transmission delays and slow feedback.

Mobile awareness introduces a new type of awareness to the domain of computer-supported cooperative work [Bürger 1999, Cheverst/Blair/Davies/Freiday 1998]. Constraints imposed by mobile environments may have effects on the cooperation abilities of group members. Some of these effects can have severe impacts on:

- reachability,
- the possibility of attaining a quorum for voting or decision making, depending on the reachability of the users,
- link quality provided by the underlying infrastructure, such as bandwidth limitations and a higher bit error probability for wireless links.

For users, mobile awareness means that group members are permanently kept informed about who is currently connected and what quality of service their communication links permit. Applications often require the flexibility to adapt their protocols to the varying properties of the group members' individual communication links. This is a well known problem in the area of Internet-based multimedia communications, and one approach is to guarantee QoS by implementing specific reservation protocols. However, since the mobility behavior of users is difficult to predict, such services are extremely difficult to establish in a mobile environment.

Another aspect that must be considered is what kind of technical support the mobile user needs to accomplish his tasks, and what sort of awareness information is required. Mobile awareness information should not only help carry out synchronous sessions and conferences, but also help with planning meetings and, more generally, with planning and coordinating cooperative work in teams including mobile members.

Mobile Collaboration Support

Support for mobile collaboration requires an infrastructure which is responsible for collecting and distributing mobile-specific awareness information.

With respect to the different kinds of mobility (see section 2), relevant awareness information can be classified into the following categories [Berghoff/Matthes/Drobnik 1999]:

- *member awareness*: information pertaining to a single user.
- *group awareness*: information about all group members and their respective reachability and working state.
- *session awareness*: information about ongoing working sessions.

Member awareness comprises the following information:

- Personal location
- Personal state (reachable, interruptible)
- Personal schedule
- Currently-available communication services and their quality.

In general, there are three different approaches to managing mobile awareness information [Burger 1998]:

- *Centralized approach*: a central system monitors and distributes information about all the group members.
- *Distributed approach*: each group member can request specific awareness notifications from any other group member.
- *Agent-based approach*: awareness agents handle the required awareness information. Awareness agents can be mobile agents which are sent to other group members in order to collect or distribute the relevant information remotely.

The agent-based approach has several advantages, especially in mobile environments. One can think of cooperating stationary and mobile agents that manage and adjust the parameters of mobile stations:

A stationary *office agent* is running in each users's home area. A user is associated with their office agent through a *personal agent* that resides on their (mobile) workstation. The personal agent sends all awareness information as well as other information about the user's state (e.g., location, link QoS) to the user's associated office agent. The office agent then distributes the aggregated information to other users. By distributing information via the office agent rather than directly by the personal agent, bandwidth on the link from/to the personal agent can be conserved. This is especially important when the group member is connected across an unreliable low-bandwidth link like a radio connection. Another advantage is that an office agent is always reachable independently of the state of associated users, whether they are in the "home" office, a remote office, or busy working.

Group members can obtain awareness information in two possible ways:

- *poll*: the personal agent asks the respective group member's office agent for specific information.
- *push*: the personal agent subscribes to notifications which are sent out continuously by the office agent.

For example, if a user just wants to know the current status of another group member (reachable, busy, away), the relevant awareness information can be polled. But in a closely-coupled group session there need to be immediate notifications during the entire lifetime of the session. Thus a group member can contact another user's office agent via its own personal agent in order to subscribe to these notifications, using filter specifications to describe the information of interest. The office agent collects these filter specifications and relays the appropriate awareness information to the original user's personal agent.

If a group member is taking a mobile station—for example, a notebook computer—to a remote place, the direct connection to the office agent is lost. A mobile *correspondent agent* moving through the wired network in parallel with the mobile user may substitute for the mobile user's office agent. Since it follows the mobile station, the mobile correspondent agent is located near the awareness information source. In this way, awareness information from the personal agent may be distributed more timely than via the office agent in the user's home area. If the mobile station is communicating over a wireless link, the mobile correspondent agent can additionally act as an gateway between the wired and wireless networks to compensate for the limited quality of wireless links. The office agent in the user's home area can provide the mobile correspondent agent with any required filtering and distribution specifications for the associated mobile station. All information from the mobile station can then be distributed by the mobile correspondent agent.

The agent-based infrastructure is not restricted to the distribution of awareness information. The office agent may be responsible for forwarding or caching data such as electronic documents. If a group member wants to submit a document he can query the receiver's office agent to find out whether the document will be forwarded or cached. In that way, workflows in the group can be supported. The actual workflow should take into account awareness information (whether someone is at their office, traveling, etc.). Awareness information was originally thought to support spontaneous and unstructured interactions between group members, but structured interactions (workflows) will also benefit from considering awareness information. Moreover, workflow management systems can supply awareness information concerning the current state of a workflow with regard to the persons involved, and its parameters.

Conclusion

In conclusion, both the desired applications and the underlying mobile (wireless) communication methods must be considered when mobility is to be supported. There are different types of working scenarios for mobile users, which are supported by different kinds of application scenarios—offline work, interactive communication, or the use of streaming applications (video, audio). In addition, quality of service aspects must be taken into account.

As applications become more advanced and make more complex requirements of the underlying network infrastructure, it will be necessary for them to interact with the network itself. The demand for mobility will also increase as people expect to be able to access their accustomed computer environment from anywhere and at any time. The interconnection of high-performance networks as well as the global interoperability of advanced mobile technologies is one of the key objectives in this area.

One of the key strengths of the Internet service model is that it hides the details of how messages are forwarded through the network. On one hand this design principle is extremely powerful, because it separates applications from the complexity of the underlying communications system. On the other hand, however, it simultaneously constrains applications because they cannot exploit a detailed knowledge of the properties of the underlying network to enhance their performance (e.g., active networks).

The integration of mobile awareness features into applications for computer-supported cooperative work is an important step towards location-independent or mobile teamwork.

It is evident that the future of networking will be governed by the convergence of mobile and fixed networking infrastructures. More research is needed to enable actors to exploit the full potential of this convergence to establish and maintain relationships as well as to adapt and utilize these technical developments to enhance business processes and evolve new business opportunities.

References

AAA (2000): IETF Working Group: *Authentication, Authorization and Accounting (AAA)*. The Internet Engineering Task Force, Active Working Groups, 2000

Barak, A./Wheeler, R. (1989): MOSIX: An Integrated Multiprocessor UNIX, in: *Proc. of the USENIX Winter 1989 Technical Conference*, 101–112, February 1989

Berghoff, J./Matthes, M./Drobnik, O. (1999): Mobile-awareness in Collaborative Learning Envrionments. *Proc. of ISAS'99*, Orlando, FL, July 1999

Berghoff, J.; Schuhmann, J.; Matthes, M.; Drobnik, O. (1998): *Communication Support for Knowledge-intensive Services*. Broadband Communications (BC'98), IFIP TC 6/WG6.2 Fourth International Conference on Broadband Communications, Stuttgart, Germany, April, 1998.

Biehl, I./Meyer, B./Wetzel, S. (1998): Ensuring the Integrity of Agent-Based Computations by Short Proofs, in: *Mobile Agents: Second International Workshop MA '98*, September 9–11, 1998, Stuttgart, Germany (LNCS 1477). Berlin, Heidelberg, New York, ...: Springer 1998

Borenstein, N./Rose, M. T. (1993): MIME Extensions for Mail-Enabled Applications: application/safe-tcl and multipart/enabled-mail, Working Draft, ftp://ftp.aud.alcatel.com/pub/tcl/code/safe-tcl-1.2.tar.gz

Borghoff, U.M./Schlichter, J.H. (1998): *Rechnergestützte Gruppenarbeit*. Berlin, Heidelberg: Springer 1998.

Bakre, A./Badrinath, B. (1997): Implementation and Performance Evaluation of Indirect TCP. IEEE Transactions on Computers, Vol. 46, No. 3, March 1997

Brand, O.; Mahalek, D.; Sturzebecher, D.; Zitterbart, M. (1999): MACS – Eine modulare Kollaborationsumgebung. *Praxis der Informationsverarbeitung und Kommunikation (PIK)* 4/1999.

Bürger, M. (1999): *Unterstützung von Awareness bei der Gruppenarbeit mit gemeinsamen Arbeitsbereichen*. Dissertation, Herbert Utz Verlag, München, Germany, 1999.

Burger, C. (1998): Team Awareness with Mobile Agents in Mobile Environments. *Proc. of the International Conference on Computer Communications and Networks*, Lafayette, Lousiana, USA, October 1998

Cabri, G./Leonardi, L./Zambonelli, F.: Reactive Tuple Spaces for Mobile Agent Coordination (1998), in: *Mobile Agents: Second International Workshop MA '98*, September 9–11, 1998, Stuttgart, Germany (LNCS 1477). Berlin, Heidelberg, New York, ...: Springer 1998

Campbell, A./Gomez, J./Valkó, A. (1999): *An Overview of Cellular IP*. First IEEE Wireless Communications and Networking Conference (WCNC'99), New Orleans, USA, September 1999.

Cardelli, L./Gordon, D. (1998): Mobile Ambients, in: Nivat, M. (ed.): *Proceedings of Foundations of Software Science and Computation Structures (FoSSaCS)*, (LNCS 1378). Berlin, Heidelberg, New York, ...: Springer 1998

Cheng, C./Yen, J. (1998): *Virtual Learning Environment (VLE) – A Web-based Collaborative Learning System*. Proc. of the 31st Hawaii International Conference on System Sciences (HICSS'98*)*, IEEE Computer Society, USA 1998.

Cheverst, K./Blair, G./Davies, N./Friday, A. (1998): Supporting Collaboration in Mobile-aware Groupware. Proc. of Workshop on Handheld CSCW (CSCW'98), Seattle, USA, November 1998.

Ciancarini, P./Rossi, D. (1997): Jada—Coordination and Communication for Java Agents, in: *Mobile Object Systems* (LNCS 1222). Berlin, Heidelberg, New York, ...: Springer 1997

Comerford, R. (2000): Handhelds duke it out for the Internet. *IEEE Spectrum*, IEEE, August 2000

Denning, P. J. (1989): The Internet Worm. *American Scientist*, March–April 1989, 126–128. Reprinted in: P. J. Denning (ed.): *Computers Under Attack—Intruders, Worms and Viruses*, New York: ACM Press/Addison Wesley 1990

Douglis, F./Ousterhout, J. (1991): Transparent Process Migration: Design Alternatives and the Sprite Implementation. *Software—Practice and Experience* **21**(8): 757–785, August 1991

Droms, R. (1997): *Dynamic Host Configuration Protocol (DHCP)*. Internet Official Protocol Standard (STD1), March 1997.

Dutta-Roy, A. (2000): The cost of quality in Internet-style networks. *IEEE Spectrum*, IEEE, September 2000

Eberspächer, J./Vögel, H.-J. (1999): GSM Global System for Mobile Communcations, Teubner, Leipzig, Germany, 1999.

Etzioni, O./Weld, D. (1994): A Softbot-Based Interface to the Internet, *Comm. ACM* **37**(7): 72–76, July 1994

Fieger, A.; Zitterbart, M.; Keller, R.; Diederich, J. (1999): Towards QoS-support in the Presence of Handover, in: *Proc. 1st Workshop on IP Quality of Service for Wireless and Mobile Networks*, Aachen, Germany, April 1999

Fünfrocken, S. (1998): Transparent Migration of Java-Based Mobile Agents—Capturing and Reestablishing the State of Java Programs, in: *Mobile Agents: Second International Workshop, MA'98*, September 9–11, 1998, Stuttgart, Germany (LNCS 1477). Berlin, Heidelberg, New York, ...: Springer 1998

Funato, D./Okada, S./Tokuda, H./Saito ,N. (1999): TCP Redirection for Adaptive Mobility Support in Stateful Applications. IEICE Trans. Inf. & Syst., Mol. E82-D, No. 4, April 1999.

Gelernter, D. (1985): Generative Communication in LINDA, *ACM Trans. Prog. Lang. Sys.* 7(1): 80–112, January 1985

General Magic: http://www.genmagic.com/technology/odyssey.html

Genesereth, M. R./Ketchpel, S. P. (1994): Software Agents, *Comm. ACM* **37**(7): 48-53, 147, July 1994

Harrison, C. G./Chess, D. M./Kershenbaum, A. (1995): Mobile Agents: Are they a good idea? IBM Research Report RC 19887, March 1995, http://www.research.ibm.com/xv-d953-mobag.ps

Hohl, F. (1998): Time-Limited Blackbox Security: Protecting Mobile Agents from Malicious Hosts, in: Vigna, G. (ed.): *Mobile Agent Security* (LNCS 1419). Berlin, Heidelberg, New York, ...: Springer 1998

Hohl, F. (2000): The Mobile Agent List, http://mole.informatik.uni-stuttgart.de/mal/mal.html

Horstmann, C. S./Cornell, G. (1997): *Core Java 1.1*, Mountain View: Sunsoft Press/Prentice Hall 1997

IEEE 802 Part 11 (1999): Wireless LAN Medium Access Control (MAC) and Physical Layer (PHY) specifications. The Institute of Electrical and Electronics Engineers, Inc. New York, USA, 1999.

IKV++: http://www.ikv.de/products/grasshopper/

Kleinrock, L. (2000): On Some Principles of Nomadic Computing and Multi-Access Communications. *IEEE Communications Magazine*, July 2000

Kristoffersen, S./Ljungberg, F. (1998): *Representing Modalities in Mobile Computing.* Proc. of the Interactive Applications of Mobile Computing (ICM'98), Rostock, Germany, November 1998.

Lassila, O./Swick, R. (1998): Resource Description Framework (RDF) Model and Syntax Specification. Technical Report, W3 Consortium, 1998. http://www.w3.org/TR/WD-rdf-syntax

Lingnau, A./Dömel, P./Drobnik, O. (1995): An HTTP-based Infrastructure for Mobile Agents, in: *Fourth International World Wide Web Conference Proceedings*, December 11–14, 1995, Boston, MA, published as issue 1 of *World Wide Web Journal*, Sebastopol, CA: O'Reilly & Associates 1995.

Lingnau, A./Drobnik, O. (1996): Making Mobile Agents Communicate—A Flexible Approach, in: *Proc. 1st Annual Conference on Emerging Technologies and Applications in Communications (etaCOM'96)*, Portland, OR, May 1996

Lingnau, A./Drobnik, O. (1998): Mobile Agents in a Mobile Communications Database, in: *Proc. 3rd IFIP TC6 Workshop on Personal Wireless Communications (Wireless Local Access)*, Tokyo, April 1998

Matthes, M./Krieger, U./Drobnik, O. (2001): *Auswirkung drahtloser Netzsegmente auf die Transporteffizienz von TCP/IP-Verbindungen.* To appear in the Proc. of Kommunikation in Verteilten Systemen (KiVS 2001), February 20-23, 2001, Hamburg, Germany, 2001.

Meyer (1971): *Meyers Enzyklopädisches Lexikon.* Mannheim: Bibliographisches Institut 1971

Milojičić, D. S./Douglis, F./Wheeler, R. (1999): *Mobility: Processes, Computers, and Agents.* New York: ACM Press/Addison-Wesley 1999

Milojičić, D. S./Zint, W./Dangel, A./Giese, P. (1993): Task Migration on the top of the Mach Microkernel, in: *Proc. of the 3rd USENIX Mach Symposium*, 273–290, April 1993

Minar, N./Gray, M./Roup, O./Krikorian, R./Maes, P. (1999): Hive: Distributed Agents for Networking Things, in: *Proc. 1st International Symposium on Agent Systems and Applications and 3rd International Symposium on Mobile Agents (ASA/MA 99)*, October 3–6, 1999, Palm Springs, CA. Los Alamitos, CA, ...: IEEE Computer Society 1999

Mitsubishi: http://www.meitca.com/HSL/Projects/Concordia/

Möbs, A. (1998): *Entwurf und Implementierung einer Laufzeitumgebung für mobile Agenten in Java.* Diplomarbeit, Fachbereich Informatik, Johann-Wolfgang-Goethe-Universität Frankfurt 1998

ObjectSpace: http://www.objectspace.com/voyager/

Ousterhout, J. K. (1994): *Tcl and the Tk Toolkit*, Reading, MA: Addison-Wesley 1994

Peine, H. (1997): Ara—Agents for Remote Actions, in: Cockayne, W. R./Zyda, M.: *Mobile Agents—Explanations and Examples*, Upper Saddle River, NJ: Manning/Prentice Hall 1997

Perkins, C.E. (1997): Mobile IP – design Principles and Practices. Addison-Wesley Wireless Communications Series, Massachusetts, USA, October 1997.

Pham, V. A./Karmouch, A. (1998): Mobile Software Agents: An Overview, *IEEE Communications*, July 1998

Picot, A./Reichwald, R./Wigand, R.T. (1998): *Die grenzenlose Unternehmung – Information, Organisation und Management.* Wiesbaden: Gabler Verlag 1998

Reichwald, R./Möslein, K./Sachenbacher, H./Englberger, H./Oldenburg, S. (1998): *Telekooperation – Verteilte Arbeits- und Organisationsformen.* Berlin, Heidelberg: Springer 1998

Remmel, K. (1996): *Entwicklung einer verteilten Terminkalenderanwendung auf der Basis objektorientierter mobiler Agenten.* Diplomarbeit, Fachbereich Informatik, Johann-Wolfgang-Goethe-Universität Frankfurt 1996

Sakamoto, T./Sekiguchi, T./Yonezawa, A. (2000): Bytecode Transformation for Portable Thread Migration in Java, in: *Proc. 2nd International Symposium on Agent Systems and Applications and 4th International Symposium on Mobile Agents (ASA/MA 2000)*, September 13–15, 2000, Zürich, Switzerland (LNCS 1882). Berlin, Heidelberg, New York, ...: Springer 2000

Sander, T./Tschudin, C. (1998): Protecting Mobile Agents Against Malicious Hosts, in: Vigna, G. (ed.): *Mobile Agent Security* (LNCS 1419). Berlin, Heidelberg, New York, ...: Springer 1998

Schneier, B. (1996): *Applied Cryptography (2nd edition)*. New York: John Wiley & Sons 1996

Shoch, J. F./Hupp, J. A. (1982): The "Worm" Programs—Early Experience with a Distributed Computation. *Comm. ACM* **25**(3): 172–180, March 1982

Sienkiewicz, M. (1998): Write Once, Run ... Where? In: *Using Java*, Usenix Association 1998. http://www.usenix.org/publications/java/usingjava10.html

Spafford, E. H./Heaphy, K. A./Ferbrache, D. J. (1989): A Computer Virus Primer, in: P. J. Denning (ed.): *Computers Under Attack—Intruders, Worms and Viruses*, New York: ACM Press/Addison Wesley 1990

Straßer, M./Baumann, J./Hohl, F. (1997): Mole—A Java-Based Mobile Agent System, in: Mühlhäuser, M. (ed.): *Special Issues in Object-Oriented Programming*. Heidelberg: dpunkt Verlag 1997

Truyen, E./Robben, B./Vanhaute, B./Coninx, T./Joosen, W./Verbaeten, P. (2000): Portable Support for Transparent Thread Migration in Java, in: *Proc. 2nd International Symposium on Agent Systems and Applications and 4th International Symposium on Mobile Agents (ASA/MA 2000)*, September 13–15, 2000, Zürich, Switzerland (LNCS 1882). Berlin, Heidelberg, New York, ...: Springer 2000

Varschney, U. (2000): Recent Advances in Wireless Networking. *IEEE Spectrum*, IEEE, June 2000

Varschney, U./Vetter, R. (2000): Emerging Mobile and Wireless Networks. *Comm. ACM* **43**(6), June 2000

Walke, B. (1998): *Mobilfunknetze und ihre Protokolle*, Band 1 und 2, Teubner, Stuttgart, 1998.

Walke, B. (2000): *Zur Realisierung eines hochbitratigen drahtlosen Internets*. DFG SPP Mobilkommunikation, Abschlußkolloquium, TU München, October 2000.

White, J. E. (1996): Mobile Agents, in: Bradshaw, J. (ed.): *Software Agents*, Cambridge, MA: AAAI Press/MIT Press 1996.

Wolisz, A. (1999): Mobility in Multimedia Communication. Proc. of 2. WAKI-Symposium „Verteilte multimediale Anwendungen und dienseintegrierende Kommunikationsnetze“, Flensburg, Germany, September, 1999.

Quality of Service Management for Middleware and Applications

Kurt Geihs and Christian Becker

Johann Wolfgang Goethe-University
Institute of Informatik
Robert Mayer Str. 11-15
D 60054 Frankfurt am Main
{geihs|becker}@informatik.uni-frankfurt.de

Summary:
Quality of Service (QoS) management is an increasing demand on distribution infrastructures. While most of the existing QoS management architectures support a fixed set of QoS only, larger distributed systems encounter a variety of QoS requirements. This leads to a mix of different distribution platforms and increased interoperability and management efforts. Generic QoS management support is needed in order to reduce this effort and to provide flexibility towards new application requirements. We present a framework for generic QoS management based on standard CORBA middleware.

Keywords:
Quality of Service, Middleware, CORBA

Introduction

The client/server model is the predominant interaction model in distributed computing systems. It distinguishes between two roles. A client is an active entity which sends service requests to a server. A server is a passive entity awaiting requests from clients. In response to a client's service request, a server performs some activity and in most cases returns results to the client. Generally, a server may have many clients, and a client may work with different servers concurrently. A server may change its role to become a client when it requests an action from some other server. In distributed systems the interaction between clients and servers is achieved by sending messages over a communication network.

A server offers to clients some functionality which is accessible via the service interface. When using a service, clients will primarily be interested in its functional properties, i.e. what the service does. Nevertheless, in many cases clients will also be interested in the quality of the service, i.e. how well the service is performed. The term Quality of Service (QoS) addresses these non-functional issues in a client-service relationship. In contrast to the functional interface which represents the service offered to clients, the non-functional issues are related to the quality of the service as perceived by its clients. Examples of quality aspects in distributed systems are real-time response guarantees, fault-tolerant behaviour, and the degree of data consistency.

QoS has become an important subject in networks and distributed systems for two main reasons: First, some applications require QoS guarantees for their proper operation. For example, multimedia applications depend on QoS provision by design, e.g. the transmission and handling of audio- and video-streams need resource reservations for transmission bandwidth and CPU processing time. Furthermore, these streams require tight synchronisation. Application QoS requirements are also evident in environments where the availability of certain components is critical for the whole system. Financial applications and control software of power plants require a very high availability. Avionic systems rely on the timeliness and order of task execution. Additionally, a new class of applications based on the Internet is emerging. While a closed network could present distinct propositions about resource availability by centralised network management, this does not hold in an inherently decentralised network like the Internet which until today has only offered a best-effort communication environment. Hence Internet based applications, such as commercial business to business solutions like eProcurement or Internet shops, have to provide support for their QoS requirements for themselves.

The second reason for the steadily increasing QoS awareness in distributed applications is related to commercial usage. Whenever clients have to pay for some service they will certainly be concerned about the quality of the service, and they will probably pay less for lower quality. Therefore, client and server need to agree on a certain QoS level before the service starts. Then the QoS needs to be monitored during the application runtime. Finally, the actual QoS performance needs to be taken into account when billing is an issue.

From the application developer perspective, QoS management is a system dependent task, and ideally the internals of QoS mechanisms should not be a concern for application developers who should not have to deal with implementation of the QoS mechanisms. Instead it is desirable that the developer reuses existing QoS management software components. Thus a strict separation of application and QoS behaviour is one of our objectives in order to facilitate the independent reuse of service and QoS functionality.

Most existing QoS architectures provide support for a certain QoS category only, e.g. real-time or fault-tolerance. However, a large distributed system is likely to face demand for a variety of QoS categories. Thus, several QoS management architectures would have to be employed, but the resulting interoperability and management efforts are not desirable. We claim that nowadays distributed systems require generic support for the flexible integration of QoS management, and we show that with appropriate extensions CORBA is well suited for generic QoS management.

In the following we present our generic QoS management framework based on CORBA. The main emphasis is put on the motivation and the overall design principles. A detailed discussion of the individual architecture components can be found in other publications [Becker/Geihs 1997, 1998, 1998, 1999, 2000, Becker/Geihs/Gramberg 1999]. First, we will give a brief overview of definitions and requirements concerning QoS management, and discuss the related work. Then we will present our architectural framework. The necessary extensions to CORBA at design and implementation time as well as at runtime are also explained. The chapter closes with an example and a look forward to future research.

Definitions and Requirements

The notion of QoS has many facets. It originated in the area of telecommunication and computer networks where it is related primarily to throughput, response time, reliability, and synchronisation issues. With the widespread use of client/server systems, the scope of QoS is broadened so that all aspects which are related to the service quality are included. Naturally, QoS is observed from the client perspective. This has been recognised and manifested already in documents such as [OMG 1997], [ITU 1993], and [ISO 1995]. The following definitions are based on this work.

Definitions

A *QoS characteristic* identifies a specific QoS concern and represents a quantifiable value from a user's perspective. QoS characteristics are rather abstract entities which do not necessarily correspond with concrete values in the system. A QoS characteristic such as "availability", for example, could be represented by the mean time to failure (MTTF).

QoS parameters are used to represent a QoS characteristic in the system. They contain values which identify the state of the QoS. They can be used to measure or negotiate a QoS level. The QoS characteristic "availability" could be represented by the number of replicas in a server group or by statistically gathered data determining the percentage of availability.

A *QoS category* is a set of QoS characteristics which relate to a common application concern. Real-time or multimedia QoS characteristics constitute such QoS categories. However, a QoS category is an abstract concept which has no direct counterpart in the system. The QoS characteristic "availability" would fit into the QoS category "fault-tolerance".

A QoS level negotiated between a client and a service leads to a *QoS agreement.*

QoS mechanisms are the engineering parts needed to perform QoS management during service interaction. They provide the required data structures and management behaviour. For example, interfaces and components for configuration and monitoring as well as for mapping between QoS parameters are part of the QoS mechanisms. A QoS mechanism for availability could be based on the replication of servers, i.e. grouping servers in a group which allows the crashing of some servers in the group without impairing the service towards clients.

A *QoS framework* provides interfaces, mechanisms, specification tools and auxiliary infrastructure services that support the development, implementation and operation of QoS-enabled applications.

QoS Properties and Requirements

QoS provision for interactions between a client and a service has to be made from end-to-end along the whole path of communication through the system. While from an application perspective only the actual service quality perceived at the top layer is relevant, implementing QoS addresses all layers and therefore is a system dependent task. The quality of the upper layers depends on the QoS of the underlying layers. In a distributed system the underlying operating system, the network and other application resources all contribute to the perceived QoS.

Our goal is to build QoS support into existing object-oriented middleware such as CORBA. Appropriate abstractions are needed in order to ease the implementation of QoS enabled clients and services. Therefore, we observe the following requirements for a generic QoS management framework that is based on an underlying object-oriented middleware architecture.

- Expandable:
  A distributed application encounters manifold QoS requirements during its lifetime. Hence, a QoS management architecture should provide the ability to grow and change with its environment. Technically, this implies genericity and multi-category support.

- Separable:
  Providing genericity and multi-category support alone is not sufficient to meet the application requirements. Separation of concerns must be an objective here. Client and service code should not be mixed unnecessarily with QoS specific behaviour, and the complexity of QoS implementations should be transparent to application developers.

- Reusable:
  The usage patterns of a certain QoS category are very similar for most applications. Therefore, design and code reuse for QoS mechanisms should be achieved in clients and services. In order to do so, appropriate general abstractions for QoS parameters, management interfaces and communication interfaces are required.

- Extensive:
  The QoS support framework should not stop at the time of design and implementation but rather provide assistance throughout the whole application lifetime. Thus, infrastructure services for e.g. trading, negotiation, monitoring and accounting should be an integral part of the framework.

Before we describe our QoS management approach that meets the above requirements, we briefly discuss the related work in order to demonstrate the motivation for our work and point out the important differences.

Middleware

The Common Object Request Broker Architecture (CORBA) [OMG 1995, OMG 1998] is an open standard for object-oriented middleware. We assume that the reader is somewhat familiar with CORBA and give only a short overview. For a more detailed presentation see [Vinoski 1997]. CORBA is attractive as a platform for QoS integration because of its availability across a multitude of different operating systems, hardware platforms and programming languages. Several implementations of CORBA exist, some of them in the public domain with source code available.

Object Interaction in CORBA

Naturally, the interaction of objects in CORBA is request/response based. Figure 1 illustrates the CORBA components involved in an interaction between a client and a service.

To invoke a service the client needs to know the object reference for the service object. There are many ways to obtain such an object reference, which we will not discuss here. To invoke a method in the service interface, the client issues a call to a co-located object – the stub (or proxy) object. In the stub object a request is created which is passed via the invocation interface to the Object Request Broker (ORB). Based on the object reference provided, the ORB is responsible for locating the target object and delivering the request.

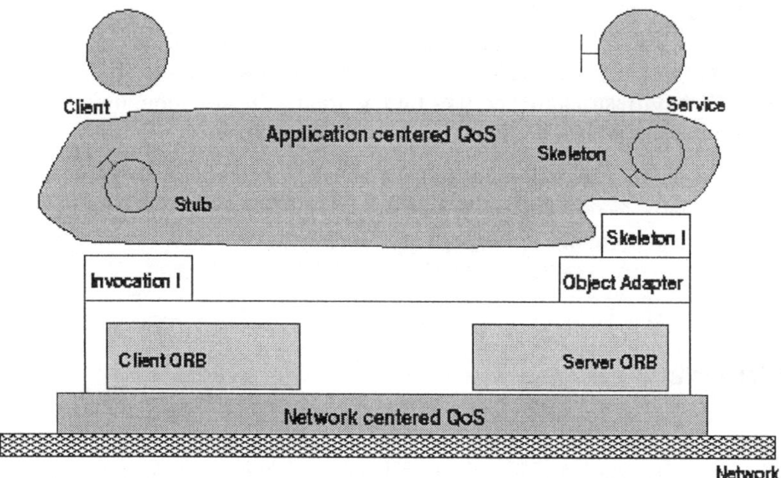

Figure 1: Middleware Architecture

On the service side the request is received by an ORB and handed over to an object adapter. The object adapter manages object implementations which serve an interface. It selects the appropriate object and delivers the request through the skeleton which dispatches the invocation to the corresponding method of the service object. A result may possibly be returned to the client on the same path.

Prior to runtime, service interfaces are defined in an interface definition language (IDL). The IDL is used to generate the stub objects and service skeletons in the individual implementation languages of the client and the service.

The CORBA Common Object Services [OMG 1995] provide functionality which is relevant for a broad variety of applications but not needed in all applications. Some of the object services require additional support from the underlying ORB, but this is transparent to the user. Some object services address distinct QoS characteristics. We will discuss this issue in the next subsection.

QoS Integration in CORBA

This subsection briefly covers different existing approaches to QoS integration in CORBA. Based on these discussions we will introduce our QoS framework.

The Ace ORB (TAO)

TAO [Schmidt/Levine/Mungee 1997][5] is a CORBA implementation that provides support for real-time QoS along with the other standard CORBA features. For real-time QoS the order of task execution and the observance of distinct task deadlines are the important issues. In order to support this, TAO provides a QoS specification in IDL through a particular data structure (`RT_Info`) which contains attributes for the runtime information of a task. This information is forwarded to an offline scheduler which calculates the priorities of the tasks. At runtime this information is used by the scheduler to guarantee the deadlines and execution order. Clearly, this is not a trivial task. The TAO runtime support is present all along the communication path between client and service.

Fault-Tolerant CORBA: Electra and Eternal

Electra [Maffeis 1995] is a CORBA extension for fault-tolerance. Diversity through majority votes can be achieved as well as masking crashes of servers in an ensemble of replicas. The QoS support is divided into two layers. The network layer (between ORB and transport) is enhanced by a group communication protocol (ISIS or HORUS), while the layer between the ORB and the application objects is supplemented with functions intended to configure object groups and retrieve sets of results. Additionally, the IDL compiler emits code for state-transfer functions an object has to provide in order to participate in an object group. There is no explicit QoS specification in Electra.

Eternal [Moser/Melliar-Smith/Narasimhan 1998] provides transparent group management of services to support fault-tolerance. Application objects can be configured for QoS provision using external management interfaces with the underlying group communication. The ORB is enhanced towards the network by a multicast protocol (Totem). Thus, users need not be aware of the group management or the invocation of a request to a group.

Quality of Service Objects (QuO)

QuO [Zinky/Bakken/Schantz 1997] is a QoS management platform that uses CORBA mainly as a transport mechanism. Explicit specification languages for QoS, i.e. resource and behaviour aspects, are translated into the target language [Loyal/Schantz/Zinky/Bakken 1998]. The ORB provides support on two layers for QoS mechanism integration. The layers correspond to the two layers sketched in Figure 1. The application centred QoS is layered in so-called delegates, while the network centred QoS is encapsulated in a specialised ORB. QuO supports generic QoS management but focuses on the application integration of QoS through spe-

---

5 Much more information about CORBA and TAO can be found under http://www.cs.wustl.edu/~schmidt

cialised languages, rather than on the extension of a middleware platform to support generic QoS provision.

QoS in Common Object Services

The Object Management Group (OMG) is aware of the growing demand for QoS support. Following the CORBA philosophy to encapsulate common behaviour in object services, this has so far resulted mainly in specifications for QoS enhanced object services. Though there is an attempt to integrate the diverse QoS management approaches into a common OMG standard [OMG 1997], this has not yet led to a comprehensive QoS architecture specification. Up to now two OMG specifications were released that directly address QoS concerns: *CORBA Messaging Service* and *Real-time CORBA*. Fault-tolerant CORBA is still on its way.

The Real-time CORBA specification [OMG 1998] addresses real-time issues in a manner very similar to TAO. The QoS support is done along the whole communication path, including interfaces to ORB resources, like threading, scheduling, request interception, pluggable protocols etc. The CORBA Messaging [OMG 1998] deals with properties of the message exchange in terms of reliability and synchronisation. A set of policy objects specified in IDL allows the customisation of the QoS offered by the CORBA Messaging. For the various synchronisation issues ORB extensions are needed.

Some of the other CORBA Services provide QoS support as well, e.g. the Audio/Video-Stream Management [OMG 1998] and the Notification Service. Both rely on a name/value representation of QoS properties and address only a specific category, i.e. multimedia transmissions and the reliability of event delivery.

Conclusions

This brief discussion of QoS integration in distributed object systems has revealed a number of specialised approaches. A generic approach for QoS integration into middleware systems is still lacking. Since the QoS requirements of distributed systems evolve, i.e. they are not known a priori, extensibility of any given architecture is desirable. Otherwise, a mix of QoS categories would lead to a mix of different platforms which would have to interoperate via some form of intermediary. We believe that a generic architecture and framework for QoS management is needed in order to ease the design, implementation and maintenance of large QoS-enabled distributed object systems.

The next section classifies QoS as an aspect in the sense of the aspect-oriented programming when it is being integrated in object-oriented environments. Subsequent sections present our Management Architecture for Quality of Service (MAQS) that provides generic QoS integration in CORBA. The presentation is organised along the lifetime phases of a distributed application: from design time through implementation issues to runtime.

Quality of Service Integration

Besides the general properties of QoS mentioned in section 2, there are additional properties arising from the QoS integration in a specific environment. In this section we look at QoS integration in object-oriented environments.

Aspect-Oriented Programming (AOP)

The design of large applications is arduous. Decisions made in early modelling stages influence later phases, i.e. implementation and maintenance. Hence much effort in the past has been made to deploy proper software analysis and design methods. Typically these methods are tied to a distinct paradigm, e.g. imperative or object-oriented. The aspect-oriented programming paradigm (AOP) [Kiczales et. al. 1997] claims that although each method tries to partition a given problem into self-contained, encapsulated entities, this kind of partitioning is not always feasible. Dependencies between modelled entities break the desired encapsulation and neglecting this fact in modelling makes the design hard to deploy and even harder to reuse. AOP aims at a conceptual understanding of the "crosscutting" of responsibilities through separate entities. For that purpose, the AOP distinguishes aspects and components.

A *component* is an entity which encapsulates a distinct responsibility. Components can be combined with other components to achieve a distinct behaviour. They interact through well defined interfaces.

An *aspect* is not encapsulated – in contrast to a component. Aspects crosscut each other preventing clear encapsulations. Aspects typically reflect non-functional issues of a system, e.g. error handling, performance tuning or synchronisation.

The proposed solution to the coexistence of aspects and components in a system is the introduction of *aspect languages* and an *aspect weaver*. Aspect languages are specialised languages, suitable for modeling and expressing the distinct properties of an aspect and its connection with other aspects. The aspect weaver is a tool which takes all aspect specifications of a system and generates a corresponding program.

Most aspect-oriented approaches have so far dealt with distribution and synchronisation aspects in distributed systems. Recently, the integration of QoS provision has become a target for AOP-based systems.

Quality of Service as an Aspect

Let us look at two examples of QoS as an aspect in the sense of the AOP. We assume that clients and services are modelled as objects which communicate using an underlying middleware as described in section 3.

As a first example let us consider fault-tolerance. In order to mask the crash of individual servers, replica groups can be built. A client sends the request to all servers in the group and as long as one server remains in the group an answer will be delivered back to the client. Neglecting the group communication problems, like delivering requests in the correct and same order to the replicas, and assuming that an underlying multicast protocol will ensure this along with deterministic replicas, the focus here is on the application specific integration of the QoS mechanism.

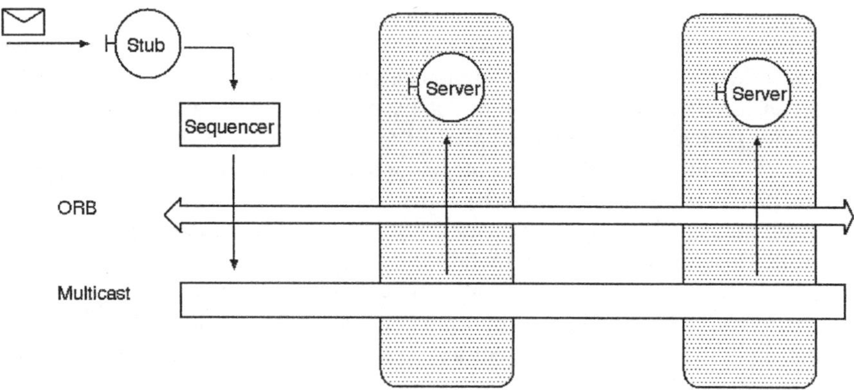

Figure 2: Replica Group

The servers are modelled as objects. Hence, they encapsulate their state through the interface. The client accesses the replica group transparently through the stub object which relies on a sequencer. The sequencer dispatches all client requests to the replica group via the multicast protocol.

The effect of the QoS integration differs from client to service side. While clients gain transparent access to the replica group through the stub object and the sequencer, servers are exposed to the QoS mechanism. In order to establish virtual synchronicity among the replicas the state of the server has to be identical. Hence, the sequencer has to transfer an initial state to each replica and the current state to each new server joining the group. This violates the encapsulation of the state. Servers have to provide methods of access to the state. Hence, the QoS mechanism and the server are no longer encapsulated and are therefore aspects in the sense of the AOP.

Our second example relates to a QoS characteristic from the performance category. Again, a group of replicated servers is offering the same service. Client requests should be load-balanced in order to reduce the mean response time. This can be easily established in a similar fashion to the above replica group. Instead of relying on a multicast protocol the sequencer can use the normal transport of the ORB. Before a request is submitted the sequencer collects the load information of the servers in the group. After determination of the least loaded server the request will be dispatched to this server. Thus, the load balancing remains transparent for the application. The servers must provide the load information. The QoS mechanism could establish a generic load-information based on the CPU utilisation. This, however, is not suitable for a wider range of applications where load depends on other factors as well, e.g. length of the request queue or some other environment data. Again, QoS mechanism and service cannot be separately encapsulated, and therefore are aspects in the sense of AOP.

In general, the necessary precautions before a service request is issued on the client side and the counterpart on the service side can be viewed as aspects that are separate from the application logic. Hence, it is desirable to specify and implement the QoS mechanisms in isolation from the application and combine them automatically. This is exactly what the AspectWeaver is supposed to do.

In our CORBA-based QoS framework called MAQS we support the integration of QoS specification and corresponding QoS mechanisms in an AOP-like manner through a relatively straightforward extension of the OMG IDL.

MAQS: A Quality of Service Framework

We have developed a QoS framework called MAQS (Management Architecture for Quality of Service). The framework is based on CORBA but because of well-known similarities between different platforms [Chung et. al. 1998] the results should be transferable to other object-oriented middleware as well. This section briefly covers the design goals and the important elements of the framework.

In terms of the requirements for QoS management as stated in section 2 as well as the general lifecycle of software systems, the following phases of QoS support can be determined for distributed object systems:

- Design and implementation time:
  Application designers build an application based on interfaces which are translated by the IDL compiler into target languages and implemented by objects. The interfaces determine which contracts the interaction within an application relies on. Interfaces reflect entities that were isolated in the application analysis stage.

- Runtime:
  During the execution of a distributed application the actually possible QoS agreements have to be established, based on the resource availability and requirements. This requires support from infrastructure services such as negotiation of QoS agreements, resource control to assign and reserve resources, and resource monitoring in order to detect violations of QoS agreements. If accounting is performed, a service charge should be raised according to the delivered QoS [Gupta/Stahl/Winston 1999]. The necessary performance data can be collected by the monitoring and resource control services.

While the runtime phase is merely an issue of system administration, the design and implementation phase needs special attention and support for the developer of QoS mechanisms. Therefore a new role is introduced in the framework in addition to the application developer: the *QoS implementer*. While middleware is introduced in order to offer an abstraction which hides the complexity and heterogeneity of the underlying platform, QoS mechanisms need to see some of this complexity and depend on the internals of the request processing. Implementing QoS mechanisms requires a fundamentally different perspective on the system than application development. The conceptual separation of concern between the QoS mechanisms and the application is reflected by this new role. The ultimate goal would be to separate application code from QoS management code as much as possible in order to increase the potential of reuse and reconfiguration.

Instead of relying on distinct runtime interfaces, e.g. design patterns, for the integration of QoS mechanisms in the application, the framework adds QoS specifications to the interface definition language. The client programmer of a service is only confronted with one specification language – the IDL. The IDL compiler can generate appropriate skeletons on client- and service-side which have to be implemented by the QoS implementer and the application developer. The skeletons are clearly separated, thus fostering the separation of concern in the implementation language. The IDL compiler becomes an aspect weaver.

The broad variety of QoS requirements justifies the effort of an augmented IDL compiler only if the applicability of the approach addresses a broad range of QoS characteristics. This meets the requirement for extensive QoS management. But specifying a QoS characteristic and offering implementation support on the application layer is not sufficient. Already existing QoS mechanisms of the operating system or the network should be integrated as well as other QoS libraries, e.g. multicast communication or encryption. Hence, the framework has to provide integration of reused QoS mechanisms as well as integration of new QoS mechanisms.

The overall objectives the framework addresses are:

- Genericity:
  specification of arbitrary QoS characteristics and integration of QoS mechanisms.

- Multi-category:
  not being tied to a distinct set of QoS categories.

- Reusability:
  fosters separation of concern in order to facilitate the reusability of QoS characteristics.

The following presentation of our QoS framework follows the two aforementioned phases.

Design and Implementation Phase

In non-generic QoS architectures, the QoS mechanisms and parameters are fixed. Generic QoS architectures have to put the application designer in a position to define QoS parameters, implement QoS mechanisms, and use them along with the application objects.

QoS Specification

QoS management has the notion of state and behaviour just like the classical object model. QoS parameters reflect the current state of the QoS provision, while the behaviour is performed by the QoS mechanisms that primarily relate to operations for QoS related activities. Obviously, a QoS framework must facilitate the specification and construction of these elements.

Elements of a QoS Specification

Let us look at the two elements in more detail.

- State:
  The state of a QoS characteristic is represented by QoS parameters. QoS parameters are exchanged between client and service during negotiation and are monitored while service interaction occurs. The transmission of QoS parameters over the network can be performed by the usual middleware communication facilities. Thus QoS parameters should be either represented in IDL, an augmented IDL, or in a separate notation that is compiled into an IDL specification.

- Behaviour:
  The behaviour of QoS mechanisms may involve many entities along the communication path. Most importantly, the interaction between client and service has to be intercepted in order to allow QoS mechanisms to do the necessary processing. Clients and services should not have to deal with additional abstractions for the interaction other than the ones that are already provided by the underlying middleware, i.e. stubs and skeletons which provide network transparent transport of requests. Nevertheless, QoS mechanisms on client and service side may have to interact as well, which is done via the underlying middleware. Furthermore, management operations for the set-up and monitoring of the QoS configuration have to be provided. The QoS framework should provide interfaces for these operations. In a generic QoS management architecture, QoS provision cannot be achieved without an interaction between the service logic and the QoS mechanism, because QoS integration results in aspects in the sense of AOP (see 4.2).

Much of the code for the QoS behaviour and the data structures for the QoS parameters can be generated automatically if an appropriate specification notation for the QoS constructs is provided.

Alternatives for QoS Specifications

There are several options for the definition of the elements of a QoS specification. We will present a brief overview of these options before our approach is explained. A deeper discussion can be found in [Becker/Geihs 1999]. With respect to the above mentioned objectives and requirements, a QoS specification could be established as follows:

- No QoS specification language:
  Neither additional syntax nor semantics are added to the existing IDL. The developer of a QoS relies on an implicit understanding that certain IDL constructs are meant to be used for QoS management. An example of such an approach is TAO, which represents its QoS parameters in plain IDL.
- Explicit IDL extension:
  Introducing new keywords into the IDL enables the IDL compiler to generate code for the QoS handling. One disadvantage is that the original IDL is exposed to changes and therefore not backward compatible. On the other hand the IDL definition contains all relevant information about the functional and non-functional aspects of the service. We have chosen this approach for our Management Architecture for Quality of Service (MAQS) [Becker/Geihs 1998]. Our newly developed QIDL [Becker/Geihs 1999] extends the standard OMG IDL with QoS specification elements.
- Implicit IDL extension:
  In order to generate code for the QoS handling without extending the IDL by new keywords, existing keywords and mechanisms can be used. Through special identifier conventions, e.g. using a "QoS" prefix for QoS specifications, the same support as with explicit IDL extensions can be achieved. Though OMG IDL is not changed explicitly, this obviously introduces implicit changes, restrictions and potential conflicts.
- Separate QoS specification language:
  Introducing a separate language for QoS specifications keeps the IDL unmodified, and the changes to the existing architecture are minimal. Two examples of this approach are QRR [Frolund/Koistinen 1998] and the QuO aspect languages [Loyal/Zinky/Schantz/Bakken 1998]. The latter introduces a set of aspect languages for the contract and structure specification of a QoS. These languages are mapped to an augmented ORB. The disadvantages are that an additional language has to be integrated and service specifications are scattered over several separate specification parts.

For generic QoS management, separate QoS specifications or an explicit extension of IDL seem to be the most appropriate way to go. We have decided to use an explicit IDL extension, which we call *QIDL - QoS Interface Definition Language*. It is easy to see that the same technical goals could be achieved by a separate QoS specification language as well. Extending the IDL offers all necessary information about a server – functional interface and supported QoS – in one single specification. Additionally, the IDL compiler can be used to generate appropriate separations of the aspects in the target language. Thus, the IDL compiler becomes an AspectWeaver.

QIDL

The Quality of Service IDL (QIDL) is a notation for QoS specifications and their assignment to interfaces. The QIDL language mapping supports an AOP-based approach to separate the QoS and service/client implementations. The key concept in QIDL is the QoS interface, which consists of the declaration of state and behaviour.

Let us consider an example of a QoS for fault-tolerance that illustrates the elements of a QoS specification in QIDL. The client requests are dispatched – transparently for the client – to a replica group. Depending on some user-defined policy the crashes of *k* servers can be tolerated. Basically the QoS definition consists of two parts. The QoS definition is prefixed by the keyword `qos` and the name of the QoS. The QoS parameter section allows the definition of arbitrary QoS parameters. This is done analogous to structs in IDL before the `interface` keyword in the QoS definition.

In the example, two parameters are declared: the number of replicas and a sequence containing the corresponding stringified object references. The interface section defines all operations affiliated with a QoS. The operations used on the client side for configuration are concerned with the policy, i.e. set the minimum of available replicas, and the group management, i.e. enter a new replica server. One QoS internal operation is offered. The service side QoS mechanism implements the `get_addr` operation, which returns the multicast address that the service side QoS mechanism is bound to. The client side QoS mechanism uses this address to configure the underlying multicast mechanism. The responsibility a service has to provide in terms of a QoS mechanism is executed via the service/QoS aspect integration which in the example is the state transfer: `get_state` and `put_state`. The state information is service specific and cannot be determined by the QoS mechanism.

```
qos replica
{
  // state
  sequence <string> replicas;
  long number_of_replica;
  // behaviour
  interface
  {
    // client side configuration
    boolean set_policy(in long hosts);
    void enter_replica(in string ref);
    // QoS internal: retrieve server's multicast
    // address
    string get_addr();
    // aspect integration: service responsibility
    any get_state();
    void put_state(in any st);
  };
};
```

The assignment of QoS to a service is achieved by simply attaching the QIDL specification to the service interface. A service interface can support any number of QoS characteristics, i.e. QoS interfaces. At runtime only one of the possible QoS characteristics can be active at a time. This is not a restriction for the claimed genericity of our QoS management approach, since arbitrary combinations of QoS characteristics can be defined as a new QoS characteristic. A deeper discussion of QIDL and its usage can be found in [Becker/Geihs 1999].

The next subsection will briefly cover the mapping of the specification to the QoS mechanisms.

QoS Mechanism Integration

The QIDL specifications for a QoS and the assignment to services have to be mapped to the implementation language, just like regular IDL definitions. Such a mapping depends heavily on the underlying QoS mechanism integration. Figure 1 illustrates two layers of possible QoS mechanism integration:

- Application centred QoS:
  The QoS provision on this layer does not depend on networking QoS issues but deals only with application specific responsibilities. Therefore it can be realised completely "above" the ORB. Examples are voting mechanisms for achieving diversity or a load balancing QoS which does not need any additional support from the underlying layers. ORB bypasses for multimedia streams can be established at this layer as well.

Network centred QoS:
If the QoS provision on the application layer relies on QoS mechanisms related to transport issues, e.g. diversity needs multicast communication on the network, this has to be established in the end to end communication path. Because the ORB encapsulates the network and platform specific properties, this layer is normally hidden from application objects. The ORB has to be extended by an interface for the access to the underlying QoS mechanisms. Our framework provides a layer within the ORB where QoS mechanisms can be integrated as well as delegated to QoS mechanisms of the operating system or network.

These two layers result from the obvious separation of application and platform specific behaviour through the ORB. While an ORB can fully encapsulate the underlying platform when QoS issues are neglected, this is not possible when QoS management is a concern. Existing CORBA based QoS management typically provides QoS mechanisms on these two layers. Additional requirements may exist depending on the particular QoS characteristic. The TAO approach to real-time QoS management shows that even some parts of the ORB (object adapter, scheduler) are affected as well.

We will now sketch our mapping approach and discuss alternative mapping possibilities that are introduced with new features in CORBA 2.2 and the CORBA Real-time standard.

QoS Parameter

QoS parameters in QIDL are mapped to the *struct* data type in IDL. All name/type pairs in the QoS definition are mapped to a struct which contains the same pairs. The struct is named identically with the QoS definition. Thus different QoS characteristics with the same QoS parameter types are distinguishable by CORBA typecodes even if they represent the same C++ type.

Application Centred QoS Mechanisms

The QoS operations in a QIDL specification are mapped to entities which cooperatively provide the application centred QoS mechanism. In order to support the end-to-end QoS view, several entities on client side and service side are generated.

- Client side:
  An interface of a service is translated to a stub object which redirects the service access for clients. In order to allow QoS enabled interaction without additional communication schemes, the stub object has to ensure the QoS provision for the application objects. In our QIDL–C++ mapping (see Figure 3) every QoS characteristic assigned to an interface is translated to a so called *mediator*. After a QoS is negotiated and accepted by the client, the corresponding mediator is instantiated and installed as a delegate of the stub object. Every request is forwarded to the mediator which can execute QoS related operations or dele-

gate QoS behaviour to the network layer. The mediator corresponds directly to the interceptors introduced in the CORBA Real-time proposal.

- Service side:
  The mapping on service side differs slightly from the client side. Instead of using a delegation based approach only, inheritance is also used to enhance the service implementation with QoS specific behaviour. The QoS behaviour definition is mapped to a skeleton class, very much in the way that interfaces are translated. The QoS implementer provides all operations in the QoS implementation except for those related to the QoS/service integration, which have to be implemented by the service implementer and are delegated through inheritance to the service implementation. In order to allow QoS specific behaviour similar to the client side mediator, an invocation request is delegated to an operation in the QoS implementation which knows about the actual QoS agreement at runtime. The delegation is done by the skeleton to the QoS implementation.

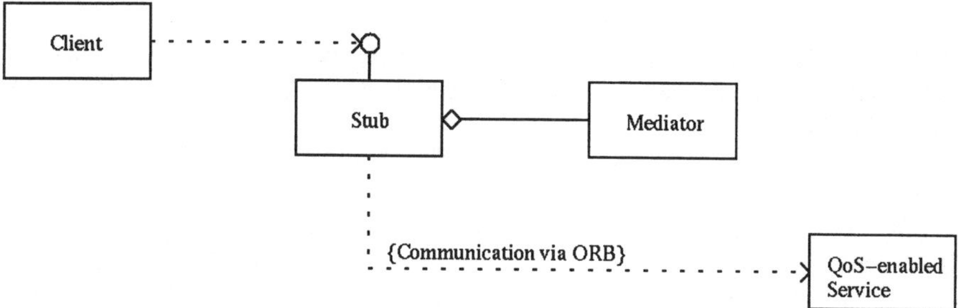

Figure 3: Client side QoS mechanism

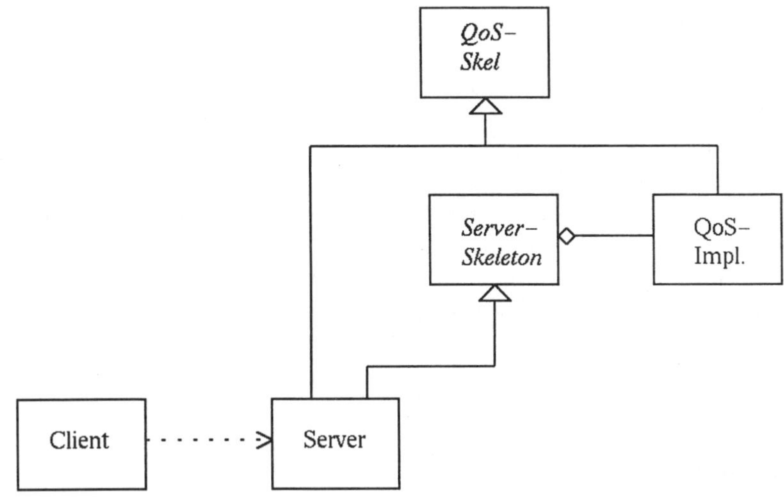

Figure 4: Server side QoS mechanisms

Network Centred QoS Mechanisms

As stated before, QoS provision is hierarchically structured along the communication path between client and service. In order to support application centred QoS mechanisms with access to network and operating system QoS management facilities or to realise such mechanisms on their own, well defined integration points and interfaces are needed. A solution to the network centred QoS mechanism integration should focus on generality rather than on support for distinct QoS categories. The actual discussion in the OMG about portable interceptors and pluggable protocols shows that a common view on the integration points has not been reached yet.

Our approach provides an interface for network related QoS implementations immediately after a request has been delivered to the ORB. This offers the maximum flexibility for a QoS mechanism integration. Since our architecture is based on a micro-kernel ORB, i.e. [Römer 1998], the functionality for marshalling, using IIOP, and transport features via TCP is available as clearly separated modules, and therefore can be used and customised by a QoS implementation. On the other hand, specific marshalling code or network transport protocols can be implemented. This demonstrates impressively the benefits and elegance of the micro-kernel approach, even in middleware systems.

Every QoS mechanism on the network layer is realised as a module that has to implement a simple interface. The customization of the QoS modules is done by means of requests with a distinct object reference. Hence each QoS mechanism module can offer an additional customised interface towards application centred QoS mechanisms or management facilities like monitoring services.

Assisting Operations

In order to assist clients and services in establishing QoS-enabled interaction, a set of operations is generated along with the language mapping of QIDL to the implementation language. These operations provide basic functionality enabling clients and services to retrieve the list of supported QoS from a service, to initiate a negotiation, and to accept an offer during a negotiation. These operations are all generated from the QIDL specification and offer necessary basic functionality for negotiation and the set-up of the application centred QoS mechanisms. If a client accepts an offered QoS level during negotiation, the corresponding mediator on client side and delegate on service side are installed.

Runtime

So far we have described those elements of a generic QoS management architecture which are relevant during design and implementation time. Since QoS management is concerned with the dynamic characteristics of distributed systems, support during runtime is clearly needed. While most of the additional functionality which is not encapsulated by the QoS mechanisms can be integrated into additional services like resource control or monitoring, negotiation is an exception here. We will briefly describe our QoS negotiation approach.

At runtime three phases of interaction have to be considered:

- Establishment:
  Clients typically use directory services or trading services to locate services. For QoS enabled systems these lookup services have to incorporate information about the QoS characteristics of a service. Prior to interaction, the QoS level has to be negotiated between client and service.
- Interaction:
  During interaction between client and service the negotiated QoS has to be monitored. If a violation is detected either adaptation to another QoS level or an abort can occur. The information about the actual delivered QoS levels can be used for accounting issues.
- Closing:
  Upon closing an interaction between client and service, the allocated resources must be freed. Clients can then be charged according to the quality delivered.

Negotiation

Negotiating a distinct QoS level for a QoS characteristic seems quite simple at first. A client sends a QoS parameter representing the desired QoS characteristic and its value to the service. The service can deny or accept the requested QoS. The situation changes if a client is willing to accept a variety of QoS levels. If a service is not capable of satisfying a requested level it can try to offer an alternative level nearby. Since the perspective of QoS-enabled interaction is client centred and different clients have different preferences about the states of a QoS, this cannot be decided by the service alone.

Consider a video transmission which has the attributes *price* and *quality*. Some clients may need high quality independent of the price while others would tend to maximise the price/quality ratio. As a result, the negotiation procedure will become more complex, since the client has to negotiate the QoS parameter states in turn according to its preferences, or a general notation for a set of different client preferences in QoS negotiations has to be supplied.

Several proposals for the specification of client preferences already exist (worth-functions) [Kostinen/Seetharaman 1998], linear embedment [Dini/Hafid 1997, Linhoff-Popien/Thißen 1997]). Worth-functions are capable of supporting preference specifications for generic QoS parameters. Such client preference specifications can become quite complex and may require a quite advanced understanding of the underlying mathematics.

We have developed a refinement based representation of QoS client preferences which eases the description of client preference ranges. This makes the definition of client preferences similar to the modelling of class hierarchies, and thus it is familiar to object designers. Our notation is independent from the underlying QoS parameter representation, and could be used in other approaches as well. For more details see [Becker/Geihs/Gramberg 1999].

Infrastructure Services

The interaction of client and service needs assistance from infrastructure services. At first, a client has to find an appropriate service that provides the desired functionality and supports the required QoS characteristic. Then negotiation takes place in order to find a QoS agreement depending on the actual availability of resources. If the resource availability changes during interaction, client and service have to adapt to the changed environment. Finally, clients should be charged according to the delivered quality. These runtime activities are facilitated by trading, monitoring, resource control and accounting services.

Trading

In distributed object systems typically two kinds of directory services exist. A naming service maps service names to service instances. A trading service maps given service properties to matching service instances. The name resolution can be used for QoS enabled services without any change. However, current traders have to be extended in order to handle QoS enabled services. Since QoS specifications in QIDL are stored in the CORBA interface repository, conventional CORBA traders based on the type definitions in the interface repository can be extended to trade QIDL specifications in a straightforward way.

Monitoring

During service interaction the agreed QoS level has to be monitored to detect violations. Upon violation of a QoS agreement the client application can either adapt its behaviour to the new situation or renegotiate. The information about the duration of a certain QoS agreement may be input for the accounting service.

Monitoring the involved components can be based on existing messaging services, like the event or notification service, or by an additional customised service. We favour the latter, since a combination of standard interfaces as well as generic interfaces can be supported. The observer object delegates a monitoring task to the monitoring service. The monitoring service offers a set of standard interfaces to monitor values of an object and check their validity against prescribed policies, e.g. retrieve a `long` value and check if it lies within a distinct interval. Upon violation, a notification is issued to the observer object. Thus the monitoring service de-couples the monitoring of components from the observer object.

Monitoring objects which do not support the standard interface of the monitoring service can be built either by using the Dynamic Invocation Interface (DII) based interface to the monitoring service or by providing appropriate object wrappers to the monitored objects.

Accounting and Resource Control

Billing clients depending on the delivered service quality introduces a new dimension to open distributed systems where flat rates prevail today. The availability of different QoS levels leads directly to accounting and charging considerations: otherwise, users will tend to always ask for the best quality. Differentiation by price according to quality and resource consumption will prevent clients from resource monopolisation and will motivate them to differentiate their service demands. Depending on the pricing policies, a pricing scheme could define minimum quality requirements for which no charges are applied, or even issue penalties if a service does not deliver the negotiated quality. A flexible QoS management architecture should have a set of different policies for resource allocation and accounting built in along with the possibility of user defined policies. Additionally, the acquired information about resource consumption is useful for capacity and configuration management of the distributed system.

Figure 5 illustrates the collaboration of the above mentioned services. The resource control service is only intended to be used by QoS mechanisms or system administrators. Application designers should not get involved with this service.

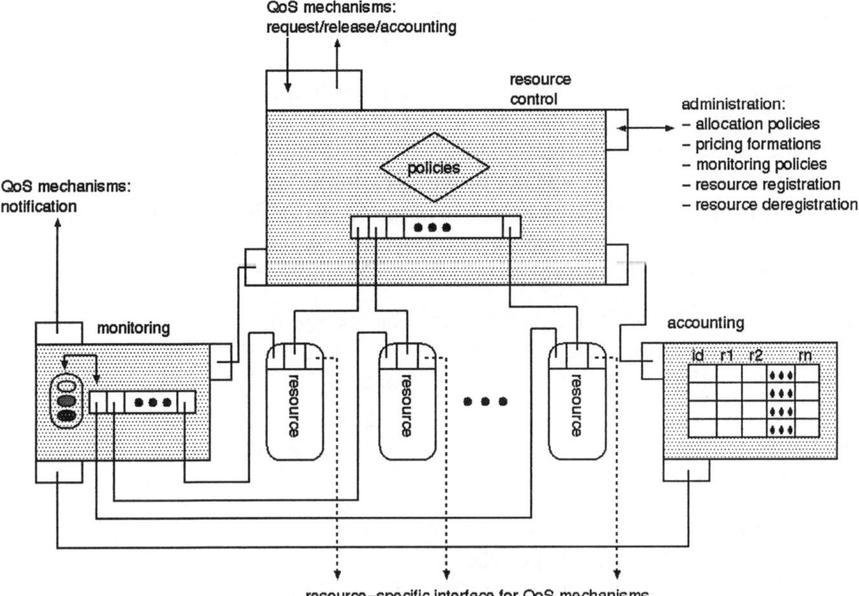

Figure 5: Collaboration of infrastructure services

QoS mechanisms can request or release resources through an interface. The decision whether a resource request is to be granted is based on policies. Policies allow the reservation of resources to distinct servers. This ensures that system relevant services will get their resources when needed. Other policies can utilise such resources by granting them until recalled to other servers. The resource control submits a message on each resource grant/return to the accounting service, which keeps track of the resource consumption a client/service interaction produces. Upon termination, clients can be charged depending on their resource consumption. In order to determine the possible violation of a QoS agreement early monitoring can keep track of the state of a resource. The monitoring service is capable of issuing notifications to the QoS mechanisms if defined thresholds are violated. Resources offer three interfaces. The first is intended to be used by resource control to request/free a resource. Monitoring is established through the second interface. While these interfaces are identical to all resources, the third interface reflects the resource specific functionality. This interface is used from QoS mechanisms to configure the resource according to the desired QoS agreement, e.g. reserve a distinct bandwidth.

Example

In this section a small example of a performance related QoS characteristic from a real-world scenario is presented to show the use of the framework. A ticker server emits stock information to clients. The clients allow subscriptions to ticker channels which provide constant updates of the stock information. In order to assist the traders – in this context a human user who performs stock trades - who use the clients, analysis functionality can be performed on the stock data. Since the analysis is time consuming it is moved to designated computers.

The "load" QoS characteristic performs load balancing of requests among a group of servers. This will reduce the average response time. The following QIDL-specification defines the QoS characteristic "load".

```
1:  qos load
2:  {
3:
4:   interface{
5:   // client qos methods
6:     // register a servers stringified IOR
7:     void enter_server(in string ref);
8:     // set policy: bind per call: 0, initial bind: 1
9:     void set_policy(in short pol);
10:  // server/qos integration methods
11:      // retrieve load information in [0,1]
12:    float get_load();
13:   };
14: };
```

The QoS characteristic is opened by the `qos` keyword followed by the name of the characteristic. The QoS declaration contains two sections: the QoS-parameters and the interface of the QoS characteristic. The QoS parameter section for the "load" characteristic is left empty since there is no QoS parameter. The interface section contains two kinds of operation. First, the operations used to configure the QoS mediator on client side are declared. Lines 7 and 9 are responsible for the operation to enter a server into the group of servers and configuring the binding policy. A client can be bound to a distinct server for a couple of invocations (initial bind) or each request is dispatched to the server with the lowest load. Second, there is the server side aspect integration operation `get_load`. Since the server load can be determined by different policies the QoS implementation delegates the implementation to the server which can determine the load due to application specific factors, e.g. length of request queue.

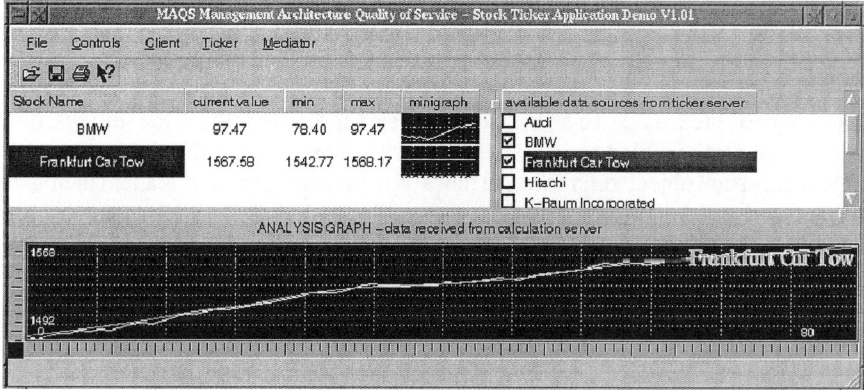

Figure 6: Ticker application: Client window

Figure 6 shows the client window. In the upper right part a user can select stocks he is interested in. These are displayed with their current values in the upper left part. If a user wants further analysis, he can select one of these stocks and the resulting graphs are displayed in the bottom of the window.

```
interface calc
{
  typedef sequence<double> doublelist;
  void simulate(in doublelist points, out doublelist
      lower, out doublelist upper, in long avglen);
};

interface calc_loadbalancing : calc withQoS load
{
};
```

The QIDL definition above shows the definition of the analysis server interface (`calc`) and the assignment of the QoS to the interface resulting in the `calc_loadbalancing` interface.

```
  CORBA::Object_var obj = o->string_to_object(
                                (const char*) ref );
  server = calc_loadbalancing::_narrow(obj);
  load_Mediator *med = new load_Mediator;
  med->orb = o;
  server->_set_mediator(med);
  server->set_policy(0); // per call is default
  ifstream refstream("ref");
  while (refstream >> ref)
  {
```

```
11:     server->enter_server(CORBA::string_dup(ref));
12:   }
```

The usage of the `calc_loadbalancing` server differs only in the initialisation from a non QoS-enabled server. Lines 1 and 2 are responsible for obtaining a stub object from an object reference. In lines 4-6 the mediator for loadbalancing is instantiated and initialised. After that the binding policy is set and the servers are entered in the group.

```
void CCalc_Server_App::calculate_load()
{
        m_current_load = m_calls / m_calls_per_second;
        if ( m_current_load > 1.0 )
        {
                m_calls_per_second++;
                m_current_load = 1.0;
        }
        m_calls = 0;
};

float CCalc_Server_App::get_load()
{
        return m_current_load;
};
```

To sum up, the separation of QoS behaviour from the application is well established. On the client side only the initialisation of the stub object has been affected. Once this was done, the application could communicate as before. The server side had to be adapted to the aspect integration forced from the QoS characteristic. While a simple implementation of the `get_load` operation could have been provided this design allows flexible integration of server specific load information.

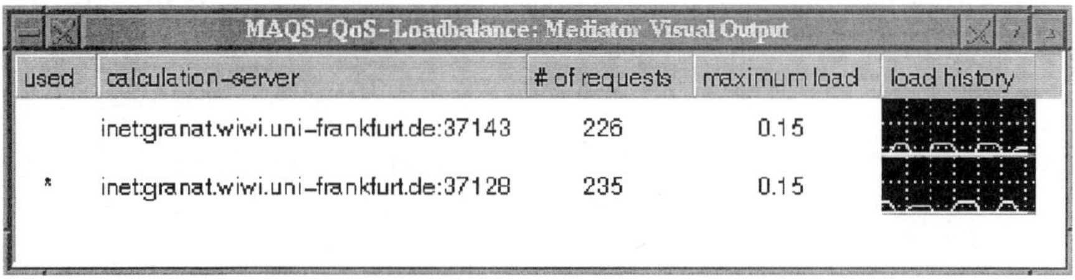

MAQS-QoS-Loadbalance: Mediator Visual Output

used	calculation-server	# of requests	maximum load	load history
	inet:granat.wiwi.uni-frankfurt.de:37143	226	0.15	
*	inet:granat.wiwi.uni-frankfurt.de:37128	235	0.15	

Figure 7: Load Mediator

The mediator was provided with a graphic output in order to demonstrate the load balancing. Figure 7 shows the load graph of two servers and their alternating usage. The same load on both servers indicates proper balancing.

Conclusions and Future Work

We have presented a generic QoS management framework for CORBA. It is interesting to recognise that the newly introduced features in CORBA 2.2 and in the Real-time CORBA conceptually have many features in common with our approach. We view this as a confirmation of our design philosophy. Although there are still many open issues the support for QoS in CORBA is increasing steadily.

As we have shown, integration of QoS management into CORBA can be achieved without any substantial architectural changes. Nevertheless, suitable means of QoS specification and additional infrastructure services are needed. A logical next step for the CORBA standardisation in respect of QoS management would thus be the definition of a QoS specification technique. We have discussed design alternatives for the QoS specification. Because of the aspect nature of QoS we favour explicit IDL extensions over the reuse of existing IDL elements such as struct data types and interfaces. The resulting clear separation of QoS and application objects as well as the support for automatic code generation justify this decision.

In future work we will extend the QoS infrastructure services. The current negotiation component is suitable for closed distributed systems under the assumption that services will not optimise their profit using the knowledge about the client's preferences. We will investigate negotiation strategies for open distributed systems where this assumption does not hold.

Accounting, billing and charging is another area where more work is needed. The specification and integration of accounting and control policies is a major issue here. It would also be worthwhile to study whether and how the QoS management for CORBA can be carried over to other middleware systems such as Java RMI.

References

Becker, C./Geihs, K. (1997): MAQS – Management for Adaptive QoS-enabled Services, in Proceedings of Workshop Middleware for Real Time Systems and Services (WMRTSS)

Becker, C./Geihs, K. (1998): Quality of Service – Aspects of Distributed Programms, in Proceedings of 2nd International Workshop on Aspect Oriented Programming

Becker, C./Geihs, K. (1998): QoS as a Competitive Advantage for Distributed Object Systems, in Proceedings of Workshop of Enterprise Distributed Object Computing (EDOC 98)

Becker, C./Geihs, K. (1999):Generic QoS Specifications for CORBA, in Proceedings of Kommunikation in Verteilten Systemen (KIVS 99)

Becker, C./Geihs, K./Gramberg, J. (1999):Representing Quality of Service Preferences by Hierarchies of Contracts, in Proceedings of Elektronische Dienstleistungswirtschaft und Financial Engineering (FAN 99)

Becker, C./Geihs, K. (2000):Generic QoS Support for CORBA, in Proceedings of International Symposium on Computers and Communications (ISCC 00)

Chung, P.E. et. al. (1998): DCOM and CORBA Side by Side, Step by Step, and Layer by Layer, C++ Report vol. 1(10), 18-29

Dini, P./Hafid, A. (1997): Towards Automatic Trading of QoS Parameters in Multimedia Distributed Applications, in Proceedings Open Distributed Processing and Platforms

Frolund, S./Koistinen, J. (1998): Quality of Service Aware Distributed Object Systems, Technical Report HPL-98-142, HP-Labs, Palo Alto

Gupta, A./Stahl, D.O./Whinston, A.B. (1999): The Economics of Network Management, Communications of the ACM, vol 42(9), 57-63

International Organisation for Standardisation (1995): Quality of Service – Basic Framework N9309

International Telecommunication Union (1993): E.800 Quality of Service and Dependability Vocabulary

Kiczcales, G et. al. (1997): Aspect-Oriented Programming, Technical Report SPL97-008P9710042, Xerox Palo Alto Research Center

Koistinen, J./Seetharaman, A. (1998): Worth-Based Multi-Category Quality-of-Service Negotiation in Distributed Object Infrastructures, in Proceedings of Workshop Enterprise Distributed Object Computing (EDOC 98)

Linhoff-Popien, C./Thißen, D. (1997): Integration QoS Restrictions into the Process of Service Selection, in Proceedings International Workshop on Quality of Service (IWQoS 97)

Loyal, J.P./Bakken, D.E./Schantz, J.A./Zinky (1998): QoS Aspect Languages and their Runtime Integration, Springer, New York

Maffeis, S. (1995): Adding Group Communication and Fault-Tolerance to CORBA, in Proceedings of the USENIX Conference on Object-Oriented Technologies (COOTS 95)

Moser, L.E./Melliar-Smith, P.M./Narasimhan, P. (1998): Consistent Object Replication in the Eternal System, Theory and Practice of Object Systems, Vol. 4(2), 81-92

Object Management Group (1995): CORBAServices: Common Object Services Specification, Framingham, MA

Object Management Group (1995): The Common Object Request Broker Architecture, Rev. 2.0, Framingham, MA

Object Management Group (1997): Quality of Service, Green Paper, Framingham, MA

Object Management Group (1998): The Common Object Request Broker Architecture, Rev. 2.3, Framingham, MA

Object Management Group (1998): CORBA Messaging, Framingham, MA

Object Management Group (1998): Real-time CORBA, Joint Submission, Framingham, MA

Object Management Group (1998): CORBAtelecoms: Telecommunications Domain Specifications, Framingham, MA

Römer, K (1998): MICO – MICO is CORBA, Eine erweiterbare CORBA-Implementierung für Forschung und Ausbildung, Master's Thesis, Computer Science Dep., Goethe-Universität, Frankfurt

Schmidt, D./Levine, D.L./Mungee, S. (1997): The Design of the TAO Real-Time Object Request Broker, Computer Communications Journal

Vinoski, S. (1997): CORBA: Integrating Diverse Applications Within Distributed Heterogeneous Environments, IEEE Communications, February, 46-55

Zinky, J.A./Bakken, D.E./Schantz, R.E. (1997): Architectural Support for Quality of Service for CORBA Objects, Theory and Practice of Objectsystems, vol. 3(1), 55-73

US-American Legislation on Digital Signatures

Johann Bizer

Johann Wolfgang Goethe-University
Institute of Public Law
Mertonstr. 17
D 60054 Frankfurt am Main
bizer@jur.uni-franfurt.de.

Anja Miedbrodt

Johann Wolfgang Goethe-University
Sonderforschungsbereich 403
(now working as a lawyer with Haver & Mailaender in Stuttgart)
am@haver-mailaender.de

Summary:
This contribution provides an overview of digital signature legislation in the US. We will show that a lack of legislative initiative on the federal level caused chaotic state legislation. Very recently, the Federal Congress reacted to this by finally enacting the Electronic Signatures in Global and National Commerce Act, harmonizing the existing body of state law. As Congress regulates only what could hinder the market from solving the problem, we expect complications for the international discussion of harmonizing digital signatures.

Introduction

Economic activity within electronic networks reacts sensitively to unresolved legal issues. If obligations based on electronic contracts cannot be legally enforced, e-commerce may be jeopardized altogether. In this respect, electronic communication raises specific problems since electronic declarations of intention can easily and unnoticeably be altered. This poses of problem of integrity for business partners. In addition, the originator may not be properly identified so that a problem of authenticity arises. These problems could possibly be overcome by means of digital signatures, provided a number of technical and organizational requirements are met.

Worldwide, specifying requirements for suppliers of digital signatures is an issue of non-state standardization (Relevant actors within the US are for example the Information Security Committee of the American Bar Association and the Internet Council of the National Automated Clearing House Association..), intended international agreements (See e.g. OECD-Crypto-Guidelines 1997, UNICTRAL Draft Uniform Rules On Electronic Signatures), transnational directives (See EC-Directive on Community Framework for Electronic Signatures dated December 13, 1999), and national legislation. Thus the legislator is only one of the actors who are outlining institutional conditions for digital signatures. This makes it even more important to look at the activities of other legislators in the world and their possibly competing regulatory models. Among these, the most influential and active is the Congress of the USA [Hain/Rieder 1997; Kuner 1996; Miedbrodt 1998; Miedbrodt 2000; Schumacher 1998].

The Approaches to Signature Regulation in the US

Legislative Power

The United States is a federal state i.e. the sum of the individual states constitutes a national state and thus establishes its sovereignty [N. Redlich, B. Schwartz, J. Attansio 1995]. Similar to Germany (Article 70 et seq., Basic Law), as a matter of principle, the individual states possess legislative power unless the *Constitution* expressly grants this right to the federal lawmaker. Article I § 8 of the *Constitution* grants Congress the right to regulate economic transactions between the individual states. Since digital signatures concern interstate commerce, the requirements for suppliers of digital signatures must be set by the federal legislative power to provide a uniform regulation across the states.

In Germany, the Constitutional Law imposes a warranty obligation on the legislator with regard to the outline conditions for evidential security. This obligation was fulfilled by regulating the requirements for digital signature procedures [Bizer 1997]. The US-American federal legislator, on the other hand, does not perceive himself to be under such a constitutional obligation. In the beginning Congress refrained from regulating a framework for digital signatures, applicable to all kinds of transactions. This point of view was expressed in its "*Global Framework For Electronic Commerce*" (see http://www.iitf.nist.gov/eleccomm/ecomm.htm). Instead, the development and implementation of digital signatures was to be left to the market. Consequently, Congress regulated only the requirements for applications concerning communication with government agencies. Two pieces of legislation were passed in this process. Firstly, the Government Paperwork Elimination Act (See http://frwebgate.access.gpo.gov) regulates the electronic filing of forms with federal agencies. Secondly, the Internal Revenue Restructuring and Reform Bill (see http://frwebgate.access.gpo.gov) allows for electronic filing of income tax returns. Obviously, the requirements set forth in tax returns. Obviously, the requirements set forth in these acts provide a standard for electronic communication even if the intention of the government was to restrict it merely to electronic communication with government agencies. As a matter of course, the standard unintentionally provided by Congress influenced the demand side of the market.

Perhaps due to the acceptance of this influence, Congress somewhat shifted its position and worked explicitly on regulating digital signatures. On October 1, 2000 the National Electronic Signatures in Global and National Commerce Act became effective. This was a decisive step towards a uniform legal basis for electronic signatures.

Regulatory Initiatives

Due to the fact that the US-American federal legislator did not initially make use of its legislative competence, the states took the initiative and either enacted or planned laws regulating digital signatures. As the concepts functioning as a basis for regulation differed very much across the states, the basic legal conditions for digital and electronic signature procedures in the US were very confusing.

While there were two basic approaches, one applicable to particular forms of communication and one applicable to all forms of communication, the latter one can again be divided into two conflicting and one hybrid model:

- The first model is meant to regulate infrastructure requirements for digital signatures by way of legislation. The lawmaker stipulates specific technical and organizational requirements for digital signatures. Compliance is verified by means of a licensing or accreditation procedure (It is not uncommon for the legislators in the US to commission a private institution with the elaboration of requirements. The draft of an *Electronic Financial Services Efficiency Act of 1997, 1997 House Bill 2937 (Baker*), which was, however, not passed, suggested that a private *Electronic Authentifications Standards Review Committee* be established to develop and control criteria that suppliers of authentication services would be subject to). This approach is called the "technical-legal model" since it contains technical and organizational requirements for the provision of evidence of the integrity and authenticity of electronic documents. Examples of this model are the *Utah Digital Signature Act*, strongly influenced by the elaborations of the *American Bar Association,* and the *Washington Electronic Authentication Act.* For this reason, the model is called the Utah/Guideline-Model. The German Digital Signature Act dated August 1, 1997 also follows this model. In conformity with the EC-Directive on a Community framework for electronic signatures, dated December 13, 1999, the German Digital Signature Act is currently being amended.

- The other basic model follows the notion that, *for the time being*, the market should regulate the specification of requirements for suppliers of digital signatures. In order to enable the development of such a market, the legislator has taken account only of regulations that could hinder electronic commerce. Those are mostly regulations regarding the recognition of digital signatures in legal relations. This approach is called the "economic model". An example for this model is the draft of the *Massachusetts Electronic Records and Signature Acts* (*MERSA*).
- The so-called " hybrid approach" combines components of both models. For instance, the *Illinois Electronic Commerce and Security Act* (*ECSA Illinois*) makes use of both models by regulating only the basic conditions for electronic and digital signatures. Another example is the EC-Directive on a Community Framework for electronic signatures.

The variety of regulations resulting from these approaches proved also to be a disadvantage in interstate legal relations. In particular, they complicated negotiations relating to the recognition of equal security in supra- or interstate agreements. In order to harmonize these various actions the *National Conference of Commissioners on Uniform State Law (NCCUSL)* has taken action and elaborated in July 1999 the *Uniform Electronic Transactions Act* (UETA). Even if the UETA supports, to a certain degree, the harmonization of the different regulation models, it provides only a harmonized model. Still, the individual states have to transform it into state law, which means, of course, that how and if the transformation takes place depends solely on the decision of individual states. Furthermore, past experience reveals that this process takes rather a long time.

Therefore the enactment of a federal act was essential in order to harmonize the different approaches taken by the states. In the following section, we supply a brief survey of the most essential regulations of the Electronic Signatures in Global and National Commerce Act and the way it is embedded in general US-law.

How are Digital Signatures Embedded in General US-American Law?

For a better understanding of the provisions of the Electronic Signatures in Global and National Commerce Act a short introduction to signatures in general US-American law is provided.

Contract Law

While the US is actually composed of 51 legal systems (50 states and the federal government), it is possible to generalize to some extent about written signature requirements. Generally speaking, contracts and obligations do not have to be in writing unless the law requires otherwise. According to US-American law, a signature is any symbol or sign that has been added by the signatory with the intention of authenticating a document (§1 *United States Code*. A similar provision is contained in § 1-201 (39) *Uniform Commercial Code*). Neither how the signature is set nor what means were used to provide the signature is relevant (Joseph Denunzio Fruit Co. v. Crane, 79 Federal Supplement 117 (District Court S.D. California 1948).

In the US, questions concerning the validity of handwritten signatures tend to arise most frequently in the context of the so called "Statute of Frauds". In order to make contracts enforceable, the "Statute of Frauds" provides for certain types of contracts (such those of a value more than $ 500 pursuant to § 2-201(1) Uniform Commercial Code), for the lease of private property pursuant to § 2A-201(1) (b) Uniform Commercial Code, and for security agreements pursuant to § 9-203 (1) (a) Uniform Commercial Code. It states that contracts must be in writing and signed by the party against whom enforcement is sought. Since this concerns an enormous number of contracts, uncertainty about this issue could hinder electronic commerce.

Evidence Law

The Rules of Evidence postulate some prerequisites, which could hinder the admissibility of electronic documents. One example is the "authentication rule". This requirement is satisfied by evidence sufficient to support a finding that the matter in question is what its proponent claims. If he claims that an electronic document was generated by a particular person, he has to prove that this person actually wrote this document. Using a digital signature the proponent has to describe the technical and organizational requirements of a public-key-infrastructure which ensures the proof of authenticity and integrity.

The same is true for the requirement of admissibility. In order to prove the content of a writing, or a recording, the original of the writing or the photograph has to be submitted, except as otherwise provided (Rule 1002 Federal Rules of Evidence). If data are stored on a computer or similar device, any printout or other output readable by sight could be provided, as long as it can be shown to reflect the data accurately (Rule 1001 (3) Federal Rules of Evidence).

The National Electronic Signatures in Global and National Commerce Act

The National Electronic Signatures in Global and National Commerce Act is based on the "economic concept". It deliberately leaves out any provisions with regard to digital signatures. Accordingly, it merely removes the above-mentioned legal obstacles to the development of electronic commerce.

The provisions of that act are applicable to all types of electronic communications. It consists in principle of four parts:

- Electronic records and signatures in general,
- Transferable records,
- Principles governing the use of electronic signatures in international transactions,
- Amendments of the Child Online Protection Act.

Electronic Records and Signatures

"Electronic signatures" according to Sec. 106 p. 5 National Electronic Signatures in Global and National Commerce Act are all electronic sounds, symbols or processes, attached to or logically associated with a contract or other record and executed or adopted by a person with the intent to sign the record.

"Electronic record" means a contract or other record created, generated, sent, communicated, received, or stored by electronic means (Sec. 106 p. 4 National Electronic Signatures in Global and National Commerce Act).

Sec. 101 National Electronic Signatures in Global and National Commerce Act is the central regulation of the first part, dealing with the following questions:

- Validity of electronic records, signatures and contracts,
- Prerequisites for electronic records to satisfy a rule of law requiring that information relating to a transaction is to be provided for a consumer in writing,
- Retention of contracts and records,
- Notarisation and acknowledgement.

In this context the regulations regarding electronic signatures and records are of importance.

According to Sec. 101 (a) National Electronic Signatures in Global and National Commerce Act, a signature, contract or other record describing a transaction affecting interstate or foreign commerce, may not be denied legal effect, validity or enforceability solely because it is in electronic form.

With respect to the content of the regulations, this is a mere clarification. According to current contract law, an electronic signature would meet the signature requirements provided the electronic signature was executed with the intention of authenticating a document. However, there are also laws stipulating additional requirements for certain communication relationships with respect to the equalisation of a signature and electronic signature. This leads to the conclusion that an electronic signature would not be able to meet the "signature-requirement" in all other cases [Hill/Bro 1999].

Furthermore, the National Electronic Signatures in Global and National Commerce Act determines that a contract relating to transactions in interstate or foreign commerce may not be denied legal effect, validity, or enforceability solely because an electronic signature or electronic record was used in its formation (Sec. 101 (a) (2) National Electronic Signatures in Global and National Commerce Act).

Furthermore, Sec. 101 (e) National Electronic Signatures in Global and National Commerce Act provides that if a statute or other rule of law requires that a contract or other record relating to a transaction be in writing, the legal effect, validity, or enforceability may be denied if such electronic record is not in a form that is capable of being retained and accurately reproduced for later reference by all parties or persons who are entitled to retain the contract or record. By these provisions the above mentioned problems regarding the "Statute of Frauds" are overcome. Thus, it is incumbent on the parties to apply a method which fulfils these requirements. The law itself does not , however, supply any clues to what technologies can fulfil these requirements.

According to Sec. 101 d (3), 101 (d) (1) National Electronic Signatures in Global and National Commerce Act the prerequisites of such regulations requiring a contract or other record relating to a transaction to be provided, available or retained in its original form are met, provided that an electronic record of the information in the contract or other record:

accurately reflects the information set forth in the contract or other record;

remains accessible to all persons who are entitled to access by statute for the period required by such a statute in a form that is capable of being accurately reproduced for later reference.

With respect to the current Evidence Law there are no reforms. The same requirements have to be fulfilled according to Rule 101 (3) Federal Evidence Rules.

In summary, the National Electronic Signatures in Global and National Commerce Act clarifies the legal status of electronic signatures and eliminates the uncertainty concerning the "Statute of Frauds". But restrictions like the "authentication rule" for the admission of electronic documents still remain.

Continuous Validity of State Law

With respect to the relationship between National and State Law, Sec. 102 (a) National Electronic Signatures in Global and National Commerce Act regulates that a state statute, regulation, or other rule of law may modify, limit or supersede the provision only if such a statute constitutes an enactment or adoption of the Uniform Electronic Transactions Act as approved and recommended for enactment in all States by the National Conference of Commissioners on Uniform State Laws in 1999. Both with respect to the approach as well as to the content of the regulation, the Uniform Electronic Transactions Act and the National Electronic Signatures in Global and National Commerce Act are basically identical.

In addition, regulations stated in the National Electronic Signatures in Global and National Commerce Act (Sec. 102 (a) (2)) are only modifiable by the State Law, if they specify alternative procedures or requirements for the use or acknowledgement or both of electronic records or signatures to establish the legal effect, validity, or enforceability of records of contracts. Furthermore Sec. 102 (a) (2) states that if such alternative procedures or requirements are consistent with the provisions of this act and such alternative procedures or requirements do not require, or accord greater legal status or effect to, the implementation or application of a specific technology must make specific reference to this act. The same is true for a technical specification for performing the functions of creating, storing, generating, receiving, communicating or authenticating electronic records or electronic signatures if enacted or adopted after the date of the enactment of this act. This means that the National Electronic Signatures in Global and National Commerce Act is preemptive especially with respect to such laws as the Utah Digital Signature Act or the Washington Electronic Authentication Act which are based on the "technical-legal concept".

Conclusion

In conclusion, the discussion of the various regulatory concepts on the state level had been decided by enacting the National Electronic Signatures in Global and National Commerce Act. This act effectively harmonizes the evolving chaos caused by different state laws on electronic signatures. But the act also displays the Congress' restraint with respect to regulating more than what is considered to hinder the development of electronic commerce. The specification of the technical and organisational requirements which are necessary to provide an evidence of integrity and authenticity have been left to the market.

Due to the fact that the European legislator modelled the Directive after the "hybrid approach", we have two competing models in the international discussions on regulating digital signatures. We expect this to complicate a harmonization between the European Union and the USA.

References

Bizer, J. (1997): Beweissicherheit im elektronischen Rechtsverkehr, in: A. Haratsch/D. Kugelmann/U. Repkewitz (eds.), Herausforderungen an das Recht der Informationsgesellschaft, Stuttgart 1996, pp. 141-161.
http://www.iitf.nist.gov/eleccomm/ecomm.htm

Hain/Rieder (1997): DuD, p. 469

Hill/Bro (1999): Moving with Change, p. 11

Kuner (1996): NJW-CoR, p. 108

Miedbrodt (1998): DuD, p. 389

Miedbrodt (2000): Signaturregulierung im Rechtsvergleich, Ein Vergleich der Regulierungskonzepte in Deutschland, Europa und in den Vereinigten Staaten von Amerika, Baden-Baden 2000

Redlich, N./Schwartz, B./Attansio, J. (1995): Understanding Constitutional Law, p. 37

Schumacher (1998): CR, p. 758

The Government paperwork Elimination Act is retrievable at http://frwebgate.access.gpo.gov

The Internal Revenue Restructuring and Reform Bill is retrievable at http://frwebgate.access.gpo.gov

III Applications

The contributions of this section are describing applications from different fields of network research. The analysis focuses on communication networks on capital markets, eContracting, and Internet based management of distributed business processes. The variety of these areas as well as the variety of the research methods gives the reader an insight concerning the different features associated with research in the broad field of network applications.

The chapter is structured as follows: In the first article, communication networks on capital markets are analyzed. The role of different actors, the information flows between them and the information processing is examined, e.g. by empirical studies. Furthermore, the respective implications of the globalization of capital markets are discussed.

Thereafter, in the second article, network coordination is examined in the field of eContracting. Economic actors, media to long-term relationships and the role of technology is studied from the perspective of Principle-Agent Theory. Existing models are reviewed and IT-based simulations are performed.

The following (third) article scrutinizes Internet based management of distributed business processes. For instance, process and document modeling concepts based on a combination of Petri nets and the document standard XML are studied. Different concepts are discussed in the context of distributed workflow management, fragmentation of workflows and allocation of workflows.

Each article clearly specifies to what kind of network it is referring, what the elements are and what kind of relationships exist between them. In addition, cross-references to other parts of the book are given where they seem to be useful.

Communication on Capital Markets

Michael Stubenrath

Johann Wolfgang Goethe-University
Institute for International Accounting
michael@stubenrath.de

Summary:
In this article, the communication network on capital markets is analyzed. The information network itself, the production of information, the actors and the sources of information for capital market decisions are discussed. Furthermore, content and technical communication standards are examined and empirical research in this area is presented. Thereafter, the globalization of capital markets is addressed. Communication problems are outlined and the way the different actors cope with these communication problems is scrutinized.

Keywords:
Capital markets, communication network, financial analysts, news agencies, annual report, globalization, communication problems, accounting diversity

Introduction

Up to now, research in the area of capital markets has only partly dealt with the communication network. Financial accounting, financial analysis and capital market reactions to certain information have been studied in depth. The way information is transferred and processed has mostly been treated as a black box. Because of the ongoing globalization of capital markets, actors are faced with several communication problems. Therefore detailed research in the area of the communication network becomes necessary in order to gain an understanding of how communication is performed and how communication problems can be solved. Capital markets are therefore analyzed from an information-economics point of view in this article.

The communication network on capital markets can be characterized by its actors who represent the elements of the network and the relationships between them. The most important actors are financial analysts, corporations and news agencies. In the context of this information network, information flows between the actors, information processing, as well as the sources of information, are analyzed. Furthermore, the role of information for capital market decisions is discussed.

One important aspect of communication on capital markets is the role of standards which to a certain degree determine the content of communication. These standards concern the financial statements of corporations, the obligation to report on certain events and also the content of personal communications, e.g. analyst meetings. In addition, technical communication standards (or formats) are analyzed. Apart from the physical distribution of printed annual reports, the Internet may become the most important medium for corporate reporting and may even in future replace printed reports which are still obligatory today. To examine this hypothesis, a new empirical study with year 2000 data [Stubenrath/Löbig 2000] comprising the one hundred corporations that form the DAX 100 (German stock market index) is presented. The results are compared with the results of a study with 1998 data and an identical research design [Deller/Stubenrath/Weber 1999a] in order to examine the dynamic developments in this area.

Thereafter, special communication problems resulting from the internationalization of the capital markets, like language barriers and, as the most important problem, internationally heterogeneous accounting information are discussed. The way actors cope with these problems is also studied. The coping mechanisms of financial analysts, corporations and news agencies are outlined. For financial analysts, the results of a few studies are described. For news agencies, anecdotal evidence is acquired by a personal case study. For corporations, a personal empirical investigation is again presented, in which the languages and financial accounting standards used for corporate reporting by the DAX 100 corporations are surveyed.

The Communication Network

Information Processing and the Actors Involved

Capital markets can be described as a network with financial flows. Therefore the primary actors are corporations asking for capital and investors providing capital. The financial relationships are prescribed by contracts in which the rights and duties of the contracting parties are outlined [Franke/Hax 1999, 30-53]. Equity securities themselves are standardized with regard to their contractual agreements and are therefore marketable. As on other markets, information about the quality of securities is essential for the functioning of capital markets [e.g. Wittich 1997, 1-2]. Information about the quality of securities in this context is financial information about the corporations. Besides the network of the financial flows there is a network of information within capital markets. This represents the informational basis of the decisions of the capital market participants [Barker 1998, 3-5]. To put it more simply, the flows of information within capital markets can be described as follows.

Investors receive information from the corporations. These are periodic reports (annual reports and interim reports) and information about specific events in press releases. Furthermore, investors (and financial analysts) on the one and enterprise representatives on the other hand communicate with each other. Examples of this communication are analyst meetings, road shows and other round-table or one-on-one discussions [Bittner 1996, 16-20]. From other information sources investors receive further information which may also be decision-relevant. Examples include market data or macroeconomic data.

On the basis of this information, investors make their decisions about security transactions. And the aggregated decisions of all investors are reflected in security prices. This market data again influences investor decisions and also management decisions. The question now is how this information is used in order to produce an investment decision.

The information production on capital markets can be described by the following steps: information search, information preparation, information processing and the investment decision or advice as the result of the information processing [Eberts 1986, 98; Hax 1998, 9]. Within the information search, different kinds of information are acquired, like annual report information, market information, industry information or macroeconomic data. Within the information preparation the different sets of data are brought together and are eventually structured in a different way, or heterogeneous information is standardized. One example of conflating different data sets is the calculation of price-earnings-ratios - data from annual reports and market information are both needed.

Within the information processing, analysts use e.g. discounted cash flow or discounted earnings models to determine the value of an enterprise and compare this value to its current market value [Chugh/Meador 1984, 47; Day 1986, 305]. Furthermore, different information sets are used in order to reach an investment decision which then represents the result of the information processing. This result is generally expressed in a buy, sell or hold strategy [Gentz 1996, 110] and is often outlined in a research report. In practice, fundamental analysis is the most important form of equity analysis [Pike/Meerjanssen/Chadwick 1993; Pankoff/Virgil 1970, 12]. Its aim is to determine an incremental value in order to discover over- or underpriced shares [e.g. Francis 1972, 307]. This knowledge can then be the basis of profitable investment strategies. But who are the actors involved in the production of this information?

The most important actors are corporations, investors, financial analysts and news agencies. Corporations provide information to investors, financial analysts and news agencies and also communicate with them. The relevant corporate strategy is called investor relations [Ellis 1985, 34; Krystek/Müller 1993]. On the one hand, regulation obliges corporations to give information to other capital market participants. On the other hand, corporations also give voluntary information in order to reduce the cost of their capital [Botosan 1997; Diamond 1985; Diamond/Verrecchia 1991]. In practice, the most important instruments of investor relations are the annual report, interim reports, the annual general meeting, press and financial analyst conferences, conference calls, and one-on-one discussions [Dürr 1995, 50-110; Günther/Otterbein 1996, 404-410].

Investors make their decisions on the basis of the information acquired. Whether they produce the needed information themselves or whether they take advice from information intermediaries is at least a make or buy decision. Portfolio managers as well as information intermediaries who carry out financial analysis are called financial analysts [Schlienkamp 1998, 216; Moizer/Arnold 1984, 341].

Information offered	**Reuters**	**Bloom-berg**	**Dow Jones Markets**	**Primark**
General Company Information	X	X	./.	X
Share Price Information	X	X	X	X
Research Reports / Forecasts	X	X	./.	X
Company Press Releases	X	X	X	X
Original Annual Reports	./.	X	./.	X
Standardized Annual Reports	X	X	./.	X
X = provided, ./. = not provided				

Table 1: Information offered by news agencies (in 1998)

News agencies on capital markets can be defined as information intermediaries who work in the information production steps 'information search' and 'information preparation'. They act as intermediaries between the corporations on the one hand and the financial analysts, intermediaries as well as portfolio managers, on the other. Examples of these news agencies are Bloomberg, Dow Jones Markets, Primark and Reuters [Kugler 1996, 92]. News agencies acquire information which may be decision-relevant for financial analysts. Examples include real time market information as well as historical company information [Kugler 1996, 92-93]. The information is typically provided via the terminals of the news agencies. Furthermore, Reuters and Bloomberg, for example, have their own technical networks. Examples of typical information products of these news agencies are given in table 1.

After having discussed the different actors of the information network, the question arises: what information is needed for capital market decisions and how important are the different information sources? Therefore table 2 offers an overview of empirical research in this area. The studies refer to Behavioral Accounting Research [for an overview of this area of research see Haller 1989] and describe the relative importance of different information sources to financial analysts (intermediaries and portfolio managers). The research design is generally based on interviews or questionnaires and the financial analysts are asked to rank the different sources of information.

Summarizing the results of the different studies, it becomes obvious that accounting information and direct contacts with management are the most important sources of information in practice (the ranks given in the studies are partly standardized in table 2).

Furthermore it seems that both information sources – direct contacts with management and accounting information - are interconnected to a certain degree. At analyst meetings details of the annual report or interim report are often discussed [Diehl/Loistl/Rehkugler 1998, 92-99; Francis/Hanna/Philbrick 1997]. Analysts get a 'picture of the corporation' by studying the annual report and discuss details that remain unclear afterwards with the management [e.g. Gniewosz 1990, 227]. One function of the annual report is explicitly seen in the preparation of meetings with company representatives [Krehl 1985, 6-7]. The next question that arises is what kind of content and technical communication standards are there on capital markets, and how do these standards influence the communication between the actors.

Study		Anderson (1981) **	Arnold/Moizer/Noreen (1984) ***		Breton/Taffler (1995) *	Chang/Most/Brain (1983) *			Hussey/Bence/Wilkie (1992) ***	Lee/Tweedie (1981) **	Pike/Meerjanssen/Chadwick (1993) ***		Vergoossen (1993) *	Yap (1997) ***
Country		Australia	USA	UK	UK	USA	UK	Germany	UK	UK	UK	Germany	Netherlands	Australia
Accounting Information	Annual Reports	1	1	1	2	1	2	1	1	1	3	2	1	1
	Interim Reports		2	2	3	4	4	2	2	2			3	
Direct Contacts to Management	Individual Contacts	3	3	3	1	3	1	3	2	3	1	3	2	5
	Analyst Meetings										2	1		
IPO-Prospectus		-	-	-	-	2	3	5	-	-	-	-	4	-
Press Releases and other Company Information		-	-	-	6	6	6	4	4	-	-	-	5	-
Newspapers		4	4	4	4	7	5	6	5	4	4	4	6	3
Statistical and Macroeconomic Reports and Forecasts		-	5	5	5	-	-	-	-	5	-	-	7	2
Information from other Brokers and Financial Analysts		2	6	6	7	5	7	7	6	-	5	5	8	4

* Information intermediaries only
** Portfolio managers only
*** Information intermediaries and portfolio managers

Table 2: Information sources ranked by financial analysts

Information Content Standards

Information content standards determine or influence the information content itself. Examples include accounting standards which determine the content of annual reports, or regulations concerning the obligation to report on certain events in press releases. In the following, the content standards required in Germany are used as an example.

Accounting information from corporations communicates financial information to investors, financial analysts and other interested parties. Financial information represents information about business transactions and status in terms of money. To be useful for capital market decisions, financial information is classified and summarized. Classified summaries (as subsets of the annual report) are the balance sheet, the profit and loss account and the cash flow statement. They inform investors and analysts in words and numbers about the financial position of an enterprise [Imdieke/Smith 1991, 2-4].

Accounting standards give answers to the following questions:

- Who or what kind of companies have the obligation to prepare annual and interim reports?
- How much information has to be published and what kind of information is obligatory?
- Which figures have to be aggregated and classified and how?

The most important accounting standard setters in Germany are the German parliament (laws are prepared by the German Ministry of Justice), the German Accounting Standards Board (*Deutsches Rechnungslegungs Standards Committee,* DRSC), and also the German Stock Exchange (*Deutsche Börse AG*) [see also Ordelheide 1999a].

Accounting standards for annual reports are regulated in the German Commercial Code (*Handelsgesetzbuch,* HGB). As a consequence of the globalization of capital markets, paragraph 292a HGB allows German corporations (for a limited period) to prepare their annual reports voluntarily according to International Accounting Standards (IAS) or according to US-Generally Accepted Accounting Principles (US-GAAP) instead of preparing them according to HGB [Böcking/Orth 1998; Ordelheide 1999a, 104]. In the exchange market segment New Market (*Neuer Markt*) the German Stock Exchange generally obliges listed corporations (under private law) to prepare their accounts according to IAS or US-GAAP [Deutsche Börse AG 1999b]. Corporations listed in the market segment SMAX have this obligation from 2001 on [d'Arcy/Leuz 2000, 391]. Besides accounting standards there are other content standards which also influence communication relationships.

The management of corporations has the obligation to report events that could be value-relevant and therefore decision-relevant for investors [Deutsche Börse AG

1995a]. According to the German Securities Act (*Wertpapierhandelsgesetz,* WpHG) the management of listed corporations has to disclose every event or fact in their sphere of influence that could seriously affect the share price of their corporation [Fülbier 1998, 33-78; Fürhoff/Wölk 1997, 450-455]. The WpHG also outlines insider trading regulation in Germany. Insiders of corporations are not allowed to use their information advantages for investment decisions or to transmit the relevant information to third parties [Caspari 1995; Hopt 1995a and 1995b].

Other examples of content standards are obligations for corporations listed in the German New Market or SMAX. Corporations have to disclose an investor calendar in which all relevant dates like the annual general meeting or analyst and press conferences are mentioned, they have to arrange one analyst meeting per year and to establish direct contact with the investor relations department [Deutsche Börse AG 1999b and 1999c; Förschle/Helmschrott 1997; Strieder/Ammedick 1999]. Besides these standards for the content of communication, there are also technical standards which determine communication on capital markets.

Technical Communication Standards

Technical communication standards play an important role in the communication network on capital markets. The efficiency of capital markets is determined by the quality of information services and the technology used [Honeygold 1998, 64]. As a portfolio manager noted: "everything depends on information technology today, and the speed and accessibility of information is paramount" [Kondo/Malakkal 1990]. Nevertheless, up to now only a few studies have dealt with technology in the context of capital markets [e.g. Garbade/Silber 1978].

An interesting question in this context is under what circumstances investors on capital markets can realize returns higher than the market return. This is only possible if actors have above-average expert knowledge and process information permanently and quickly for their investment decisions [Hax 1998, 62]. For fast information processing, the services of a news agency with its own technical network or information services provided via the Internet may be essential. If we concentrate on time lags, it becomes clear that electronic information delivery may create comparative advantages for financial analysts in comparison with postal delivery. The information can be processed one or several days earlier and capital market decisions (or advises) can be made earlier as well. And postal delivery still seems to be the primary (and is the obligatory) way of disseminating annual reports [Deller/Stubenrath/Weber 1999a and 1999b], although it is expected that corporate reporting via the Internet will become the most important way to disseminate financial information in the near future [Ordelheide 1999b, 244]. Therefore it seems that it would be very interesting to study Internet usage in investor relations activities in practice. In recent years academics have already started on empirical investigations in different countries [for an overview see Lymer 1999] and analyzed in detail the potential applications of the Internet as a medium for investor relations activities [Deller/Stubenrath/Weber 1997 and 1998]. To get an impression of current Internet usage in this area and relevant developments in recent years, the subsequent empirical study surveys the Internet investor relations activities of 100 German corporations.

The 1998 data of a study conducted by Deller, Stubenrath and Weber [1999a] are compared with year 2000 data of a study by Stubenrath and Löbig [2000]. The two studies are chosen because both have the same sample which comprises the 100 corporations that form the DAX 100 (German stock market index). Using this comparison we can analyze both current Internet use within the investor relations activities of corporations as well as corresponding developments in recent years. The primary focus of the investigations is the question of how many corporations use the Internet, and to what extent they use it as a medium for the delivery of accounting information. Furthermore, the question of whether the Internet is used to disseminate further information for investors and whether it is also used as a communication tool was examined.

The first question was how many corporations have their own homepage and whether they make web sites with information for investors and financial analysts available. The results are as follows.

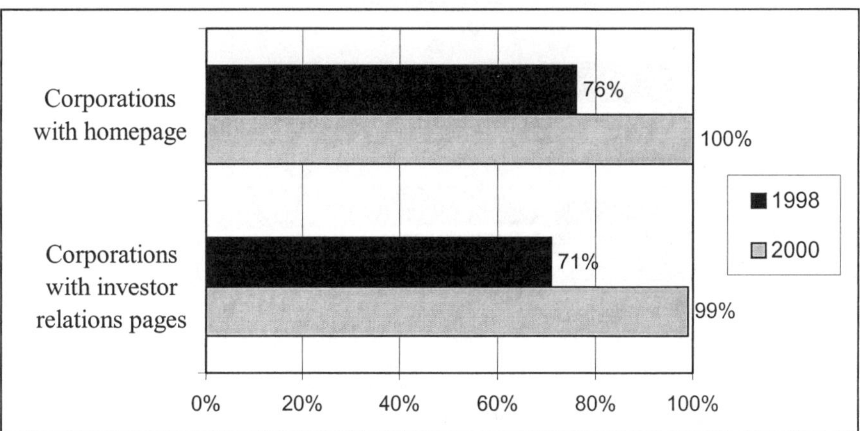

Figure 1: Internet use

Figure 1 shows that in 1998 76 per cent of the corporations had a homepage on the Internet. In comparison, 100 per cent had a company homepage in 2000. The results are very similar with respect to investor relations pages: In 1998 71 per cent of the corporations had web pages with information for investors and financial analysts, compared to 99 per cent in 2000. The results indicate that the use of the Internet as an investor relations medium is already standard today. Nevertheless, the results above do not allow any statements concerning the quality or quantity of the information presented to be made.

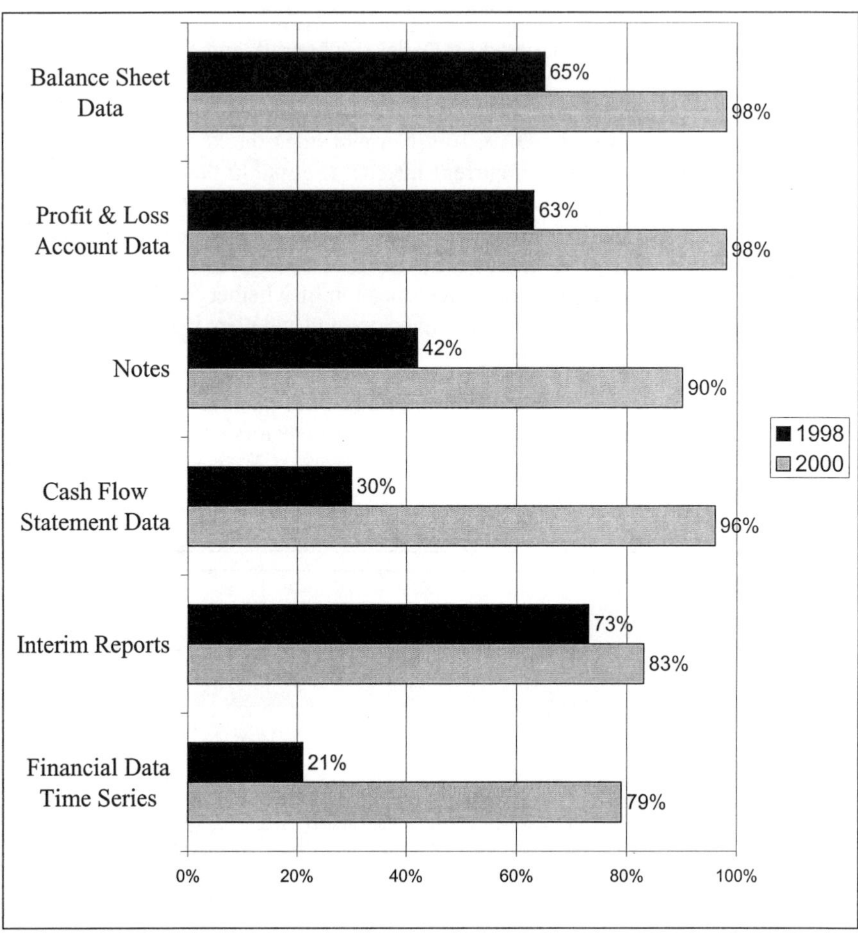

Figure 2: Scope of the accounting information reported

Therefore the next question is: to what extent the Internet is used and what features are used. To obtain more meaningful results all percentages from now on are calculated in relation to the number of corporations that use the Internet for their investor relations activities (in the relevant year). Figure 2 shows the findings concerning accounting information.

In 1998, accounting information, namely balance sheet data and profit and loss account data, was offered by approximately 65 per cent of the corporations. In 2000 almost all corporations which had investor relations pages gave this accounting information (98 per cent). But in 1998 as well as in 2000 only some of the corporations added the notes to the accounts (42 per cent and 90 per cent respectively). Interim reports were offered by 73 per cent in 1998 and 83 per cent in 2000. With respect to cash flow statement data and financial data time series the findings were extremely dissimilar. In 1998 only a few corporations made cash flow statement data (30 per cent) and financial data time series (21 per cent) available. In 2000 both features occur frequently with 96 and 79 per cent respectively. The results clearly show the improvements made in recent years.

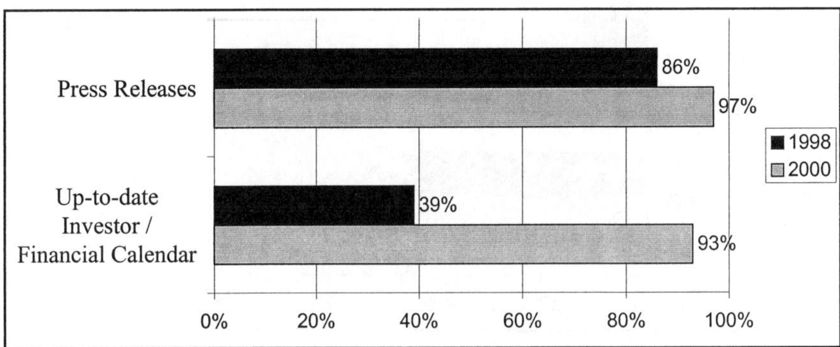

Figure 3: Further information

Figure 3 gives an overview of whether press releases and an up-to-date investor / financial calendar were provided. Press releases, which were already common in 1998 with 86 per cent, are now offered by 97 per cent. An up-to-date investor / financial calendar was offered by only 39 per cent of the corporations in 1998, and had become a standard feature by 2000 (with 93 per cent). Furthermore, the possibilities of contacting the investor relations department via e-mail and related features were scrutinized. The results are shown in figure 4.

The possibility of sending electronic mails directly to the investor relations department varies considerably between 1998 and 2000. In 1998 31 per cent of the corporations provided this possibility in contrast to 96 per cent in 2000. Only a few corporations offered answers to so-called frequently asked questions on their web sites in 1998. This feature had only increased to 20 per cent by 2000. An online investor information order service was offered by 46 per cent of the corporations in 1998 and by 64 per cent in 2000 respectively.

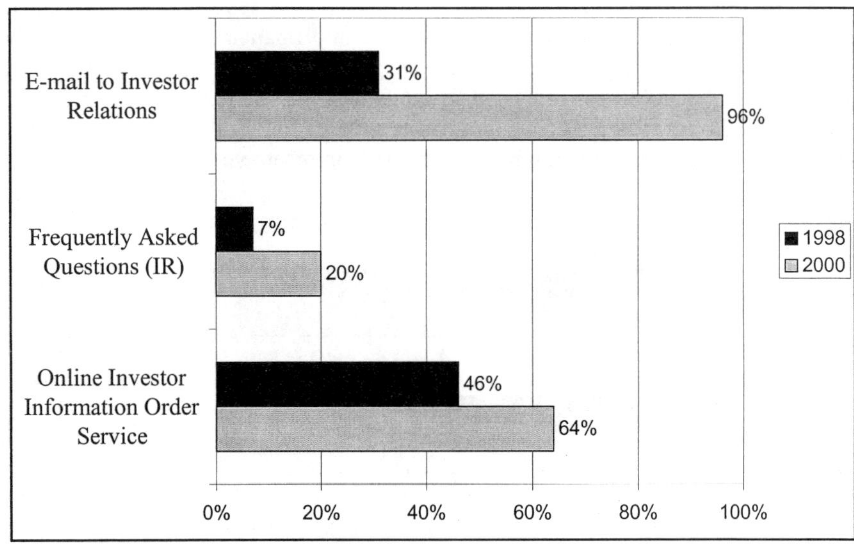

Figure 4: E-mail and other features

All in all, the results show that the Internet is becoming the most important communication standard in communication between corporations and other capital market participants. In terms of accounting information, the Internet already seems to be a standard medium, although it has to be kept in mind, that some security problems still exist and the presentation formats used are still partly heterogeneous [Westarp/Ordelheide/Stubenrath/Buxmann/König 1999].

Globalization of Capital Markets

Internationalization of Capital Flows

The internationalization of capital flows is not a new phenomenon, although its importance increased in the 1990s [e.g. Glaum/Mandler 1996, 45-48; Ziegler 1992, 26]. This internationalization became possible as a consequence of the removal of controls on the movement of capital and the fast technological developments of recent years. Today, securities can be traded around the globe 24 hours a day [Gyohten 1993, 17; Earle/Fried 1993].

Indicators for this ongoing globalization are, for example, increases in foreign listings or increases in foreign shareholdings. Another indicator is the development of the turnover in foreign equities, which is presented for German financial centers in figure 5. The calculations are based on data published by the German Stock Exchange [Deutsche Börse AG 1995b, 1996, 1997, 1998, and 1999a].

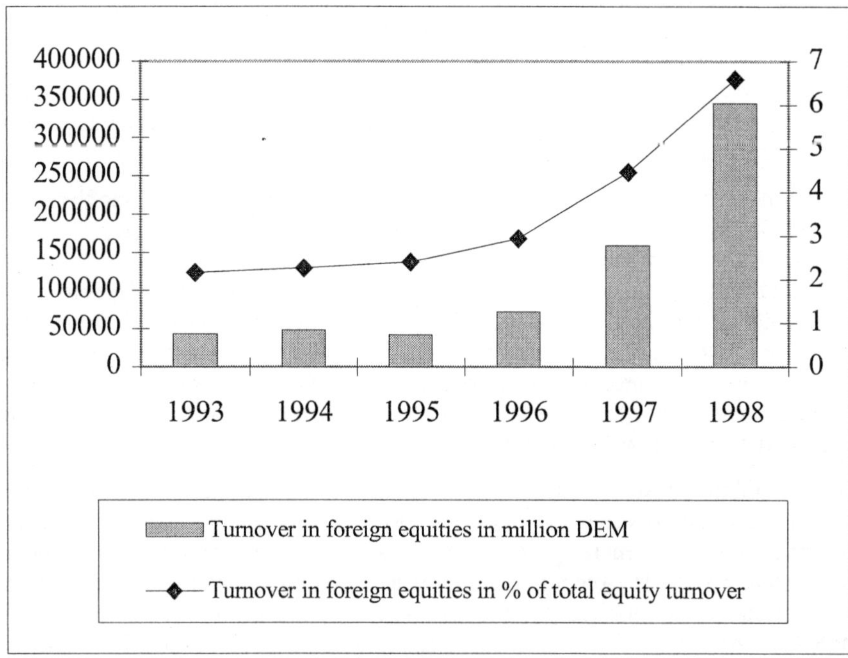

Figure 5: Turnover in foreign equities in German financial centers

The turnover in foreign equities increased from 43,000 million DEM (2.2 per cent of the total equity turnover) in 1993 to 345,000 million DEM (6.6 per cent of the total equity turnover) in 1998. From 1996 to 1998 in particular the increases were very sharp.

Communication Problems

The internationalization of capital markets discussed above is leading to an internationalization of the communication network. Information has to be transmitted across national borders and time zones, which leads to communication problems.

General problems on international markets are language and cultural barriers, although the English language is used widely on capital markets and therefore actors often communicate in the same language [Iqbal/Melcher/Elmallah 1997, 359-360]. But communication also occurs between persons who have different mother tongues and different cultural backgrounds. And there are still communication problems between persons who come from different English speaking countries [Jandt 1995, 110]. E.g. expressions used in accounting countries [Jandt 1995, 110]. E.g. expressions used in accounting standards as well as in annual reports differ across English-speaking countries [Choi/Mueller 1992, 414; Laswad/Mak 1994].

Besides verbal communication problems, there are also problems with para- and non-verbal communication [Jahnke 1996, 34-36]. During face-to-face communication, e.g. at analyst meetings or road shows, gestures and facial expression may be the most important means of communication if there are questions about insider knowledge and the company representatives are not allowed (by law) to answer the particular questions [more generally: Apeltauer 1996, 14].

Furthermore, there are communication problems arising from geographical distance [Nitschke 1996, 20-21]. On international capital markets, distances between actors are generally much greater in comparison with national capital markets. Communication using printed documents takes several days more. Therefore the importance of the Internet will increase with the globalization of capital markets. But even if persons communicate by e-mail, you have time lags as a consequence of different time zones. When actors meet each other physically, e.g. at annual general meetings or road shows, it takes much more time for the journey. Some costs may therefore increase exponentially.

But one of the most important problems on international capital markets is accounting diversity [Ordelheide 1999c, 83-84], which means that corporations from different countries generally prepare their annual reports according to different accounting standards. Accounting figures are then aggregated in different ways which leads to the problem that they are no longer comparable [Krisement 1997, 466-469]. And the problem of accounting figures is that they cannot be translated into another accounting system by external users. To perform such a translation would mean aggregating all the events and transactions of a time interval again and according to another accounting system. Other examples for this accounting diversity between different accounting standards are: different time intervals for interim reports, or different quantities of information that have to be disclosed.

To provide an understanding of this accounting diversity, a study undertaken by Böttcher [1997] is presented. Böttcher's sample consists of 74 US subsidiaries of German corporations. These subsidiaries have to prepare their original annual reports according to US-GAAP. In addition, they have to prepare an annual report according to German accounting principles (HGB), which is needed to prepare the consolidated accounts of the parent company. Böttcher compares the equity ratios based on German accounting principles to the equity ratios calculated on the US-GAAP basis. The results are given in figure 6.

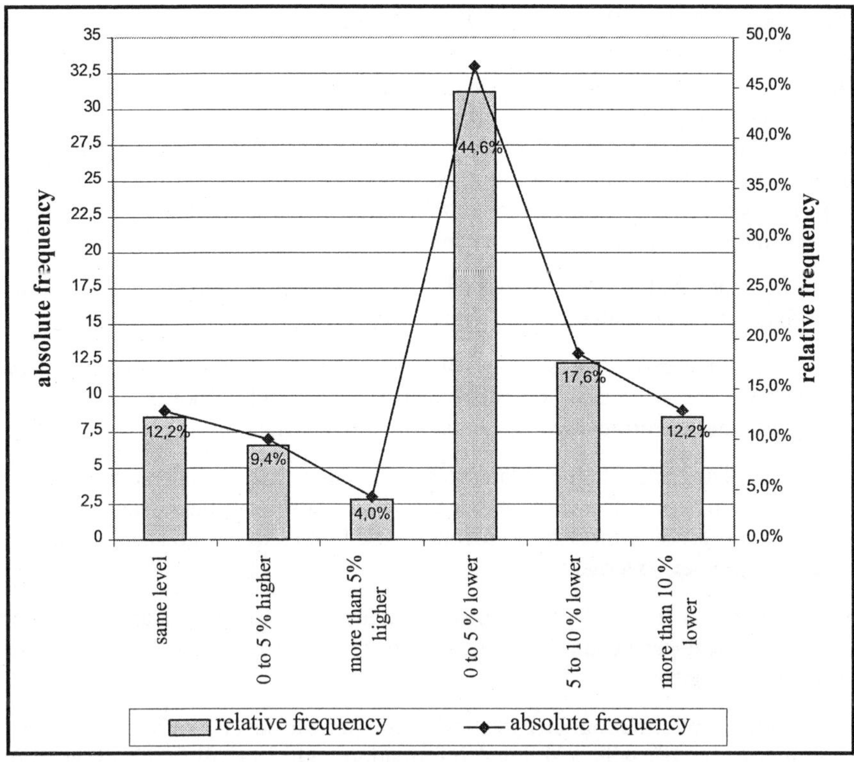

Figure 6: Equity ratios according to German accounting principles in comparison with equity ratios according to US-GAAP [data from Böttcher 1997, 38-40]

12.2 per cent of the corporations have an equity ratio according to HGB that is equal to the equity ratio according to US-GAAP. 9.4 per cent of the corporations have an equity ratio according to HGB that is 0 to 5 per cent higher than that according to US-GAAP, 4 per cent of the corporations have an HGB equity ratio that is more than 5 per cent higher than that according to US-GAAP. 74.4 per cent of the corporations have an equity ratio according to HGB that is lower than that according to US-GAAP: 44.6 per cent of the corporations from 0 to 5 per cent lower, 17.6 per cent of the corporations from 5 to 10 per cent lower and 12.2 per cent of the corporations more than 10 per cent lower.

The results clearly show that different corporations that have an identical economic situation may appear differently in their annual reports if they prepare their accounts according to the accounting standards of different countries. Therefore, financial analysts have big problems in comparing corporations across borders, which may lead to less profitable investment decisions. How actors cope with these communication problems is addressed in the following sections.

Financial Analysts' Coping Mechanisms

There are three studies that deal in depth with the coping mechanisms of financial analysts with respect to international accounting differences. These are Bhushan and Lessard [1992], Choi and Levich [1990], and Miles and Nobes [1998]. In order to give a brief overview of the coping mechanisms, the results of the three empirical studies are summarized in the following. The studies have samples comprising portfolio managers and/or intermediaries.

When financial analysts are confronted with accounting differences, they use the following coping mechanisms:

- Changing the investment strategy: the analysts diversify their portfolio in some countries, e.g. according to a stock market index, and do not invest in single equities and therefore do not process company information.
- Standardizing annual reports: analysts try to standardize the accounting figures to a certain degree. Some of them make some adjustments dependent on the information given. Others try to reconcile the figures from one accounting system to another (externally).
- Interpretation from a local perspective: analysts try to analyze annual reports from a local perspective and interpret them in the economic context of the relevant country.
- Additional information: analysts try to compensate for the deficiencies of accounting figures with additional information and especially with direct contacts with the management of corporations.
- Enlisting the services of financial analysts in other countries: analysts contact foreign intermediaries in the country of interest in order to receive certain information or investment advice.

Summarizing these results, it becomes obvious that information production costs are higher on international capital markets in comparison to national capital markets. Other actors who help financial analysts with the production of information on international capital markets are news agencies.

News Agencies' Coping Mechanisms

By looking at the information services outlined in section 2.1 of this article, it becomes apparent that news agencies may give support to financial analysts by providing a lot of information about corporations and markets in many countries. Therefore information provided by news agencies can help analysts with their coping mechanisms in terms of 'additional information', 'standardizing annual reports' (additional information may be useful for some adjustments to some extent) and 'interpretation from a local perspective' (news agencies also provide country background information to some extent).

Furthermore, news agencies themselves standardize annual reports to a certain degree [Ordelheide 1998]. Because these standardizations have not been studied up to now, the results of a personal empirical case study (undertaken in 1997) are briefly summarized in the following. The standardizations used by the news agency Bloomberg were analyzed from October to November 1997. The online manuals describing the standardization of annual reports were scrutinized and unclear items were discussed with Bloomberg employees. The results were then reviewed by reconstructing the standardizations of the 1996 annual reports of Siemens and General Electric.

The results show that Bloomberg makes standardizations that can be compared to the adjustments of financial analysts. The adjustments concentrate on standardizations of the format and classification of the accounts. The resulting company-specific accounting standards are similar to US-GAAP. Nevertheless, standardizations concerning recognition and valuation of balance sheet or profit and loss account items are scarce. One example of standardizations concerning the recognition and valuation of balance sheet items is the reclassification of the minority interests of German corporations according to US-GAAP. Another example is the elimination of accumulated losses brought forward within the assets and the corresponding reduction of retained earnings.

Coping Mechanisms Used by Corporations

On international capital markets, corporations also try to reduce communication problems. On the one hand, corporations have the obligation to disclose additional information in certain cases, e.g. if they are listed in other countries [Saudagaram/Biddle 1994, 164-165]. On the other hand, corporations also voluntarily provide additional information in order to reduce their cost of capital [Verrecchia 1999, 278-279].

In order to reduce communication problems, corporations may publish their information in several languages to attract foreign investors [Choi/Mueller 1992, 27]. To test this hypothesis in the face of actual practice, an analysis of whether the 100 largest German corporations (DAX 100) offer their annual reports or short versions of the annual report in several languages was carried out. The first step of the research was to examine the homepages of the corporations to discover whether annual reports were provided online in different languages or whether annual reports in different languages could be ordered online. The second step was to analyze the 100 printed 1998 (German) annual reports in order to find clues for the existence of, or for the possibility of ordering, annual reports in other languages. Figure 7 summarizes the results.

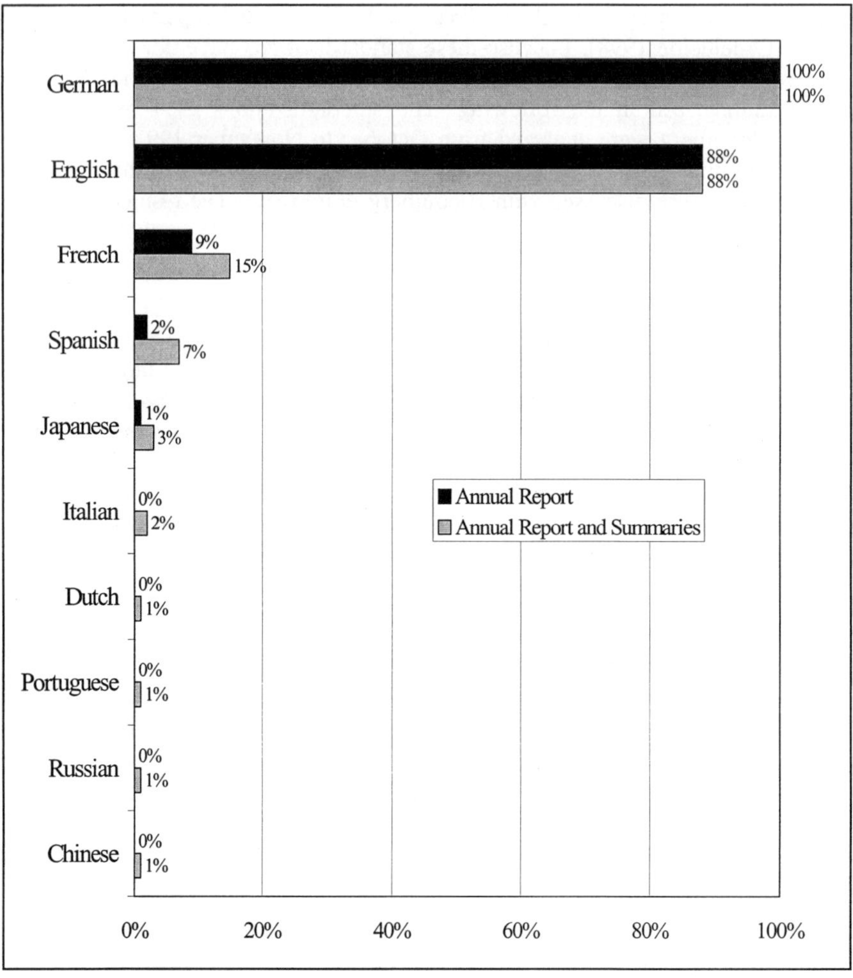

Figure 7: Languages in which annual reports are offered by German corporations

Besides the obligatory German annual report, 88 per cent of the corporations provide an annual report in English. Complete annual reports in French are offered by 9 per cent, French complete or short versions are offered by 15 per cent of the corporations. 7 per cent of the corporations offer a complete or short version of their annual report in Spanish. Other languages represent an exception. The results clearly show that the English language is the language of investor relations on international capital markets.

As outlined in section 2.2 of this article, German corporations are now allowed to prepare their annual reports voluntarily according to International Accounting Standards (IAS) or according to US-Generally Accepted Accounting Principles (US-GAAP) instead of preparing them according to (German) HGB. Therefore, it seems to be an interesting question whether this internationalization of German accounting regulation is reflected in accounting practice. To answer this question the accounting standards used by the 100 largest German corporations (DAX 100) to prepare their annual reports were examined. Again, the 100 printed annual reports were analyzed.

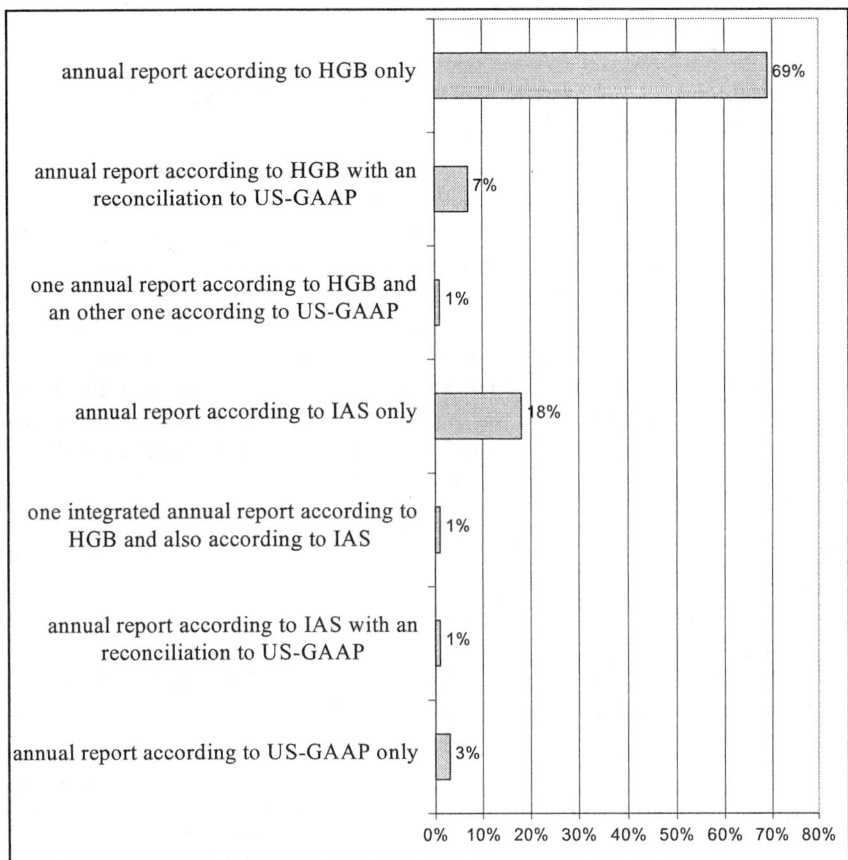

Figure 8: 1998 annual reports of German corporations

Figure 8 shows that 69 per cent of the corporations still prepare their accounts to HGB only – 31 per cent take the opportunity to provide more international accounting information. Within this group, IAS with 19 per cent (18 + 1) seems to be more popular than US-GAAP with 11 per cent (7 + 1 + 3), one corporation gives accounting information according to IAS and US-GAAP.

Summary

In this article, capital markets are studied from an information-economics point of view. The communication network, which is represented by actors and the relationships between them, is studied. Furthermore, information flows and the information production on capital markets is addressed and standards concerning the content of information and technical communication standards are discussed. With this discussion it becomes obvious that technical developments have changed the way communication occurred in the past and that corporate reporting via the Internet is already standard.

Within a discussion of the globalization of capital markets it is shown that the internationalization of capital flows is accompanied by an internationalization of the communication network and that different actors develop different mechanisms to cope with the international communication problems. Financial analysts develop different coping mechanisms for their information production and in doing so get helped by news agencies. Corporations themselves offer additional or more international information in order to communicate with international investors. Examples include annual reports of German Corporations in English and partly in other languages or annual reports prepared according to International Accounting Standards or according to US-Generally Accepted Accounting Principles.

References

Anderson, R. (1981): The Usefulness of Accounting and Other Information Disclosed in Corporate Annual Reports to Institutional Investors in Australia, in: Accounting and Business Research, Vol. 16, pp. 259-265.

Apeltauer, E. (1996): Körpersprache in der interkulturellen Kommunikation, Flensburger Papiere zur Mehrsprachigkeit und Kulturenvielfalt im Unterricht, No. 16/17, Flensburg.

Arnold, J./Moizer, P./Noreen, E. (1984): Investment Appraisal Methods of Financial Analysts - A Comparative Study of U.S. and U.K. Practices, in: International Journal of Accounting, Vol. 19, Spring, pp. 1-18.

Barker, R.G. (1998): The market for information – evidence from finance directors, analysts and fund managers, in: Accounting and Business Research, Vol. 29, No. 1, pp. 3-20.

Bhushan, R./Lessard, D.R. (1992): Coping with International Accounting Diversity - Fund Managers' Views on Disclosure, Reconciliation, and Harmonization, in: Journal of International Financial Management and Accounting, Vol. 4, pp. 149-164.

Bittner, T. (1996): Die Wirkungen von Investor Relations-Maßnahmen auf Finanzanalysten, Köln.

Böcking, H.-J./Orth, C. (1998): Neue Vorschriften zur Rechnungslegung und Prüfung durch das KonTraG und das KapAEG – Ergebnisse eines kapitalmarktinduzierten Reformzwangs, in: Der Betrieb, Vol. 51, pp. 1241-1246.

Böttcher, B. (1997): Eigenkapitalausstattung und Rechnungslegung - US-amerikanische und deutsche Unternehmen im Vergleich, Frankfurt.

Botosan, C.A. (1997): Disclosure Level and the Cost of Equity Capital, in: The Accounting Review, Vol. 72, pp. 323-349.

Breton, G./Taffler, R.J. (1995). Creative Accounting and Investment Analyst Response, in: Accounting and Business Research, Vol. 25, pp. 81-92.

Caspari, K.-B. (1995): Die Problematik der erheblichen Kursbeeinflussung einer publizitätspflichtigen Tatsache, in: Insiderrecht und Ad-hoc-Publizität – Was bedeuten die neuen Regelungen für Unternehmenspublizität und Finanzanalyse, ed. by J. Baetge, Düsseldorf, pp. 65-78.

Chang, L.S./Most, K.S./Brain, C.W. (1983): The Utility of Annual Reports - An International Study, in: Journal of International Business Studies, Vol. 14, pp. 63-83.

Choi, F.D.S./Levich, R.M. (1990): The Capital Market Effects of International Accounting Diversity, New York.

Choi, F.D.S./Mueller, G.G. (1992): International Accounting, 2nd edition, Englewood Cliffs.

Chugh, L.C./Meador, J.W. (1984): The Stock Valuation Process: The Analysts' View, in: Financial Analysts Journal, Vol. 40, Nov.-Dec., pp. 41-48.

d'Arcy, A./Leuz, C. (2000): Rechnungslegung am Neuen Markt – Eine Bestandsaufnahme, in: Der Betrieb, Vol. 53, pp. 385-391.

Day, J.F.S. (1986): The Use of Annual Reports by UK Investment Analysts, in: Accounting and Business Research, Vol. 16, Autumn, pp. 295-307.

Deller, D./Stubenrath, M./Weber, C. (1997): Die Internetpräsenz als Instrument der Investor Relations - Rechnungslegungsdaten deutscher Unternehmen im Internet, in: Der Betrieb, Vol. 50, pp. 1577-1583.

Deller, D./Stubenrath, M./Weber, C. (1998): Investor Relations and the Internet - Background, Potential Application and Evidence from the USA, UK and Germany, SFB 403 Research Report, Frankfurt.

Deller, D./Stubenrath, M./Weber, C. (1999a): A survey on the use of the Internet for investor relations in the USA, the UK and Germany, in: The European Accounting Review, Vol. 8, No. 2, pp. 351-364.

Deller, D./Stubenrath, M./Weber, C. (1999b): Inter*net*ional Investor Relations, in: Investor Relations Quarterly, Vol. 2, No. 2, pp. 27-32.

Deutsche Börse AG (1995a): Insiderhandelsverbote und Ad hoc-Publizität nach dem Wertpapierhandelsgesetz, Frankfurt.

Deutsche Börse AG (1995b): Fact Book 1994, Frankfurt a.M.

Deutsche Börse AG (1996): Fact Book 1995, Frankfurt a.M.

Deutsche Börse AG (1997): Fact Book 1996, Frankfurt a.M.

Deutsche Börse AG (1998): Fact Book 1997, Frankfurt a.M.

Deutsche Börse AG (1999a): Fact Book 1998, Frankfurt a.M.

Deutsche Börse AG (1999b): Regelwerk Neuer Markt, Stand: 01.01.1999, Frankfurt a. M.

Deutsche Börse AG (1999c): SMAX-Teilnahmebedingungen, Stand: 27.01.1999, Frankfurt a.M.

Diamond, D.W. (1985): Optimal release of information by firms, in: Journal of Finance, Vol. 19, pp. 1071-1094.

Diamond, D.W./Verrecchia, R.E. (1991): Disclosure, Liquidity, and the Cost of Capital, in: Journal of Finance, Vol. 46, pp. 1325-1359.

Diehl, U./Loistl, O./Rehkugler, H. (1998): Effiziente Kapitalmarktkommunikation, Stuttgart.

Dürr, M. (1995): Investor Relations – Handbuch für Finanzmarketing und Unternehmenskommunikation, 2nd ed., München.

Earle, D.M./Fried, J.F. (1993): Twenty-Four Hour Trading, Clearance, and Settlement: The Role of Banks, in: Regulating International Financial Markets - Issues and Policies, ed. by F.R. Edwards and H.T. Patrick, Boston et al., pp. 209-224.

Eberts, M. (1986): Das Berufsbild des Finanzanalysten in der Bundesrepublik Deutschland, Darmstadt.

Ellis, C.D. (1985): How to Manage Investor Relations, in: Financial Analysts Journal, March-April, pp. 34-41.

Förschle, G./Helmschrott, H. (1997): Der Neue Markt an der Frankfurter Wertpapierbörse, in: Wirtschaftsprüferkammer-Mitteilungen, Vol. 36, No. 3, pp. 188-194.

Francis, J.C. (1972): Investments: Analysis and Management, New York et al.

Francis, J./Hanna, J.D./Philbrick, D.R. (1997): Management communications with security analysts, in: Journal of Accounting and Economics, Vol. 24, No. 3, pp. 363-394.

Franke, G./Hax, H. (1999): Finanzwirtschaft des Unternehmens und Kapitalmarkt, 4th ed., Berlin et al.

Fülbier, R.U. (1998): Regulierung der Ad-hoc-Publizität – Ein Beitrag zur ökonomischen Analyse des Rechts, Wiesbaden.

Fürhoff, J./Wölk, A. (1997): Aktuelle Fragen zur Ad hoc-Publizität, in: Zeitschrift für Wirtschafts- und Bankrecht, Vol. 51, pp. 449-500.

Garbade, K.D./Silber, W.L. (1978): Technology, Communication and the Performance of Financial Markets: 1840-1975, in: Journal of Finance, Vol. 33, pp. 819-832.

Gentz, M. (1996): Investor Relations im Spannungsfeld zwischen den Erwartungen der Finanzanalysten und den Vorschriften zur Vermeidung von Insidertrading, in: Globale

Finanzmärkte: Konsequenzen für Finanzierung und Unternehmensrechnung, ed. by Schmalenbach-Gesellschaft Deutsche Gesellschaft für Betriebswirtschaft e.V., Stuttgart, pp. 107-112.

Glaum, M./Mandler, U. (1996): Rechnungslegung auf globalen Kapitalmärkten: HGB, IAS und US-GAAP, Wiesbaden.

Gniewosz, G. (1990): The Share Investment Decision Process and Information Use: An Exploratory Case Study, in: Accounting and Business Research, Vol. 20, pp. 223-230.

Günther, T./Otterbein, S. (1996): Die Gestaltung der Investor Relations am Beispiel führender deutscher Aktiengesellschaften, in: Zeitschrift für Betriebswirtschaft, Vol. 66, pp. 389-417.

Gyohten, T. (1993): Global Financial Markets - The Past, the Future, and Public Policy Questions, in: Regulating International Financial Markets - Issues and Policies, ed. by F. R. Edwards and H.T. Patrick, Boston et al., pp. 13-20.

Haller, A. (1989): Behavioral Accounting, in: Die Betriebswirtschaft, Vol. 49, pp. 383-385.

Hax, G. (1998): Informationsintermediation durch Finanzanalysten - Eine ökonomische Analyse, Frankfurt.

Honeygold, D. (1989): Internationale Finanzmärkte, translated by U. Bischoff, Landsberg and Camebridge.

Hopt, K.J. (1995a): Ökonomische Theorie und Insiderrecht, in: Die Aktiengesellschaft, Vol. 40, No. 8, pp. 353-362.

Hopt, K.J. (1995b): Wie sinnvoll sind rechtliche Regelungen über Insidergeschäfte? – Ökonomische und rechtliche Überlegungen zum europäischen und deutschen Insiderrecht, in: Insiderrecht und Ad-hoc-Publizität – Was bedeuten die neuen Regelungen für Unternehmenspublizität und Finanzanalyse, ed. by J. Baetge, Düsseldorf, pp. 1-21.

Hussey, R./Bence, D./Wilkie, C. (1992): A Comparison of the Views of Private Shareholders, Investment Analysts and Institutional Investors on the Wellcome plc Annual Report 1991.

Imdieke, L.F./Smith, R.E. (1991): Financial Accounting, 2nd ed., New York.

Iqbal, M.Z./Melcher, T.U./Elmallah, A.A. (1997): International Accounting - A Global Perspective, Cincinnati/Ohio.

Jahnke, R. (1996): Wirtschaftlichkeitsaspekte interkultureller Kommunikation – Interkulturelle Kommunikation in international tätigen Unternehmen unter besonderer Berücksichtigung von Führungskräften, Berlin.

Jandt, F.E. (1995): Intercultural Communication – An Introduction, Thousand Oaks et al.

Kondo, A./Malakkal, I. (1990): New Way in Data Feeds Sweeps Away Old Limits, in: Wall Street Computer Review, Vol. 4, No. 7, pp. S80-S88.

Krehl, H. (1985): Der Informationsbedarf der Bilanzanalyse – Ableitung und empirische Validierung eines Fragenkatalogs von Jahresabschlüssen, Kiel.

Krisement, V.M. (1997): An approach for measuring the degree of comparability of financial accounting information, in: The European Accounting Review, Vol. 6, pp. 465-485.

Krystek, U./Müller, M. (1993): Investor Relations – Eine neue Disziplin nicht nur für das Finanzmanagement, in: Der Betrieb, Vol. 46, pp. 1785-1789.

Kugler, R.A. (1996): Wie Profis schnell an Kurse kommen, in: Börse Online, No. 27, pp. 92-93.

Laswad, F./Mak, Y.T. (1994): An International Comparison of Uncertanty Expressions in Accounting Standards, in: The International Journal of Accounting, Vol. 29, pp. 1-19.

Lee, T.A./Tweedie, D.P. (1981): The Institutional Investor and Financial Information, London.

Lymer, A. (1999): The Internet and the future of corporate reporting in Europe, in: The European Accounting Review, Vol. 8, No. 2, pp. 289-301.

Miles, S./Nobes, C. (1998): The Use of Foreign Accounting Data in UK Financial Institutions, in: Journal of Business Finance and Accounting, Vol. 25, pp. 309-328.

Moizer, P./Arnold, J. (1984): Share Appraisal by Investment Analysts: Portfolio vs. Non-Portfolio Managers, in: Accounting and Business Research , Vol. 14, pp. 341-348.

Nitschke, U.K. (1996): Mediatisierte interne Kommunikation in internationalen Unternehmungen – Möglichkeiten und Auswirkungen von Informations- und Kommunikationssystemen für globale Netzwerkorganisationen, Bamberg.

Ordelheide, D. (1998): Wettbewerb der Rechnungslegungssysteme IAS, US-GAAP und HGB - Plädoyer für eine Reform des deutschen Bilanzrechts, in: Controlling und Rechnungswesen im internationalen Wettbewerb, ed. by C. Börsig and A.G. Coenenberg, Stuttgart, pp. 15-53.

Ordelheide, D. (1999a): Germany, in: Accounting Regulation in Europe, ed. by St. McLeay, London, pp. 99-146.

Ordelheide, D. (1999b): Rechnungslegung im digitalen Zeitalter, in: Rechnungswesen und Kapitalmarkt, ed. by G. Gebhardt and B. Pellens, ZfbF-Sonderheft 41, Düsseldorf, pp. 229-253.

Ordelheide, D. (1999c): Rechnungslegung im Zeichen globaler Finanzmärkte, in: Globale Finanzmärkte und Europäische Währungsunion, ed. by J.P. Krahnen and B. Rudolph, Frankfurt, pp. 81-99.

Pankoff, L.D./Virgil, R.L. (1970): Some Preliminary Findings from a Laboratory Experiment on the Usefulness of Financial Accounting Information to Security Analysts, in: Journal of Accounting Research, Vol. 8, Supplement, pp. 1-48.

Pike, R./Meerjanssen, J./Chadwick, L. (1993): The Appraisal of Ordinary Shares by Investment Analysts in the UK and Germany, in: Accounting and Business Research, Vol. 23, pp. 489-499.

Saudagaran, S.M./Biddle, G.C. (1994): Financial Disclosure Levels and Foreign Stock Exchange Listing Decisions, in: Inernational Capital Markets in a World of Accounting Differences, ed. by F.D.S. Choi and R.M. Levich, New York, pp. 159-201.

Schlienkamp, C. (1998): Shareholder Value – Anforderungen aus Analystensicht, in: Shareholder Value Reporting: Veränderte Anforderungen an die Berichterstattung börsennotierter Unternehmen, ed. by M. Müller and F.-J. Leven, Wien, pp. 213-224.

Strieder, T./Ammedick, O. (1999): Die Informationsverpflichtungen der Teilnehmer am SMAX, in: Finanz Betrieb, Vol. 1, No. 7, pp. 143-149.

Stubenrath, M./Löbig, M. (2000): Zur Notwendigkeit von Rechnungslegungsstandards für die Internet-Berichterstattung, SFB-403 working paper, Frankfurt.

Vergoossen, R.G.A. (1993): The Use and Perceived Importance of Annual Reports by Investment Analysts in the Netherlands, in: The European Accounting Review, Vol. 2, pp. 219-244.

Verrecchia, R.E. (1999): Disclosure and the cost of capital: A discussion, in: Journal of Accounting and Economics, Vol. 26, pp. 271-283.

Westarp, F.v./Ordelheide, D./ Stubenrath, M./ Buxmann, P./ König, W. (1999): Internet-Based Corporate Reporting – Filling the Standardization Gap, in: Proceedings of the 32nd Hawaii International Conference on System Sciences, Maui/Hawaii, January 1999, pp. 1-10.

Wittich, G. (1997): Erfahrungen mit der Ad hoc-Publizität in Deutschland, in: Die Aktiengesellschaft, Vol. 42, pp. 1-5.

Yap, C. (1997): Users' Perceptions of the Need for Cash Flow Statements – Australian Evidence, in: The European Accounting Review, Vol. 6, pp. 653-672.

Ziegler, S.B. (1992): Integration der europäischen Kapitalmärkte – Konsequenzen für die schweizerische Geldpolitik, Bamberg.

Contracts and eContracting: The Case of Forwarding Agents and Carriers

Dorit Bölsche

Schüllermann Consulting,
Hauptstraße 38a, 63303 Dreieich, Germany
boelsche@wiwi.uni-frankfurt.de

Christian Becker

Johann Wolfgang Goethe-University
Department of Computer Science
PO Box 11 19 32
D 60054 Frankfurt am Main
becker@informatik.uni-frankfurt.de

Summary:
In this investigation we analyze networks from an economic point of view. Incentive problems arise in networks which are characterized by an asymmetry of information between opportunistic actors with different objectives. In a network which consists of forwarding agents and carriers we focus on the contractual principal-agent relationships. Thinking about new information technologies one central question arises: Can new information technologies be used to reduce the asymmetry of information and to produce a better payoff for the economic actors in the network? One important result is that contracts can generally be improved if new information technologies, e. g. a tracking and tracing system or an electronic coordination system, are used to obtain additional valuable information.

Keywords:
Contracts, electronic coordination, incomplete information, moral hazard, new information technologies, principal-agent, valuable information

Introduction

From the range of themes concerning networks we analyze incentive problems and their contractual decrease. The networks considered consist of economic actors (principals and agents) and their contractual relationships. It has long been recognized that incentive problems arise in networks which are characterized by an asymmetry of information between opportunistic actors with different objectives. In these networks individual actions cannot be observed and hence contracted upon. Thinking about new information technologies, e. g. making ebusiness feasible, one central question arises: can new information technologies be used to reduce the asymmetry of information and to produce a better payoff for the economic actors in the network? This question leads to eContracting. With the term eContracting we refer to contractual coordination among economic actors which is basically and essentially influenced by new information technologies [Becker/Bölsche 2000]. In the following we analyze two different dimensions of eContracting. On the one hand, we use valuable information from new information technologies which construct sharing rules as one part of a contract. On the other hand, we use a new information technology as an intermediary between principals and agents initiating, concluding and modifying a contract.

In support of the idea of contracts and eContracting, we refer to a case from the haulage business. Physical streams in a logistic chain from a supplier to a producer of clothes are described in section 2 to explain logistic quality requirements which have to be fulfilled by the logistic service providers in the network. After describing what is required of industrial firms who charge logistic service providers, the case is reduced in section 3 to the core reflecting the initial problem, consisting of two economic actors: a forwarding agent who is charged by the supplier; and a carrier who transports the clothing materials on behalf of the forwarding agent to the producer. Even in this simple network incentive problems arise. The forwarding agent can not observe every action of an opportunistic carrier whose reduction of costs may result in a reduced payoff for the forwarding agent. We draw up a principal-agent model to analyze these incentive (or principal-agent) problems and to give recommendations for constructing a contract. This model is applied to the construction of contracts without eContracting in section 4 as well as to the construction of agreements with eContracting in section 5 and 6. With that, contractual solutions and their effects on both the profit remaining to the forwarding agent and the carriers' remuneration with and without eContracting can be compared. In section 5 we refer to one dimension of eContracting: using valuable information from new information technologies to construct sharing rules as one part of a contract. Afterwards we extend the idea of eContracting in section 6 by thinking about how to convert the analyzed principal-agent models into an electronic coordination system (ECS). Whereas up to section 5 we considered a network consisting of two actors and their contractual relationships, we enlarge the network in section 6. An intermediary who is independent of forwarding agents and carriers and provides the ECS which can be used initiating, concluding and modifying a contract is introduced. The ECS can be occupied by several economic actors from the haulage business. Thus the network is composed of several forwarding agents, several carriers, the ECS provider as well as the contractual and informational relationships among these actors.The article closes with concluding remarks and a surveyof the interesting questions concerning eContracting in networks left unanswered in this investigation.

The Case: Contracts and Physical Streams in the Haulage Business

To describe the content of eContracting, let us look at a simple case. First, four economic actors are considered. One actor who is located in Frankfurt supplies materials for the clothing industry. This supplier assigns a forwarding agent to deal with the delivery of materials to a business customer who produces clothes in London. The forwarding agent himself assigns a carrier to deliver the shipment to the producer in London. In this case we assume that the carrier possesses a tracking and tracing system. In addition, the carrier is able to scan the shipment at several locations, especially at the dispatch department of the supplier in Frankfurt and at the producer's incoming goods department in London. Up to now we have emphasized the physical flow of goods in the simple supply chain. In the following we will focus on the contractual relationships between the different firms pictured in figure 1.

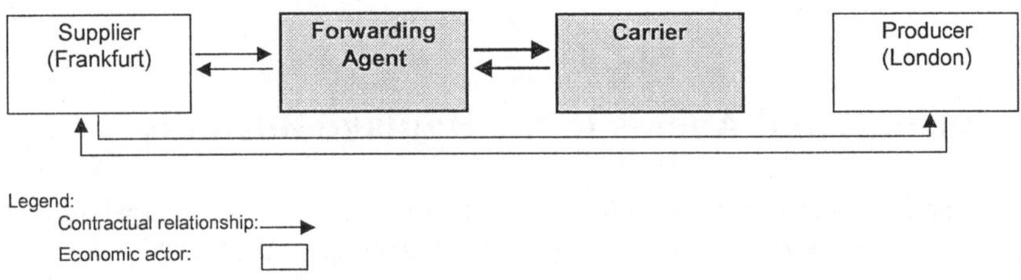

Figure 1: Contractual relationships between actors

Note that the forwarding agent, the carrier, and their contractual relationships are described in figure 1. That is to say that these elements are the focus of the investigation. The supplier and producer are also considered in our case because their (contractual) requirements influence the subject terms of the contract in the haulage business.

Essential subject terms in freight contracts are the requirements of suppliers and producers concerning logistical aspects. The specific logistical requirements have to be fulfilled by the logistic service providers from the haulage business. We define the logistical quality requirements as the characteristics including their permitted parameter values which have to be realized by the logistic service providers [Houtman 2000, 7]. Such characteristics include in particular physical characteristics (e. g. the quantity of goods, the observance of packaging instructions) and time factors (e. g. delivery time, delivery date reliability). In our case we take time factors into particular consideration. Later on we will see that information about how the parameter values of the time factors are realized can be obtained from the tracking and tracing system.

Nowadays carriers are often paid by the forwarding agent based on the delivered tonnage and the distance between the sender and recipient of the shipment (e. g. based on ton-kilometers or ton-miles). Contracts between a forwarding agent and a carrier typically include a monetary contractual penalty, which has to be paid by the carrier in the case of non-compliance with contracted logistical quality requirements. It is obvious that the contractual penalty is payable only if the forwarding agent observes the non-compliance. This presumes that the forwarding agent is able to monitor the carrier's decisions and actions in the logistic chain.

In the following section we will think about incentives derived from the haulage business. In a situation of imperfect information about the carriers actions, the following questions arise: when can the imperfect information about actions be used to improve on a contract which is initially based on the payoff alone? Can we acquire additional information using new information technologies (e. g. the tracking and tracing system)? How can such additional information best be used? By answering these questions we hope to improve the financial output for both the forwarding agent and the carrier.

Principals and Agents in the Haulage Business

The mathematical model we refer to in the next section is a principal-agent (or agency) model. With that we first explain principal-agent problems in the principal-agent relationship between the logistic service providers in our case. "We will say that an agency relationship has arisen between two or more parties, when one, designated as the agent, acts for, on behalf of, or as a representative for the other, designated the principal, in a particular domain of decision problems" [Ross 1973, 134]. In figure 1 we showed the contractual relationship between the forwarding agent and the carrier. In this relationship the carrier is the agent who conveys the clothing materials on behalf of the principal (the forwarding agent). This relationship is figured below.

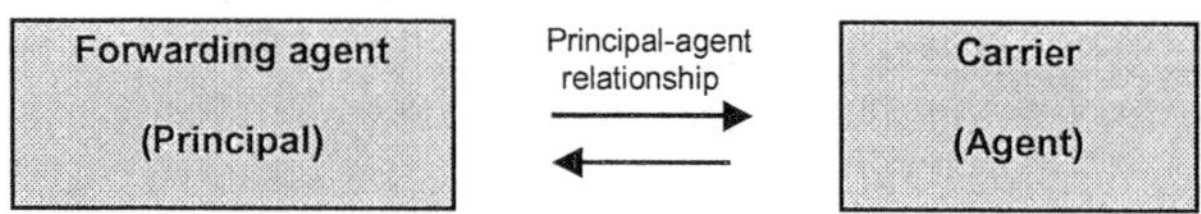

Figure 2: The principal-agent relationship between the forwarding agent and the carrier

Note that one and the same actor can be the agent in one relationship and the principal in another. The designated principal in figure 2 is not called the forwarding *agent* for nothing: this logistic service provider is the agent in the agency relationship with the clothing supplier (principal), and this supplier acts on behalf of the clothing producer in a further relationship. In a logistic chain, logistic quality requirements are given through the chain from principals to agents (in this simple case from the producer to the supplier, from the supplier to the forwarding agent, and from the forwarding agent to the carrier).

After representing principal-agent relationships we can examine the problems in these relationships. In the following we are especially concerned with one class of principal-agent problems – moral hazards. The source of moral hazard "is an asymmetry of information among individuals that results because individual actions cannot be observed and hence contracted upon" [Holmström 1979, 74]. As explained above, a natural remedy to this problem is to invest resources in monitoring of actions and use this information in the contract. In simple situations complete monitoring may be possible. In such a situation an initial solution can be achieved by employing a forcing contract that penalizes dysfunctional behavior. But in our case full monitoring of the carrier's actions by the principal would be prohibitively costly. To give an idea of dysfunctional behavior and its consequences, we give an example from our case in connection with the mathematical model. In this example we compare possible solutions with and without eContracting.

The Basic Model Without eContracting

Introducing the basic principal-agent model [Holmström 1979] in a situation of moral hazard, we extend our case from the haulage business. Imagine that the producer and the supplier have agreed upon a 72-hour-service (as one value parameter of logistic quality requirements). That means that the clothing materials have to be delivered at the producer's incoming goods department in London not later than 72 hours after the materials have been ordered. The forwarding agent is interested in punctuality because he has arranged a payoff depending on compliance with the time factor with the supplier. To secure punctuality the forwarding agent and the carrier have laid down physical requirements in a contract: based on the time remaining when the carrier picks up the clothing materials in Frankfurt, the two actors from the haulage business have agreed upon permitted routes, handling requirements, and means of transport for each logistic process in the supply chain. These physical requirements give some but not full security in terms of the time factor (72-hour-service): e. g. the carrier is not responsible for congestion caused by a strike or an accident. In connection with this extended case we will analyze the employment of a moral hazard principal-agent model with and without eContracting. In this case we would (not) use the term eContracting if the information which can be acquired from the carrier's tracking and tracing system were (not) included in the contract.

- In the principal-agent relationship, the agent (the carrier) takes an action $a \in A$, where A is the set of all possible actions. In the contract the principal and the agent agree on requirements in the logistic chain which determine the set of A. The carrier has some latitude in his decisions and actions concerning the carrying-out of the transport from Frankfurt to London.

- The financial outcome or payoff $x \in [x-, x+]$ is determined by the agents action as well as by a random state of nature θ, such that $x = x(a, \theta)$. In the case from the haulage business, the supplier and the forwarding agent agreed on a payoff $x \in [x-, x+]$ determined by punctuality of delivery. The forwarding agent receives an amount of $x+$ ($) in the case of punctuality but not less than $x-$ ($), e. g. 0 $. This payoff is determined by the carriers decisions and actions concerning the transport as well as by the random state of nature θ (congestion, an accident or a strike). The problem is to determine how this payoff should be shared optimally between the principal and the agent.

- The share of x that goes to the carrier is denoted by $s(x)$, *with* $s(x) < x$ *and* $s(x) \geq 0$. Thus, $x - s(x)$ is the share that goes to the principal.

- a is productive input with direct disutility for the agent and this creates an inherent difference in objectives between the principal and the agent. In our case it is convenient to think of a as costs arising from the developed logistic chain. The connection of an asymmetry of information (the forwarding agent can not observe the carrier's actions), the carrier's opportunism and the inherent difference in the objectives of the principal and the agent resulting in the problem of moral hazard can be explained as follows: if the principal is not able to observe the carrier's actions, the carrier could violate the agreed physical requirements, e. g. lowering his logistic costs (and maximizing his financial utility). The principal's utility function is $G(x)$, defined by the payoff alone, and the agent's utility function is $H(x,a)$, defined by the payoff with respect to his action. $H(x,a)=U(s(x))-V(a)$ denotes that the agent's utility function is the difference between the payment from the principal ($U(s(x))$) and his own costs for the related action ($V(a)$). Unpunctuality which lowers the principal's monetary utility (his profit) would be explained by an opportunistic carrier by congestion. Since the problem of moral hazard can be avoided when the agent is risk-neutral, we shall assume $U'' < 0$. The principal may or may not be risk-neutral ($G'' \leq 0$). Summing up we assume that $H(x,a) = U(s(x)) - V(a)$, with

$$V' > 0, \; V'' > 0,$$
$$U' > 0, \; U'' < 0,$$
$$G' > 0, \; G'' \leq 0,$$
$$x_a \geq 0.$$

- We first assume (without eContracting) that the principal observes only the outcome he receives from the supplier (and not the actions taken by the agent). Thus, the sharing rule has to be a function of x alone. x is used as a signal for the action which is not directly observed.

- Furthermore it is assumed that both parties agree on the probability distribution of θ. E. g. the carrier and the forwarding agent possess much the same information about the probability distribution of congestion between Frankfurt and London. The agent chooses a, e. g. the route, before θ is known.

In this case pareto-optimal sharing rules $s(x)$ are generated by the model:

(1) $\max_{s(x)} \{G(x - s(x))\}$ (The principal's objective)

subject to

(2) $H(s(x), a) \geq \overline{H}$ (Participation constraint)

(3) $a \in arg \max_{\hat{a} \in A} \{H(s(x), \hat{a}\}$ (Incentive constraint)

Constraint (1) describes the principal's objective of maximizing his (financial) utility. Constraint (2), the participation constraint, guarantees the agent a minimum expected utility $\overline{H}$, *with* $0 \leq \overline{H} \leq H(x,a)$. $\overline{H}$ can be attained for example via the negotiation process. Constraint (3), the incentive constraint, reflects the restriction that the principal is not able to observe $\hat{a}$, the action actually taken by the agent. If the principal could also observe $\hat{a}$ (symmetric information), a forcing contract could be used to guarantee that the agent selects a proper action even when $s(x)$ is chosen to solve (1) and (2), ignoring (3). In the described case of symmetric information, the result is the best possible solution, entailing optimal risk sharing and profit sharing. It differs in general from the solution of (1) subject to (2) and (3), which is called the second-best solution.

Given a distribution of θ, $F(x,a)$ is the distribution induced on x via the relationship $x = x(a,\theta)$. We assume that F has a density function $f(x,a)$ with f_a and f_{aa} well defined for all (x,a). With these assumptions the incentive constraint can be replaced by the first-order constraint [Jewitt 1988, 1177-1190]. The sharing rules $s(x)$ are now generated by the following model [Holmström 1979, 75-77]:

(4) $\max_{s(x)} \int_{x-}^{x+} G(x - s(x)) f(x,a) dx$ (The principal's objective)

subject to

(5) $\int_{x-}^{x+} [U(s(x)) - V(a)] f(x,a) dx \geq \overline{H}$ (Participation constraint)

$$\int_{x-}^{x+} U(s(x)) f_a(x,a)dx = V'(a) \qquad (6) \quad \text{(Incentive constraint)}$$

Let λ be the multiplier for the participation constraint and μ the multiplier for the incentive constraint in the Lagrangian optimization (7). Pointwise optimization of the Lagrangian yields the following characterization of an optimal sharing rule:

$$\frac{G'(x-s(x))}{U'(s(x))} = \lambda + \mu \frac{f_a(x,a)}{f(x,a)} \qquad (7)$$

Holmström shows and proves in his article [Holmström 1979] that with given assumptions (especially $V' > 0$ *and* $F_a \leq 0$ with strict inequality for some x-values):

- μ>0. That means, the principal would like to see the agent increase his effort given the second-best sharing rule.
- The second-best solution is strictly inferior to the best possible solution.

Commenting on (7) $\frac{f_a(x,a)}{f(x,a)}$ is interpreted as a benefit-cost ratio for deviation from optimal profit sharing. (7) states that such deviations should be made in proportion to this ratio. In other words $\frac{f_a(x,a)}{f(x,a)}$ measures how strongly one is inclined to infer from x that the agent did not take the assumed action, and (7) expresses that penalties or bonuses should be paid in proportion to this measure.

eContracting in the Basic Model

With these first results one central question arises: can we identify a contract approaching the best possible solution? This leads us to the deployment of eContracting. As described in the introduction, eContracting is used to refer to the contractual coordination among economic actors, which is influenced basically and essentially by new information technologies. In the basic principal-agent model introduced above, x is used as a signal (as information) for the action a which is not directly observed by the forwarding agent. In a first application of eContracting we analyze if further information about the action can be gained by using new information technologies (e. g. the carrier's tracking and tracing system). In particular we will analyze whether this further information can be considered in the contract which is concluded before the carrier delivers the shipping. In so doing, it is not only the payoff x that is considered as a signal for the carrier's actions, but also the information y, which is the information from the tracking and tracing system. This signal is observed by both parties and hence can be used in constructing the sharing rule. Let $F(x,y,a)$ be the joint distribution of x and y given a. The following extension of (7) obtains for an optimal sharing rule $s(x,y)$ [Holmström 1979, 82]:

$$\text{(8)} \qquad \frac{G'(x-s(x,y))}{U'(s(x,y))} = \lambda + \mu \frac{f_a(x,y,a)}{f(x,y,a)}$$

A new, important feature is that $\frac{f_a(x,y,a)}{f(x,y,a)}$ may change with y. Thus, for the same value of x, but under different contingencies signaled by y, the agent should receive different remuneration $s(x,y)$. Equation (8) would predict that contracts elaborate and contain a variety of provisions for unexpected events. Considering y the contract becomes more detailed. Furthermore, the contract is efficient because the signal y is "valuable" in our example. In general a signal y is said to be valuable (or good news) if the principal and the agent can be made better of with a contract of the form $s(x,y)$ than they are with a contract of the Form $s(x)$ [Milgrom 1981]. Consequently, we can give a precise answer to the preliminary question put in this chapter: with additional information from a valuable signal (from new information technologies) we draw nearer to the best possible solution.

Disregarding the mathematical model, some thoughts about the conversion of eContracting into practice are necessary. Currently, tracking and tracing systems are often used by the sender (supplier) or recipient (producer) of a belated shipment to obtain information about the delay. Information from a tracking and tracing system often has no implication for the remuneration of a forwarding agent or carrier, particularly if the shipment is on time. In our case from the haulage business it is now imaginable that the forwarding agent and the carrier have agreed on a contract including the information from the tracking and tracing system. The shipment is scanned at each transloading location , especially at the dispatch department of the supplier in Frankfurt and at the producer's incoming goods department in London. In addition, the shipment is scanned at agreed locations, so that the forwarding agent receives further information about the carrier's actions and thus about their compliance with logistic quality requirements. Both parties have now additional information, generated by the new information technology, about the agent's decisions and activities which they can include in the sharing rule. This information concerns the route in the first place. In addition, information about handling and transloading time can be obtained. The number and location of scanning points result from the value of information which is received by a scanning process. On this occasion, the costs resulting from the scanning process have to be considered as well. In terms of both value and costs, the information from each scanning location should be valuable: information from scanning a shipment at a location is said to be valuable if the forwarding agent and the carrier can be made better off with a contract including the information from the scanning process into the sharing rule. With the information from the tracking and tracing system the problem of moral hazard is reduced if the information is valuable: the carriers opportunities of acting in an opportunistic way are reduced because he could not explain a route diverging from the contractual agreement if the principal monitors the chosen route. The monitoring takes place automatically if the information from the tracking and tracing system is transferred into the calculation of the carrier's remuneration. Departing from the set of possible routes results in a lower share of the payoff for the carrier. With that, the carrier has an incentive to comply with contractual agreements which can now be monitored by the principal. In the case of valuable information from the tracking and tracing system, the principal's payoff will rise because of an increase in punctuality. The difference between the payoff with and without the information from the tracking and tracing system does not necessarily go totally to the principal. In comparison to the previously situation without eContracting, the carrier receives at least the same utility determined by his remuneration and his disutility (costs) from transporting the clothing materials from Frankfurt to London. It is also imaginable that the carrier becomes better of with eContracting because the additional amount of remuneration exceeds his additional costs.

When first considering the idea of eContracting one might think that the carrier would defend himself against this form of monitoring by the principal, especially against the recommended construction of a sharing rule. But with the given representations it is obvious that the introduction of eContracting can be initiated by both the forwarding agent and the carrier: we are approaching the best possible solution, so that both of them receive at least the same utility as without eContracting and one of them can be made better off.

We have now described one dimension of eContracting: valuable information from new information technologies is used in constructing sharing rules as one part of a contract. We will devote the following section to a further dimension of eContracting: using new information technology as an intermediary between principals and agents in initiating, concluding and modifying a contract (electronic contracting). In this connection we introduce an independent actor who develops and uses a new form of information technology which we call an electronic coordination system (ECS).

Converting the Model into an Electronic Coordination System (ECS)

Extending the Basic Model

It was important to realize in a mathematical principal-agent model that there is a difference in the principal's payoff and the agent's remuneration with and without eContracting. Furthermore, we have an important result in mind: with valuable information from the tracking and tracing system we draw nearer to the best possible solution, so that both actors from the haulage business receive at least the same utility as without eContracting and one of them can be made better off. Devoting to the electronic coordination system we keep up the example from the haulage business. Furthermore, we do not put the principal-agent model aside. We pursue the idea of converting the model or extended models into the electronic coordination system (ECS). In many respects the model we have analyzed is very primitive. One unrealistic feature is the assumption that the agent chooses his action on the basis of the same information as the principal, that is before anything about θ is revealed. Commonly this will not be the case. At least after the sharing rule is fixed, the agent learns something new about the difficulty of the environment in which his task, transporting clothes from Frankfurt to London, is to be performed. Holmström considers other realistic features in an extended model [Holmström 1979, 88-89]. In this section we will not describe extended mathematical principal-agent models in detail. The results from section 4 and 5 give us an idea that principals and agents from the haulage business may achieve better results using information from new information technologies constructing a sharing rule. In the following we give some ideas about suggested extensions of the basic model. Such extensions are necessary to bring the principal-agent models closer to what exists in practice:

- In the principal-agent model described above it is assumed that the carrier acts opportunistically. Opportunistic behavior on the part of the forwarding agent is not considered. In an extended case it is possible that a forwarding agent possesses information that is not available to the carrier. A problem of *double moral hazard* may emerge [Gupta/Romano 1998].

- In many cases a forwarding agent charges not only one agent with delivering shipments from a supplier to a producer, but rather several carriers. Shipments from Frankfurt to London can also be transported in a logistic chain including air traffic or water transport. The forwarding agent has to decide on the transport mode(s) in the logistic chain and beyond that on the agent(s) he charges with transport services. The forwarding agent has to decide about the *number of agents* in the logistic chain and beyond that about the number of tasks one agent is to execute in the logistic chain [Holmström/Milgrom 1991]. If many logistic service providers work together in a logistic chain, the payoff derives from the joint contributions of all these agents. With that, a situation of *team production* with the danger of free riding occurs. One team compensation scheme is peer pressure, which gives the logistic service providers incentives to monitor one another. If the cost of such monitoring is sufficiently low, this can obviate the free-rider problem [Prendergast 1999, 39-44].

- Agents can "game" the compensation system when they have multiple instruments at their control. This incentive problem has become known as *multi-tasking*, where compensation for any subset of tasks will result in a reallocation of activities toward those that are directly compensated and away from uncompensated activities [Holmström/Milgrom 1991; Prendergast 1999, 22-29]. Since it is difficult to specify all aspects of logistic quality requirements in an explicit contract, a common way of providing incentives is to use *subjective performance evaluation*, perhaps in addition to objective assessments [Gibbons 1998, 115-132]. Imagine that the supplier and the producer are questioned concerning the fulfillment of logistic or other requirements. This subjective impression can be integrated into the calculation of the agent's remuneration in the logistic chain.

- Often not only can the forwarding agent choose between several carriers but also carriers are able to decide in favour of a particular principal out of a set of several forwarding agents. If this is the case this must be considered when determining the agent's minimum expected utility $\overline{H}$.
- Finally, we address *repeated relationships* (in long-term contracts or repeated short-term contracts). They may possibly allow for honest behavior where opportunistic behavior occurs in a static (or single) relationship. Such dynamic contracting issues have to be considered. Forwarding agents and other logistic service providers often work together for long periods of time. In such relationships, intertemporal links in contracts are suggested, where the contract offered in one period depends on the last period's contracts and their carrying out [Prendergast 1999, 45-55].

In developing the electronic coordination system, one should have an idea of these extended principal-agent models. It is important to perceive that these models do not exclude each other. They should rather be considered as complementary.

Developing the Electronic Coordination System (ECS)

After bringing the basic principal-agent model nearer to what happens in practice we now turn to the second dimension of eContracting, the electronic coordination system. With the ECS we pursue the idea that this new information technology can be used as an intermediary between principals and agents in initiating, concluding and modifying a contract. The core of the electronic coordination system is transferable principal-agent models.

Actors in the ECS-Network

Whereas we referred in the preceding sections to a network consisting of two economic actors (the forwarding agent and the carrier) and their relationship, we now enlarge the network as illustrated in figure 3 and as explained in detail below.

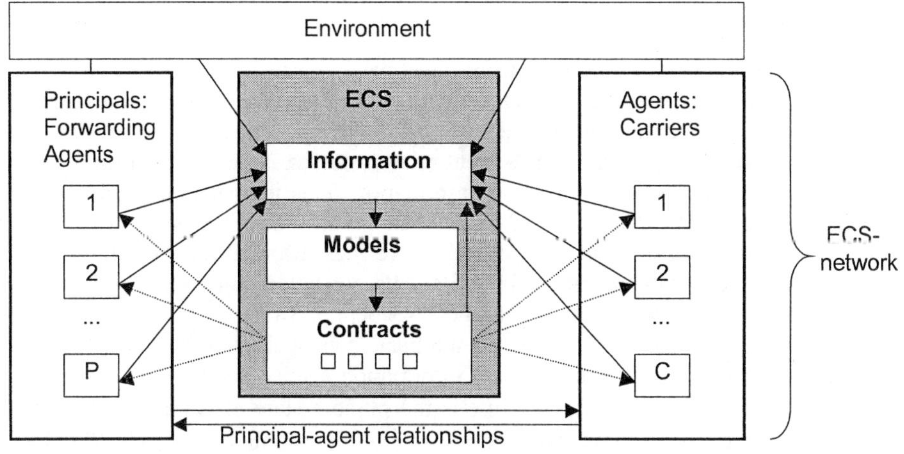

Figure 3: The ECS-network

As we have indicated already in our suggested expansion of the basic principal-agent model, we now consider several principals and agents. We assume that *P* forwarding agents (principals) and *C* carriers (agents) are interested in participating in the ECS. To Characterize a forwarding agent, we introduce the index *p=1,...,P*, and the index *c=1,...,C* is introduced to characterize a carrier. Furthermore, it is assumed that the ECS is developed and provided by an independent actor. This actor does not pursue monetary objectives and does not act in an opportunistic way. With these assumptions the investigation is easier to survey: otherwise additional principal-agent relationships with resulting problems would occur between the forwarding agents and the ECS provider as well as between the carriers and the ECS provider. The assumptions concerning the behavior of the ECS provider are not unrealistic if one thinks of the provider as researchers or an association analyzing the influence of new information technologies on economic principal-agent relationships (eContracting). Thus the actors in the ECS-network are *P* forwarding agents, *C* carriers and the independent ECS provider. Note that the environment is also depicted in figure 3. Since it has relationships to the environment, the ECS-network can be characterized as an open and dynamic system. With the passage of time principals and agents as actors (elements) in the ECS-network can leave the network and other economic actors can enter the network [Bertalanffy 1976, 548].

Characterizing the ECS and Relationships in the ECS-Network

The core of the ECS-network is the ECS which is a subsystem of the ECS-network. The ECS itself consists of elements and relationships between these elements. In figure 3 three ECS-elements are illustrated, designated as information, models and contracts. In characterizing the ECS and the relationships in the ECS-network we refer to these elements:

- ECS-element *information*: from a technical point of view, the element *information* is a database. In the following we characterize contents and sources of the information with respect to informational relationships in the ECS-network. Before a principal-agent relationship can emerge, the principals and agents need several pieces of information. This information concerns information about principals and agents belonging to the ECS-network (e. g. their behavior, tasks, objectives, assets as well) as information about the environment (e. g. about principals and agents not belonging to the ECS-network, about the legal environment, about senders and recipients with their quality requirements). With respect to the basic principal-agent model described in section 4, one essential item of information needed about the environment in order to identify a sharing rule is the random state of nature θ. This is because the payoff is determined not only by the action a but also by θ. The database is essential for support by the ECS in initiating, modifying and concluding a contract between principals and agents. Thus the informational relationships in figure 3 between the actors of the ECS-network and the ECS are explained as well as informational relationships between the environment and the ECS. The information about the economic actors belonging to the ECS (forwarding agents and carriers) has to be supplied mainly by these actors. Because forwarding agents and carriers are assumed to act opportunistically they may transfer false information to the ECS. In this investigation we do not extend this problem of adverse selection [Akerlof 1970; Baron/Myerson 1982]. But it has to be said that the ECS provider has either to give the economic actors of the ECS incentives to transmit true information or to select their own information about these economic actors. Beyond that the ECS provider has to select information about the environment.

- ECS-element *models* (or ECS-models): as has been said before, the models are the core of the ECS. ECS-models are those principal-agent models explained in sections 4, 5 and 6.1 which can be transferred into the ECS. The models have already been described and analyzed in detail, so that we can turn to the relationships with the other ECS-elements. Employing the ECS-models in practice presupposes that information has been supplied by the ECS-element *information.* Often information from different sources has to be compressed. Let's refer to θ again: if a forwarding agent and a carrier do not agree on the distribution of θ, the ECS-provider can conflate the information from both, the principal and the agent. The results of calculations in the ECS-models using information from the ECS database are recommended contracts.

- ECS-element *contracts*: the recommended contracts are the result of calculations in the ECS-models. Correspondingly, each contract is determined by the quality and quantity of information available (from the database) and by the applied model(s). In our first case from the haulage business, information is required to work out the principal's objective, the participation constraint and the incentive constraint in order to give recommendations for the sharing rule *s(x)*. In this case *s(x)* can be interpreted as the contract recommended to one principal and one agent (see outgoing arrows in figure 3). Imagine that the ECS provider has additional information about the tracking and tracing system in his database. In this case of eContracting, the contract or sharing rule *s(x,y)* gives a better prediction for both the forwarding agent and the carrier. This short reflection on the investigation in section 4 and 5 shows us that different models can be used for developing alternative contracts. In this example, the decision seems to be very easy: if the bonuses increase for both parties by choosing the contract *s(x,y)* they would both decide for this alternative. But we can also consider the more complex contracts indicated in section 6.1. The economic actors will then possibly have to decide between long, middle or short term contracts, implicit or explicit contracts, one or several tasks in and parties to a contract, objective or subjective performance measurements. The ECS is fed with data (available in the ECS-element information)by forwarding agents and carriers which determines the parameters and variables. With this information one (or several) model(s) from the available ECS-model(s) can be chosen. It depends on the inquiries addressed from principals and agents to the ECS which models are applied to constitute a contract, and thus which contracts are generated by the ECS. The ECS-element *contracts* can be characterized as an aggregation of single contracts. Because several forwarding agents and several carriers participate in the ECS, the ECS has more information available to it when initiating a contract than one single principal or one single agent. We will refer to these informational advantages in the next section.

With these short comments on the ECS-elements the initiation of contractual principal-agent relationships by the ECS is explained. An extended ECS can also be used as an intermediary for closing contracts between principals and agents. We do not go deeply into this theme because we regard the legal environment as fixed where. Digital contracts are concerned. In figure 3 existing and emerging principal-agent relationships among the economic actors of the ECS-network are indicated but not worked out in detail. From the technological point of view, an extension from an ECS initiating contracts to one supporting the conclusion of contracts is very easy. It is more difficult to convince economic actors of their advantages and of the unequivocal administration of the law and thus of using the ECS as an intermediary in concluding contracts.[6]

---

6 One possibility to deal with this problem is to start the development of an ECS by empirical data gathering, e. g. about possible actors as elements of an ECS-network and about the environment. This brings ECS-models near to practice. Over that contracts can be created by simulation (using the empirical databasis and the ECS-models) and the ECS can be evaluated and improved [Becker/Bölsche 2000]. Hopefully, resulting contracts from simulation with effects on the actors benefits can convince actors from the haulage business to participate in the ECS-network.

Note that there is feedback from the ECS-element *contracts* to the ECS-element *information.* This arrow in figure 3 characterizes the fact that the ECS can be improved by evaluation: recommended and concluded contracts can be compared with the realization of these contracts. Correspondingly, expected benefits can be compared with realized benefits. As a result the database will be extended (e. g. an extended database may contain detailed information about the actors' real behavior and thus about their reputation), dynamic ECS-models will be developed and contracts can be modified [Becker/Bölsche 2000].

Applications of the ECS

When reading through the preceding section some questions arise: why should economic actors participate in the ECS-network? Do economic actors derive (financial) advantages or benefits from participation in the ECS-network? The answers to these questions are comparable with some explanations in section 5. In section 5 we have described the fact that the first dimension of eContracting can be initiated by both the principal and the agent: adopting eContracting we draw nearer to the best possible solution, so that both of them receive at least the same benefit as they would without eContracting and one of them can be made better off. This effect has been explained with respect to the value of information. This explanation is transferable to the second dimension of eContracting. But we have to distinguish between the information available in contractual principal-agent relationships initiated in the environment of the ECS-network and those initiated by using the ECS. In general, a signal or information is said to be valuable if all economic actors obtain at least the same benefit and at least one of them can be made better off when this information is available when designing contractual relationships. It is now important to recognize that the initiation of one and the same principal-agent relationship is based on different valuable information within the ECS-network rather than in its environment. For example, information about the environment, e. g. the random state of nature θ, is more detailed and often more valuable within a network of several forwarding agents and carriers. Moreover, the reputation of each actor becomes more important in a network with direct competitors. As a result one can imagine that opportunistic behavior decreases in the ECS-network and the contractual solutions in the ECS may draw nearer to the best possible. With the restrictive assumption that the database of the ECS embraces at least all the valuable information that principals and agents would possess outside the ECS, we would obtain the following result: with valuable information available in the ECS-element *information* which can not be used by principals and agents outside the ECS-network, principals and agents draw nearer to the best possible solutions when participating in the ECS. But a more detailed investigation about the value of information outside and within the ECS is needed. We have to consider the costs of generating information within and outside the ECS as well as those information available outside the ECS-network but not in the ECS-database (e. g. the facial expressions of the other party when initiating a contract face-to-face). Correspondingly, we do not suggest that all forwarding agents and all carriers should participate in an electronic coordination system like the ECS described in this investigation. We would prefer to make principals and agents aware that it can be efficient to participate in such a network. It is especially important to recognize that an electronic coordination system is not part of a network with winners and losers, but a network in which each actor benefits from their participation.

Finally, we will indicate one promising practical application of the ECS: an ECS can be used to connect the advantages of long term skeleton agreements with the short term contracts found in contractual eBusiness relationships.[7] One important advantage of long term contracts in the haulage business and other businesses is that they give the economic actors some certainty in their expectations. But on closer inspection, contractual flexibility is lost with detailed arrangements. As an open dynamic system, the ECS-network has to react to changes and changing needs inside the ECS and in its environment and therefore flexibility is needed. "Businessmen may welcome a measure of vagueness in the obligations they assume so that they may negotiate matters in the light of actual circumstances" [Macaulay 1963, 64]. With regard to the ECS we can think about the following connection between long and short term contracts:

- Long term skeleton agreements between forwarding agents and carriers which are initiated and closed face to face give the actors the certainty they need to participate in the ECS-network. These agreements embrace e. g. capacities which have to be available to other actors in the network, minimum quality requirements which have to be fulfilled, minimum appointed time participation in the network and penalties in the case of transferring false information to the ECS.
- Short and middle term arrangements concerning those parts of contractual relationships which have not been specified in the skeleton agreements are designed within the ECS. The ECS permits swift reaction to actual circumstances like the changing quality requirements of suppliers or producers. Moreover, short term contracts closed within the ECS are well founded if the incentive problems arising in principal agent relationships can be modeled and solved by the ECS models.

Concluding Remarks and Survey

Principal-agent relationships are prevalent in economic networks. The analysis presented here improves our understanding of the functioning of basic principal-

---

7 The "e" in the term eContracting alludes to other terms like eBusiness. Those readers who engaged in the development of eBusiness have recognized that eBusiness is in many cases limited to the purchase of goods or services. Correspondingly the coordination within eBusiness can be characterized by short term contracts emerging from selling goods or services (contracts of purchase or sale).

agent models in those principal-agent relationships which are basically and essentially influenced by new information technologies. We have referred to networks consisting of forwarding agents and carriers and their contractual (principal-agent) relationships. We have first studied efficient contractual agreements in a network with one forwarding agent, one carrier and their relationship. Throughout the investigation we have enlarged the network to an ECS-network consisting of several principals, several agents and an ECS-provider. We analyzed what can be observed, and hence contracted upon, by the parties from the haulage business. When the payoff alone is observed, optimal contracts will be second-best owing to a problem of moral hazard. By using or creating additional information systems (the tracking and tracing system or the electronic coordination system) contracts can generally be improved. We have characterized optimal contracts which use such information (eContracting). Valuable information generated by new information technologies allows more accurate judgment of the performance of the agent without loss of flexibility in contracts.

Of course, the investigation presented here leaves many interesting questions in contracting and eContracting unanswered. We will address some of these questions in a short survey. First we refer to the extended models described in section 6.1. Many promising extensions of the basic model of moral hazard have been developed, but an integration of these extended models has not been achieved. Correspondingly we have to analyze if combinations of the described extended models can be developed and transferred into the ECS. Another important research field not analyzed here is the problem of adverse selection. As well as moral hazards, the problem of adverse selection is another central part of the principal-agent theory. The problem of adverse selection occurs in relationships with an asymmetry of information before a contract is concluded. These problems need to be considered before an ECS-network can be built up. E. g. it is important to give those carriers who are interested in participating in the ECS-network incentives to transmit true information about their ability and their desire to provide logistic services to the ECS-provider. A third class of interesting questions arises in connection with the value of information: what valuable information is available in the ECS-network but not in its environment and vice versa? Can we measure the value of valuable information? Finally in this survey, we have to address the development of the ECS. We pursue the idea of developing an ECS, knowing that we first have to find answers to these open questions. However, the isolation of an appropriate principal-agent model and analyzing its scope – as presented in this chapter – is a very first step. The feasibility of the principal-agent models for extensibility provides a methodological approach here and for future research.

References

Akerlof, G. A. (1970): The Market for „Lemons“: Quality Uncertaincy and the Market Mechanism, Quarterly Journal of Economics, Vol. 84 (1970), pp. 488-500.

Baron, D. P./Myerson, R. B. (1982): Regulating a Monopolist with unknown Costs, Econometrica, Vol. 50 (1982), pp. 911-930.

Becker, C./Bölsche, D. (2000): New Means for ERP-Systems by eContracting, in: Proceedings of AMCIS 2000, Advanced ITApplications in ERP-Systems, Long Beach, USA.

Bertalanffy, L. (1976): Zu einer allgemeinen Systemlehre, in: Organisationstheorie, published by E. Grochla, Stuttgart, pp. 542-553.

Gibbons, R. (1998): Incentives in Organizations, Journal of Economic Perspectives, Vol. 12 (1998), No. 4, Fall, pp. 115-132.

Gupta,S./Romano, R. E. (1998): Monitoring the principal with multiple agents, Rand Journal of Economics, Vol. 29 (1998), pp. 427-442.

Holmström, B. (1979): Moral Hazard and Observability, Bell Journal of Economics (1979), pp. 74-91.

Holmström, B./Milgrom, P. (1991): Multitask Principal-Agent Analyses: Incentive Contracts, Asset Ownership, and Job Design, The Journal of Law, Economics and Organization, Vol. 7, Spring 1991, pp. 24-52.

Houtman, J. (2000): Regelungsbasiertes Qualitätsmanagement logistischer Leistungen, will be published in: Zeitschrift für Betriebswirtschaft 2000.

Jewitt, I. (1988): Justifying the First-Order Approach to Principal-Agent Problems, Econometrica, Vol. 56 (1988), No. 5, pp. 1177-1190.

Macaulay, S. (1963): Non-contractual Relations in Business: A Preliminary Study, American Sociological Review, Vol. 28 (1963), pp. 55-69.

Milgrom, P. R. (1981): Good news and bad news: representation, theorems, and applications, Bell Journal of Economics, Vol. 12 (1981), pp. 380-391.

Prendergast, C. (1999): The Provision of Incentives in Firms, Journal of Economic Literature, Vol. 37 (1999), March, pp. 7-63.

Ross, R. A. (1973): The Economic Theory of Agency: The Principal's Problem, American Economic Review (1973), Vol. 63, pp. 134-139.

Internet Based Management of Distributed Business Processes

Kirsten Lenz, Andreas Oberweis

Johann Wolfgang Goethe-University
Institute of Information Systems
Mertonstr. 17
D 60054 Frankfurt am Main
{lenz|oberweis}@wiwi.uni-frankfurt.de

Summary:
Due to the fast growth of internet based electronic business, languages for modelling as well as methods for analyzing and executing distributed business processes are becoming more and more important.
This paper surveys some of the results of a project which aimed at providing support for planning and introducing telework in decentralized organizations. The main focus of the paper is on process and document modelling concepts, which are based on a combination of Petri nets and the document standard XML (Extensible Markup Language). These so-called XML nets are a formal, graphical modeling language that allows the modeling of both the flow of XML documents and the coordination of the underlying business process. XML nets are based on GXSL, a graphical XML schema definition language, and its related graphical XML document manipulation language (XManiLa). They can be directly executed by an appropriate workflow engine. Advantage can be taken of the formal foundation of XML nets, e.g., when analyzing a geographically distributed inter- or intra-organizational workflow model: XML nets support the process of identifying relevant process fragments, assigning them to the appropriate organizational units, and thus help to derive an improved, process-oriented organizational structure.

Introduction

Distributed inter- or intraorganizational business processes require the integration of electronic document interchange and interorganizational processes. From a document point of view, there is a need for electronically interchanging structured documents and data between the organizations involved. From a process-oriented perspective, modeling, analysis, and automated execution of distributed workflows are gaining more and more in importance. Moreover, the advantages of workflow driven electronic document interchange are relevant for intraorganizational process management, especially with the emerging integration of mass data in databases and document management.

In this paper, XML nets, a new kind of high-level Petri nets, are proposed for the modeling of both the flow of XML documents and the coordination of the underlying business process. They are based on GXSL, a graphical XML schema definition language, and the XML document manipulation language XManiLa.

XML nets can be directly executed by an appropriate workflow engine and therefore allow for the detailed analysis and simulation of distributed business processes. Additionally, XML nets support the process of identifying relevant process fragments and assigning them to the appropriate organizational units, thus helping to derive an improved, process-oriented organizational structure.

Related concepts for graphical XML data modeling languages and XML query languages can be found for example in [Bonfati/Ceri 2000, Ceri et al. 1999, Deutsch et al. 1999, Robie/Lapp/Schach 1998]. Many of the XML net concepts proposed in this paper rely on so-called SGML nets [Weitz 1998], a variant of high-level Petri nets for the modeling of workflows based on SGML documents.

Our paper is structured as follows: First, we give a brief introduction to XML, Petri nets, and workflow management. In the next section, we present a graphical XML schema definition language and propose a graphical XML document manipulation language. Finally, we introduce XML nets for the intra- and interoganizational workflow driven document interchange.

Extensible Markup Language

The Extensible Markup Language (XML) [XML 2000] is a document declaration standard proposed by the World Wide Web Consortium (W3C, http://www.w3.org/). It is a simplification of the Standard Generalized Markup Language (SGML, ISO 8879). An XML document type definition (DTD) allows the specification of a document type with problem-specific markups as a class of XML documents conforming to that specific DTD, i.e. a set of documents that follow these document design rules. Figure 1 shows a simple DTD for an employee document with personnel information, a list of projects she or he works in and a list of the skills. A corresponding valid document for the employee Mary L. Miller is shown in Figure 2.

```
<!-- DTD for employee documents-->
<!ELEMENT employee (empname,
          work_in_proj*, skill*)>
<!ATTLIST employee empid ID #REQUIRED
          sex (male|female) "female">
<!ELEMENT empname (title?,
          (firstname|abbreviation)+,
          lastname)>
<!ELEMENT title (#PCDATA)>
<!ELEMENT firstname (#PCDATA)>
<!ELEMENT abbreviation (#PCDATA)>
<!ELEMENT lastname (#PCDATA)>
<!ELEMENT work_in_proj (#PCDATA)>
<!ATTLIST work_in_proj projid
           IDREF #IMPLIED>
<!ELEMENT skill (#PCDATA)>
```

Figure 1: Document type definition for employee documents

```
<?xml version="1.0"?>
<!DOCTYPE employee SYSTEM "http://...empdoc.dtd">
<employee empid="0815" sex="female">
  <empname>
    <firstname>Mary</firstname>
    <abbrevation>L.</abbrevation>
    <lastname>Miller</lastname>
  </empname>
  <work_in_proj projid="328">20</work_in_proj>
  <work_in_proj projid="85">10</work_in_proj>
  <skill>Java</skill>
  <skill>C++</skill>
  <skill>Oracle 8</skill>
</employee>
```

Figure 2: Valid employee document

In the near future, XML DTDs may be complemented by XML schemas [XML Schema 2000], a new standard promoted by W3C which attempts to overcome the limits of a DTD, e.g., concerning the data-oriented role of XML in e-commerce applications. XML schemas, a functional superset of DTDs, are written in XML and can therefore be parsed and validated like XML documents. Moreover, they provide a concept for specifying data types and thereby ensure data integrity for valid XML documents.

Petri Nets

For the modeling of business processes several more or less formal description languages have been proposed [van der Aalst/Desel/Oberweis 2000]. In contrast to other languages, Petri nets [Brauer/Reisig/Rosenberg 1986, Reisig 1985] combine the advantages of the graphical representation of processes with a formal semantics. As well as visualization of processes, Petri nets allow for the analysis and validation of business processes [Desel/Erwin 2000]. A simple example of a low-level Petri net is shown in Figure 3, which describes the following (simplified) process:

> *A planned project is initialized. Afterwards, employees can be assigned to the project. At the beginning of a project the project is assigned to the department. After finishing the project, the employee information must be updated: new skills learned in the project have to be added, whereas the project has to be removed from the list of projects the employee works in.*

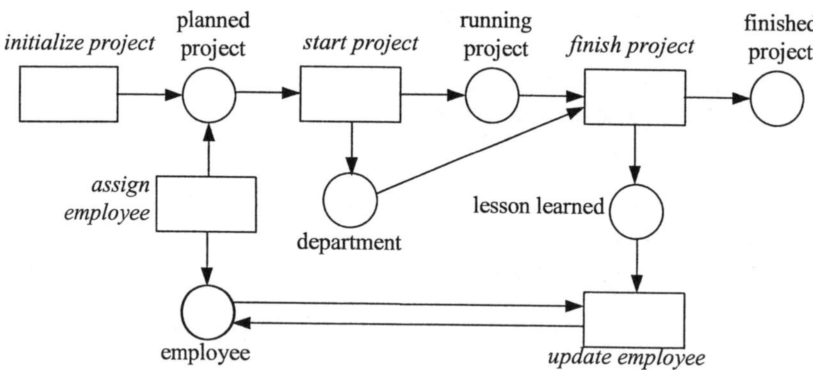

Figure 3: Simple Petri net for the process of project execution

High-level Petri nets such as predicate/transition nets (Pr/T-nets) [Genrich 1986, Oberweis 1996] or nested relation/transition nets (NR/T-nets) [Oberweis/Sander 1996] integrate behavior- and object-related aspects of workflows. In Pr/T-nets or NR/T-nets the places represent relation schemes according to which the marking of the net assigns a relation to each place. A transition represents a class of operations on the relations in the adjacent places. When a transition occurs, tuples are removed from its input places and inserted into its output places according to the respective edge inscriptions.

Workflow Management

Workflow management supports business process management by the automatic execution of (parts of) business processes: business processes can be modeled by more or less formal or graphical modeling languages like event-driven process chains [Scheer/Nüttgens 2000] or Petri nets. The workflow itself, i.e. a concrete process execution, can be interpreted as an instantiation of the workflow model. The main tasks of workflow management include the specification of the workflow model, its analysis and verification, the execution of the workflow by a suitable workflow architecture, and the development of workflow applications [Jablonski 2000].

Petri nets are well suited and frequently proposed for workflow modeling and execution [Janssens/Verelst/Weyn 2000]. they provide a restricted number of graphical modeling concepts and possess at the same time formal semantics. Their formal foundation enables the application of theoretical analysis techniques (e.g. to find out whether a certain system state can be attained or not) and the model-driven execution of the workflow. Moreover, they integrate data and behavior aspects and therefore meet the need to model for example interorganizational workflows based on electronic document interchange. The use of Petri nets at different formalization levels allows for a stepwise refinement of a workflow model. A survey of different approaches for Petri net based business process and workflow management can be found for example in [van der Aalst/Desel/Oberweis 2000].

Graphical Languages for XML Document Management

In this section, we introduce the graphical XML schema definition language (GXSL) for graphically specifying XML schemas that represent a DTD. XManiLa, an extension to the graphical XML schema definition language, is proposed for the retrieval and manipulation, especially insertion and deletion, of XML documents.

XML Schema Definition with GXSL

The XML document type definition represents a grammar for the declaration of documents. It consists of a set of markup declarations of different types: element, attribute list, entity or notation declaration. Unfortunately, this grammar is textual so that the DTDs for complex objects may often become quite unreadable. The advantages of a graphical schema definition language (like the entity/relationship model for the database design) are lacking.

In the following, we propose a graphical schema definition language for the design of XML document types, that we call *graphical XML schema definition language* (GXSL). The version of GXSL presented is DTD-based, i.e. a DTD can be unambiguously derived from the *graphical XML schema* (GXS).

Instead of creating a completely new graphical modeling language for XML document types, we rely on well known data modeling concepts (of the E/R-model and other semantic data models), which all had their impact on the static object modeling concepts of the Unified Modeling Language (UML) [Booch/ Rumbaugh/Jacobson 1999]. The main advantage of UML is that it is a highly accepted integration of well-known modeling concepts and guidelines and that it comprises a generic notation for the derivation of new graphical modeling languages for specific purposes. Due to space limitations, we focus on the logical structure of XML document types and omit XML entity declarations, internal subsets and `INCLUDE` or `IGNORE` markups. We also introduce a simplification of the GXS conforming to UML which has been adapted to the quick, rather intuitive modeling of XML document types.

The main principles of XML DTDs are classification of documents with similar structure and aggregation of document components. We represent XML documents and their elements by UML classes, hierarchically (i.e. non-recursively) structured by composition or aggregation. In the following, the UML concepts for GXSL are explained in detail.

Simple Element Types:

In general, element declarations of the XML DTD are represented by classes in GXSL. By simple element types we understand element types without children (i.e. they are not composed of other element types), namely the `EMPTY`-element type, the `ANY`-element type and the predefined `#PCDATA`. When the element declaration contains the keyword `ANY`, both other tags and general characters are allowed within the element tags. Empty elements have no content at all. See Figure 4 for the GXSL representation of simple element types in a GXS by stereotyped «any»- and «empty»-classes.

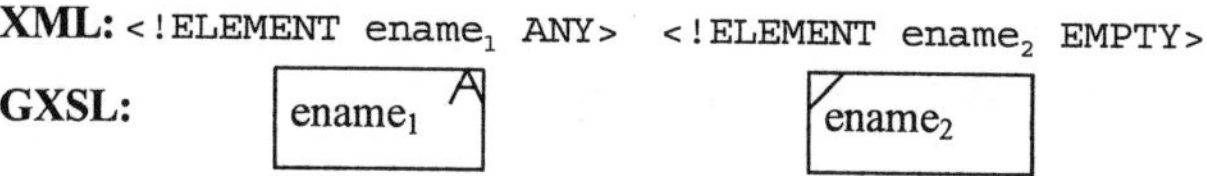

Figure 4: GXSL class representation of the `ANY`- and `EMPTY`-element type declaration

`#PCDATA` stands for *parsed character data* and symbolizes any sequence of general characters that does not contain any tag. The GXSL class «pcdata» has no name and provides its own icon as shown in Figure 5.

XML: #PCDATA

GXSL:

Figure 5: GXSL icon for the «pcdata»-class

In addition to element declarations, a DTD may include attribute list declarations in order to specify element types. The attribute list declaration for an element type ename has the following pattern:

```
<!ATTLIST ename aname1 atype1 defaultdecl1
 ...
 anamen atypen defaultdecln>.
```

aname is the attribute name, atype the attribute type and defaultdecl an optional default declaration. In a GXS, the attribute list is added to the element type (see Figure 6).

The default declaration consists of a default value and/or a default modifier. In Figure 6, the second attribute of the element type has a default value. Table 1 shows the translation of XML default modifiers into GXSL.

ename
$aname_1$: $atype_1$ $aname_2$: $atype_2$ = $default_2$ ... $aname_n$: $atype_n$

Figure 6: Element class with attribute list

It is possible to restrict the GXS class representation to the element name with or even without the list of the attribute names in a survey diagram.

XML	GXSL	
#IMPLIED	aname: atype	attribute value may remain unspecified
#REQUIRED	aname [1]: atype	mandatory attribute value, specified by the occurrence indicator
#FIXED "dvalue"	aname: atype = dvalue {frozen}	attribute value must not be changed; default value required

Table 1: GXSL class attribute for XML attribute declaration with default modifier

Nested Element Types:

Element types in XML can be nested in order to describe hierarchically structured documents, i.e. the element declaration refers to other element declarations of the DTD:

```
<!ELEMENT ename (...)>.
```

UML offers two special kinds of association to adequately model the hierarchical relationship between different element types: composition and aggregation. Composition, represented by a filled diamond, is used to express the fact that the child element is a component of exactly one element of the parent element type with existence dependency (e.g. a car consists of four wheels). Aggregation, the weaker form of composition and represented by an open diamond in the GXS (see Figure 7), can be used to express a loose, non dependent 'consists of'-relationship (e.g. a discussion group consists of four people). Additionally, a name and a name direction can be assigned to each association.

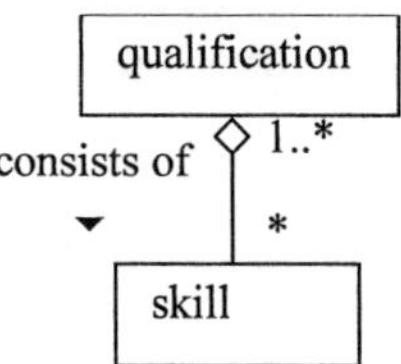

Figure 7: GXS for a nested element type

XML occurrence indicators as an appendix of an element name or a group of elements can be translated into cardinality values that can be assigned to the associated subclass(es), see Table 2.

XML occurrence operator	GXSL cardinality	
none	1	mandatory
?	0..1	optional
*	*	occurs zero or more times
+	1..*	occurs one or more times

Table 2: GXSL cardinality values for XML occurrence indicators

The cardinality value corresponding to the parent element types is always 1 for the composition and 1..* for the aggregation. For example, the element declaration `<!ELEMENT qualification (skill*)>` for the qualification of an employee as a set of skills has the GXS shown in Figure 7.

Choice:

The element type can be defined as a choice between two or more element types. For example, the DTD contains the element declaration <!ELEMENT $ename_1$ ($ename_2$|$ename_3$)> and element declarations for $ename_2$ and $ename_3$ respectively. Within a document which is valid for this DTD either an $ename_2$ element or an $ename_3$ element has to appear inside the $ename_1$ element (and must not appear in both). With GXSL, choice can be expressed by a constraint with {or}-condition between the relevant alternative subclasses (see Figure 8).

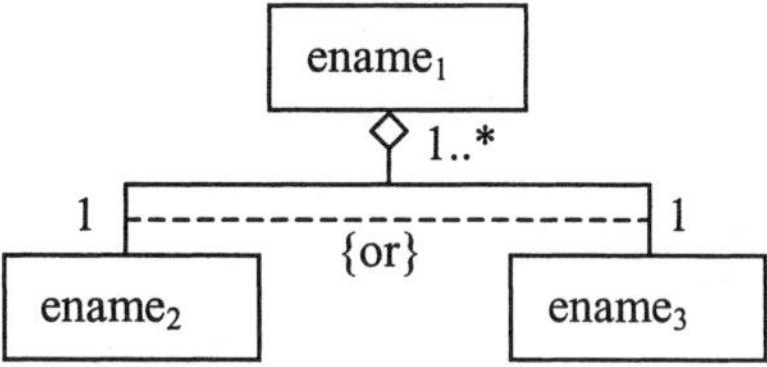

Figure 8: GXS for alternative element types

Sequence:

A sequence of elements that have to appear in a predefined order within another element can be declared as a list of element names, separated by commas:

<!ELEMENT ename ($ename_1$, $ename_2$, ..., $ename_n$)>.

We use the dependency modeling concept of UML to model a sequence with GXSL. Dependency is a (possibly directed) association and indicates a user/used relationship between elements. In GXSL we introduce a directed dependency including the label {precedes} to order the subclasses of a superclass (see Figure 9) with the following semantics: the document elements must follow the same order as their element types.

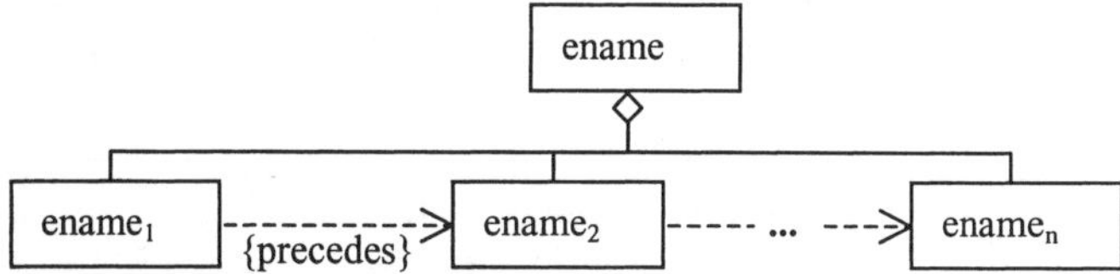

Figure 9: GXS for a sequence of element types

Cascading Nesting:

XML allows for element declarations with cascading nesting, i.e. elements are not declared explicitly but are implicitly given by an expression enclosed in parenthesis. For example, we can declare by `(ename₁,(ename₂|ename₃)+)` that an element of type $ename_1$ must be followed by an iteration of either an $ename_2$ element or an $ename_3$ element. In this case, we have to introduce an abstract class to model the hierarchy of the element type (see Figure 10). This can be compared to splitting the expression into $(ename_1,abstract+)$ and the supplementary element declaration $<!ELEMENT\ abstract\ (ename_2|ename_3)>$.

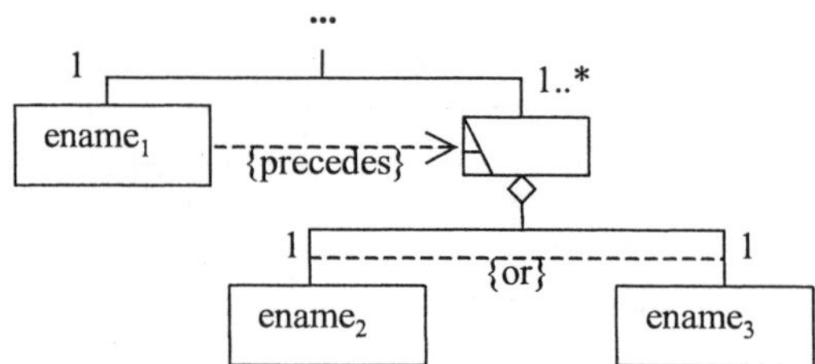

Figure 10: GXS for nested element types with an abstract class

The abstract class is a stereotyped class and has its own icon with an "A"-symbol in it. It is possible to name it but not to assign attributes to it. However, the abstract class may have a cardinality.

Referential Integrity:

Attributes may be of type `IDREF` or `IDREFS`. Its values must be included in (or be a subset of) the set of `ID` attribute values of the referenced element type. The attribute types `IDREF` and `IDREFS` therefore implicitly define referential integrity constraints between elements of XML documents that are valid for this DTD. The GXSL even allows for explicit referential integrity constraints by {ref}-dependencies (see Figure 11). {ref}-dependencies are labeled by the referencing and the referenced attribute and the *-cardinality for attributes of type `IDREFS`.

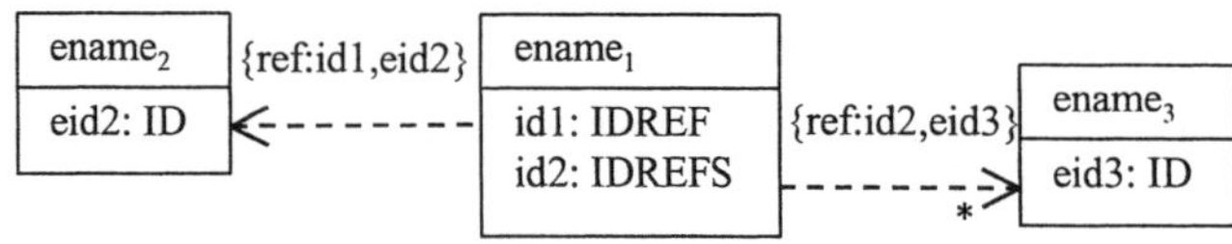

Figure 11: GXSL dependencies for referential integrity constraints

Simplifications of GXSL:

In this section, we present some simplifications of the GXSL concepts we have described so far. With these simplifications, GXSL no longer completely coincides with UML. But a simplified GXS still provides all necessary information without notational overload and the GXS design becomes more intuitive for those who are familiar with XML.

- The association name and direction can be omitted.
- Cardinality of the superclass of composition or aggregation is fixed and thus can be omitted.
- For GXSL, we declare the default cardinality to be '1' (instead of '*' for the UML), which is identical to the default occurrence indicator of XML.
- We propose a stereotyped class and a special icon for the element declaration `<!ELEMENT ename (#PCDATA)>` (Figure 12b) instead of the GXS conforming to UML (Figure 12a). Note that the `#PCDATA`-element type is not identical to the `#PCDATA`-class introduced before.

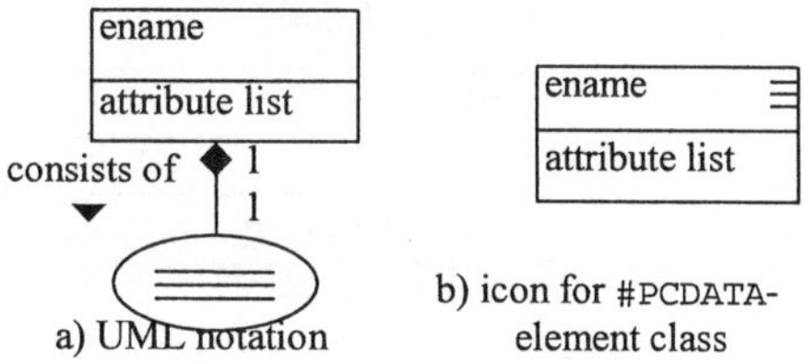

Figure 12: Simplification for `#PCDATA`-element types

- The constraint for a choice is expressed only by a dashed line. The {or}-condition can be omitted.
- The GXS for a sequence is simplified by omitting the {precedes}-dependencies. Nevertheless, elements of a valid document must appear in the same order as the respective classes in the GXS.
- The label of a {ref}-dependency may be omitted either if class attributes have not been specified in the GXS or if both referencing and referenced attributes can be uniquely identified without any label.

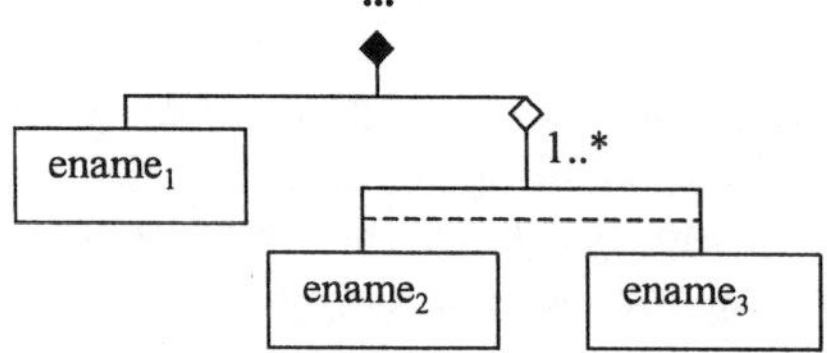

Figure 13: Simplification for cascading nesting of element types referring to Figure 10

- Cascading nesting of elements is represented without any abstract class. We allow for a tree structure of composition and/or aggregation (see Figure 13). The cardinality of the abstract class is written above the respective branch.

Example:

Figure 14 shows a GXS which represents the employee DTD of Figure 1.

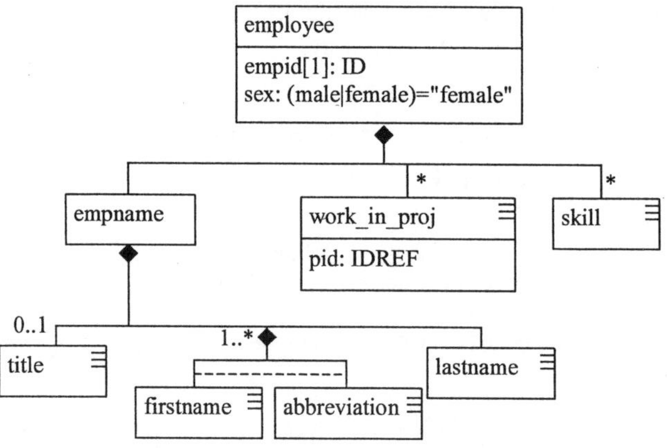

Figure 14: GXS for the employee DTD of Figure 1

Compared with the textual representation in Figure 1, the graphical representation gives a better overview of the defined element types and the logical structure of a valid employee document.

Manipulation of XML Documents with XManiLa

We can also use GXSL with some extensions for querying and manipulating XML documents. The GXSL-based XML document manipulation language is called XManiLa. A GXS can be interpreted as a template for a set of XML documents that specifies the structure of matching documents. In order also to enable content based queries, we allow for assigning constants or variables to an element or an attribute. For example, we may want to search for all female employees that have a firstname followed by an abbreviation and the lastname "Miller". The GXS in

Figure 15 describes this query. Unnamed ANY-classes express parts of the document that are not relevant for this query. e.g., a document that matches the GXS in Figure 15 must first contain an element `empname`, no matter what follows.

XManiLa is not only suited for document retrieval, but also for insertion and deletion (and thereby also for updating). These operations either concern a whole document or elements on lower hierarchy levels. Elements to be inserted or deleted are depicted by a solid line on the left side of the element type's rectangle. The insert- and delete-qualification is inherited by all subclasses. For examples of insert and delete operations on the employee documents see Figure 16.

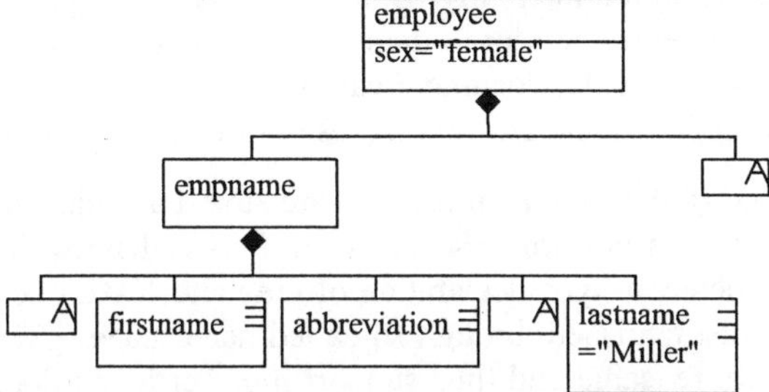

Figure 15: Female employees named Miller with a firstname followed by an abbreviation

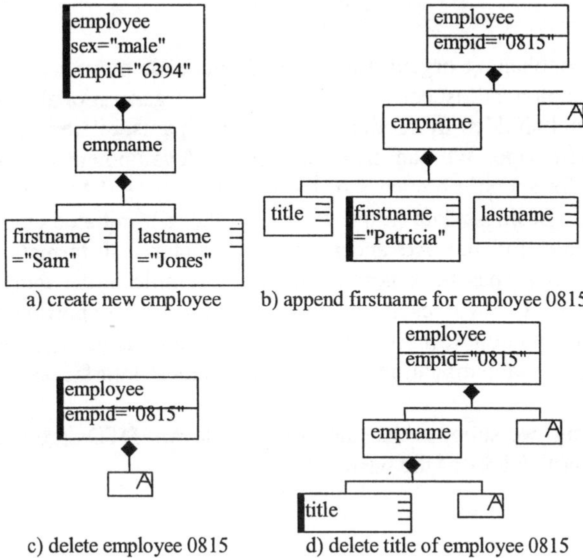

Figure 16: Insert and delete operations on the employee documents

Interorganizational Data Interchange Based on XML

The exchange of XML documents between organizations can be handled in different ways:

- The XML document can be sent to another organization without any DTD. From the recipient's point of view the document only fulfills the weaker requirements of being well-formed (i.e. has a correct syntax), supplementary information is missing.
- The DTD can be stored internally within the document type declaration of the document and therefore be sent to the recipient together with the document itself. In this case the XML document can be processed anywhere without any supplementary information. However, reuse of the DTD is not supported.
- External DTDs (either public or private) are stored as independent files. They can be identified via uniform resource identifiers (URIs) which must be contained in the document type declaration of the valid XML document. External DTDs can be distinguished through so called namespaces [XML Namespaces 1999]. They are reusable and thus support more efficient document management.

For a short introduction into XML and namespaces see for example [Eckstein 1999].

The extent of publishing organizational DTDs depends on many aspects, for example on technological aspects as well as on the organizational strategy. DTDs can be completely hidden from other process participants, bilaterally exchanged or published world wide. We can also observe the development of standard XML specifications for specific branches of the industry, e.g. ebXML for the exchange of all electronic business data (http://www.ebxml.org/), initiated among others by the Organization for the Advancement of Structured Information Standards (OASIS, http://www.oasis-open.org/). Another example is the independent consortium RosettaNet (www.rosettanet.org) which aims at supporting supply chain partners in information technology, electronic components and semiconductor manufacturing by standardization of electronic business interfaces.

In the following, we suppose that the process relevant DTDs are known and accepted by all participants of the business process.

XML Nets

In the previous sections, we have described how to graphically model XML DTDs with GXSL and how to specify document retrieval and document manipulation with XManiLa. We can now combine both techniques for the definition of XML nets.

XML nets, a new kind of high-level Petri nets, are a formal, graphical modeling language that allows the modeling of both the flow of XML documents and the coordination of the underlying business process. The static components of XML nets (i.e. the places of a Petri net) are labeled with GXSL-schemas representing a DTD. Places can be interpreted as a container for XML documents which are valid for the corresponding DTD. The flow of XML documents is defined by the occurrences of transitions which thereby manipulate (create, change or delete) documents in their adjacent places. The enabledness of a transition, which is prerequisite for the transition's occurrence, depends on the labels of the adjacent edges constructed with XManiLa and on an optional transition inscription. XML nets have the following characteristics:

- A place is represented by a GXS which identifies the type of documents contained in the place.
- An edge between a place and a transition is labeled with an extended GXS of the XManiLa that fits to the schema of the adjacent place. For each instantiation of the variables of the edge label it is possible to decide whether a document of the adjacent place matches the extended GXS or not.
- A transition may be inscribed by a logical expression over all variables that appear in the labels of the adjacent edges. The expression evaluates to either `true` or `false` for an instantiation of the variables.
- The initial marking assigns to each place of the XML net a set of valid XML documents.

The behavior of XML nets is defined by the following rule for a transition being enabled for an instantiation of variables (If a variable appears more than once in the vicinity of a transition it must be instantiated with the same value for the same transition occurrence.): all places in the preset of the transition, i.e. with an outgoing edge to the transition, contain (at least) one document that matches with the schema of the adjacent edge under the given instantiation of the variables. All places in the postset of the transition, i.e. with an edge from transition to place, contain (at least) one document that matches with the label of the adjacent edge under the given instantiation of the variables in the case of document manipulation or do not contain a matching document in the case of document creation. The transition inscription validates to `true` for these documents and the instantiation of the variables.

An enabled transition may occur. If a transition occurs, it removes the matching documents or parts of the documents as specified by the edge label from the places in the preset of the transition and inserts new documents into the places in the postset of the transition or new elements into the matching documents.

To continue the example of Figure 3, we can now assign to each place a GXS and to each edge an extended GXS as label. Figure 17 shows the schemas for planned, running and finished projects, the department, and the lessons learned. The schema for the employee is shown in Figure 14.

Besides the definition of all process relevant document type definitions, the behavior of the XML net has to be specified in detail for all transitions.

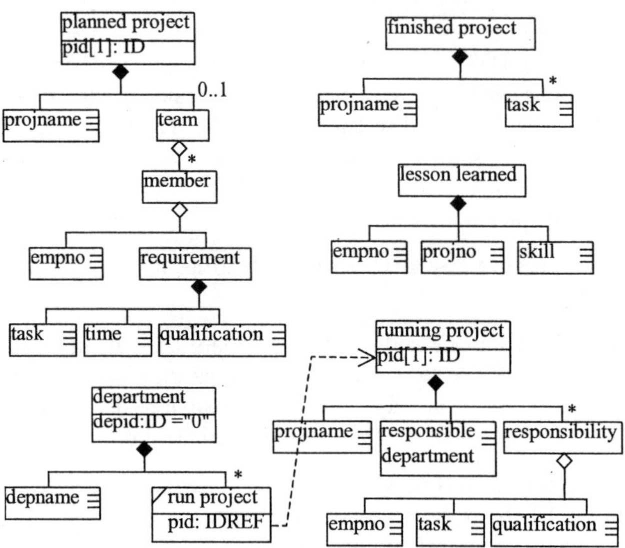

Figure 17: Graphical XML schemas for the project execution

- *initialize project*: A new document of type `planned project` is created.
- *assign employee*: The assignment consists of inserting the employee ID as team member for the project and the time required for the task execution together with the project ID for the employee.
- *start project*: When a project is started, a responsible department is chosen for the project. This is only possible for departments with an identifier that differs from the default identifier 0. The document of type `planned project` is deleted and a new document of type `running project`, including the department ID, created. The project ID is added to the department's list of running projects.
- *finish project*: Delete the relevant document from the list of running projects and create a new document with the information about the finished project. Moreover, delete the project ID from the department document. Create a new document that contains all information about the skills that an employee has learned from the project.
- *update employee*: Finally, the information about project participation is deleted in the employee document. At the same time, the new skill is appended to the employee's list of skills.

The XML net corresponding to the simple Petri net of Figure 3 is shown in Figure 18. For the sake of better readability, we omitted the GXS place labels. Furthermore, no initial marking is specified.

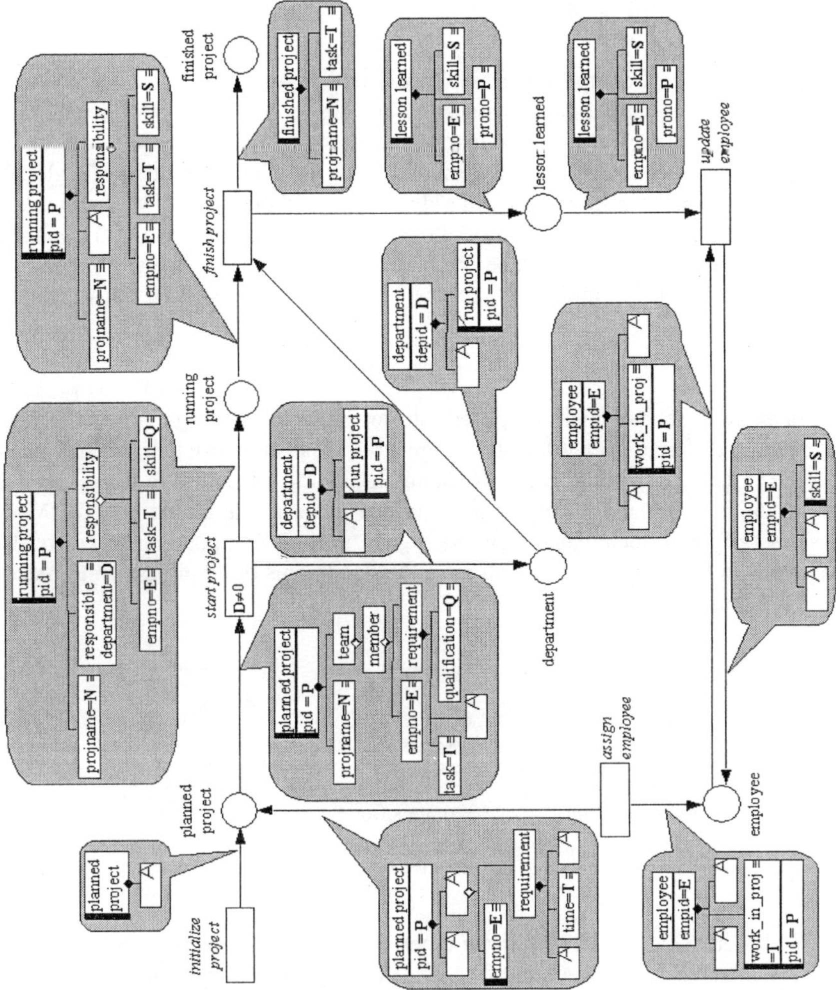

Figure 18: XML net for the process of project execution

An interorganizational workflow management system should be able to deal with both simply structured data and documents. Although places of predicate/transition nets are interpreted as containers for relations, i.e. structured data of relational databases, predicate/transition nets can also be modeled as XML nets: the GXS corresponding to a relation schema or an edge inscription is a diagram with a one level hierarchy of all attributes. This allows the combining of both concepts, data based workflow modeling with predicate transition nets, and document based workflow modeling with XML nets.

Fragmentation of XML Nets

The globalization of companies, flexibilization of organizational structures, cooperation between companies and business-to-business e-commerce, mobile computing, and the development towards distributed business processes require the application of distributed information system technologies. The distribution of a global, interorganizational workflow implies a distribution of the workflow management system on the execution level and on the design level methods for the fragmentation of centralized workflows. The fragmentation of predicate/ transition nets has been introduced in [Guth/Lenz/Oberweis 1998] and can easily be transferred to XML nets.

A global XML net can be decomposed into several local net fragments that can be allocated to different execution sites. In general, we decompose Petri nets by splitting the places, i.e. by duplicating them and assigning the copies to the respective fragments. The initial marking of an interface place in the global net (for XML nets a set of valid documents) can be assigned to the corresponding places of the fragments in two ways: by replication of the documents or by allocation to one of the fragments.

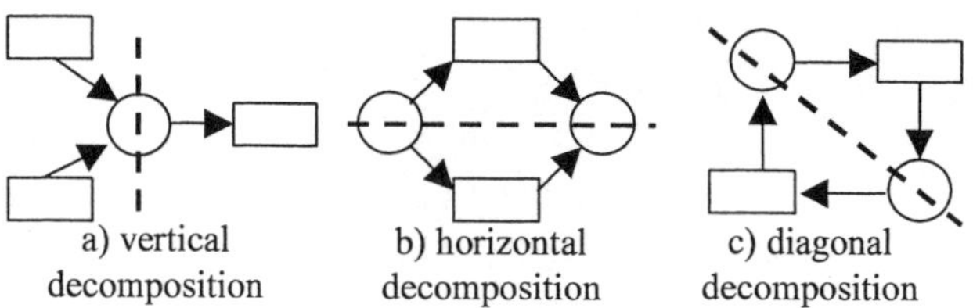

Figure 19: Vertical, horizontal, and diagonal decomposition of Petri nets

In [Guth/Lenz/Oberweis 1998] three types of decomposition are described based on the dependencies between the fragments (i.e. the data or document flow in the global net): vertical, e.g. for sequential processes, horizontal for alternative processes, and diagonal for decomposition into processes with mutual dependency (see Figure 19 for examples).

Returning to our workflow example for the project execution, we can identify three different organizational units involved in the execution of the workflow: the management, the department that is responsible for the execution of the specific project, and the human resources department (see Figure 20). The arcs describe the document flow and thus the dependencies between the workflow fragments. For example, the project department needs documents from the management for the execution of its part of the workflow (the running project document).

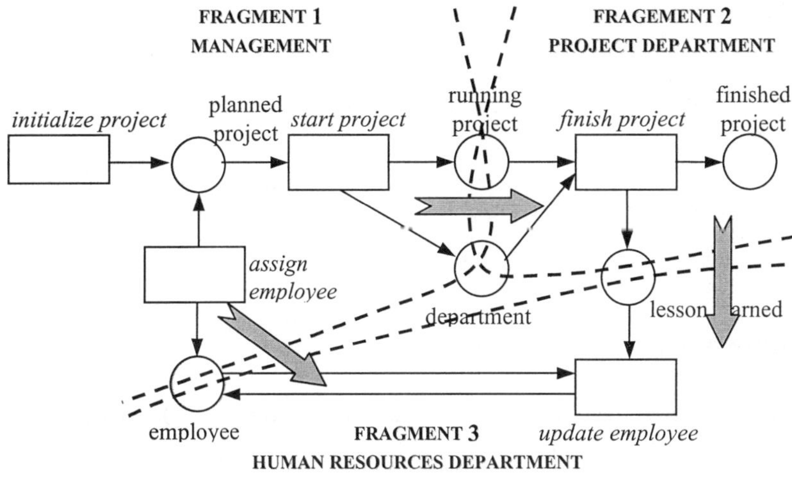

Figure 20: Workflow fragments for the distributed project execution

For the execution of a distributed workflow based on a Petri net several architectures are conceivable, with the degree of distribution ranging from centralized to completely distributed. Organizational structures, the distribution of workflow-relevant data and documents, as well as technical restrictions are crucial criteria for an efficient allocation of the workflow fragments. Whether a workflow engine runs in a central place, is installed at all process participants' sites, or is sent to the site on demand (together with the workflow fragment) depends for example on the size of the workflow engine in relation to the size of the workflow fragments, the average number of workflow fragments to be executed at the site, the maintenance and update cost of the workflow engine, and the flexibility of the workflow fragment allocation. For example, distribution of the workflow engine is a suitable architecture for the workflow support of business-to-business applications because of the rather small number of participating organizations in contrast to workflows e.g. for business-to-consumer applications like internet shopping malls.

Summary and Outlook

In this paper, we have introduced XML-nets, which integrate behavior- and document-related aspects of distributed workflows. In the future, XML schema specific aspects will be integrated into GXSL. Moreover, XManiLa will be extended to querying the sequential order of elements of the same element type.

For the geographical distribution of XML net based workflows, principles of distributed database management systems may be transferred to the management of distributed XML documents, focussed for example on the management of document replication. Finally, criteria for the allocation of workflow fragments depending on the allocation of documents, mass data and other relevant resources must be found.

We plan to extend an existing Petri net simulation tool in order to simulate and validate distributed workflows which are modeled as XML nets.

References

Bonifati, A./Ceri, S. (2000): Comparative Analysis of Five XML Query Languages, in: SIGMOD Record 29(1), pp. 68-79

Booch, G./Rumbaugh, J./Jacobson, I. (1999): The Unified Modeling Language User Guide, Addison Wesley

Brauer, W./Reisig, W./Rozenberg, G. eds. (1986): Advances in Petri Nets, Part I, Lecture Notes in Computer Science, Vol. 254, Springer-Verlag

Ceri, S./Comai, S./Damiani, E./Fraternali, P./Paraboschi, S./Tanca, L. (1999): XML-GL: a Graphical Language for Querying and Restructuring XML Documents, in: Proc. 8th Int. World Wide Web Conference, Toronto, Canada (http://www8.org/w8-papers/1c-xml/xml-gl/ xml-gl.html)

Desel, J./Erwin, Th. (2000): Modeling, Simulation and Analysis of Business Processes, in [van der Aalst/Desel/Oberweis 2000], pp. 129-141

Deutsch, A./Fernandez, M./Florescu, D./Levy, A./Suciu, D. (1999): A Query Language for XML, in: Proc. 8th Int. World Wide Web Conference, Toronto, Canada (http://www8.org/w8-papers/1c-xml/query/query.html)

Eckstein, R. (1999): XML Pocket reference, O'Reilly

Genrich, H.J. (1986): Predicate/Transition Nets, in [Brauer/Reisig/Rozenberg 1986], pp. 207-247

Guth, V./Lenz, K./Oberweis, A. (1998): Distributed Workflow Execution Based on Fragmentation of Petri Nets, in: Traunmüller, R.; Csuháj-Varjù, E. (eds.): Proc. 15th IFIP World Computer Congress 'Telecooperation – The Global Office, Teleworking and Communication Tools', Vienna, Budapest, pp. 114-125

Jablonski, S. (2000): Workflow Management Between Formal Theory and Pragmatic Approaches, in: [van der Aalst/Desel/Oberweis 2000], pp. 345-358

Janssens, G.K./Verelst, J./Weyn, B. (2000): Techniques for Modeling Workflows and Their Support of Reuse, in: [van der Aalst/Desel/Oberweis 2000], pp. 1-15

Oberweis, A. (1996): An Integrated Approach for the Specification of Processes and Related Complex Structured Objects in Business Applications, in: Decision Support Systems, 17, pp. 31-53

Oberweis, A./ Sander, P. (1996): Information System Behavior Specification by High-Level Petri Nets, in: ACM Transactions on Information Systems, 14(4), pp. 380-420

Reisig, W. (1985): Petri Nets: an Introduction, EATCS monographs 4, Springer-Verlag

Robie, R./Lapp, J./Schach, D. (1998): XML Query Language (XQL), in: Proc. of the Query Language Workshop , Cambridge, Massachusetts (http://www.w3.org/TandS/QL/QL98/pp/xql.html)

Scheer, A.-W./Nüttgens, M. (2000): ARIS Architecture and Reference Models for Business Process Management, in [van der Aalst/Desel/Oberweis 2000], pp. 376-389

van der Aalst, W./Desel, J./Oberweis, A., eds. (2000): Business Process Management – Models, Techniques and Empirical Studies, Lecture Notes in Computer Science, Vol. 1806, Springer-Verlag

Weitz, W. (1998): Combining Structured Documents with High-level Petri-Nets for Workflow Modeling in Internet-based Commerce, Int. Journal of Cooperative Information Systems (IJCIS), 7(4), pp. 275-296

XML (2000): Extensible Markup Language (XML) 1.0 (Second Edition), World Wide Web Consortium Recommendation, Technical Report (http://www.w3.org/TR/2000/REC-xml-20001006)

XML Namespaces (1999): Namespaces in XML, World Wide Web Consortium Recommendation, Technical Report (http://www.w3.org/TR/REC-xml-names-19990114)

XML Schema (2000): XML Schema Part 1: Structures, Part 2: Datatypes, World Wide Web Consortium Candidate Recommendation, Technical Report (http://www.w3.org/TR/2000/xmlschema-1-20001024 and http://www.w3.org/TR/2000/xmlschema-2-20001024)

Druck: Strauss Offsetdruck, Mörlenbach
Verarbeitung: Schäffer, Grünstadt